G000320390

SUPER COOKERY

Quick & Easy

p

This is a Parragon Book
This edition published in 2001

Parragon
Queen Street House
4 Queen Street
Bath BA1 1HE, UK

Copyright © Parragon 2000

ISBN: 0-75255-268-6

All rights reserved. No part of this publication may be reproduced,
stored in a retrieval system or transmitted, in any form or by
any means, electronic, mechanical, photocopying, recording or
otherwise, without the prior permission of the copyright holder.

A copy of the CIP data for this book is available from the British
Library, upon request.

Printed in China

Note
Cup measurements used in this book are for American cups.
Tablespoons are assumed to be 15 ml. Unless otherwise stated,
milk is assumed to be full fat, eggs are medium and pepper is
freshly ground black pepper.

Contents

Introduction   4

Soups & Starters   8

Salads & Snacks   112

Meat & Poultry   200

Fish & Seafood   330

Desserts & Puddings   440

Index   510

Introduction

This book is designed to appeal to anyone who wants a wholesome but quick and easy diet, and includes many recipes suitable for vegetarians and vegans. Its main aim is to show people that, with a little forethought, it is possible to spend very little time in the kitchen while still enjoying appetizing food.

The recipes collected together come from all over the world; some of the Indian and barbeque dishes featured require marinating, often overnight, but it is worth remembering that their actual cooking time is very short once the marinade has been absorbed. The more exotic dishes on offer are balanced by some traditional dishes which are sure to firm family favourites. If you want fast food for everyday meals, or you are short on time and want to prepare a tasty dinner party treat, there is something for everybody in this book.

To save time in the kitchen, always make sure that you have the requisite basics in your cupboard. By keeping a stock of staple foodstuffs such as rice, pasta, spices and herbs, you can easily turn your hand to any number of these recipes.

KEEPING A FULL STORE-CUPBOARD

Flour

You will need to keep a selection of flour: Self-raising and Wholemeal (Wholewheat) are the most useful. You may also like to keep some rice flour and cornflour (cornstarch) for thickening sauces and to add to cakes, biscuits and puddings. Buckwheat, chick pea (garbanzo bean) and soya flours can also be bought. These are useful for combining with other flours to add different flavours and textures.

Grains and Rice

A good variety of grains is essential. For rice, choose from long-grain, basmati, Italian arborio, short-grain, and wild rice. Look out for fragrant Thai rice, jasmine rice and combinations of different varieties to add colour and texture to your dishes. When choosing your rice, remember that brown rice is a better source of vitamin B1 and fibre.

Other grains add variety to the diet. Try to include some barley millet, bulgur wheat, polenta, oats, semolina, sago and tapioca.

Pasta

Pasta is very popular nowadays, and there are many types and shapes to choose from. Keep a good selection, such as basic lasagne sheets, tagliatelle or fettuccine (flat ribbons) and spaghetti. For a change, sample some of the many fresh pastas now available. Better still, make your own – handrolling pasta can be very satisfying, and you can buy a special machine for rolling the dough and cutting certain shapes.

Pulses (legumes)

Pulses (legumes) are a valuable source of protein, vitamins and minerals. Stock up on soya beans, haricot (navy) beans, red kidney beans, cannellini beans, chick peas (garbanzo beans), lentils, split peas and butter beans. Buy dried pulses (legumes) for soaking and cooking yourself, or canned varieties for speed and convenience.

Herbs

A good selection of herbs is important for adding variety to your cooking. Fresh herbs are preferable to dried, but it is essential to have dried ones in stock as a useful back-up. You should store dried basil, thyme, bay leaves, oregano, rosemary, mixed herbs and bouquet garni.

Chillies

These come both fresh and dried and in many colours. The 'hotness' varies so use with caution. The seeds are hottest and are usually discarded. Chilli powder should also be used sparingly. Check whether the powder is pure chilli or a chilli seasoning or blend, which should be milder.

Nuts and seeds

As well as adding protein, vitamins and useful fats to the diet, nuts and seeds add important flavour and texture to vegetarian meals. Make sure that you keep a good supply of nuts such as hazelnuts, pine kernels (nuts) and walnuts. Coconut is useful too.

For your seed collection, have sesame, sun-flower, pumpkin and poppy. Pumpkin seeds in particular are a good source of zinc.

Dried fruits

Currants, raisins, sultanas (golden raisins), dates, apples, apricots, figs, pears, peaches, prunes, paw-paws (papayas), mangoes, figs, bananas and pineapples can all be purchased dried and can be used in lots of different recipes. When buying dried fruits, look for untreated varieties: for example, buy figs that have not been rolled in sugar, and choose unsulphured apricots, if they are available.

Oils and fats

Oils are useful for adding subtle flavourings to foods, so it is a good idea to have a selection in your store-cupboard. Use a light olive oil for cooking and extra-virgin olive oil for salad dressings. Use sunflower oil as a good general-purpose oil. Sesame oil is wonderful in stir-fries; hazelnut and walnut oils are superb in salad dressings. Oils and fats add flavour to foods, and contain important fat-soluble vitamins A, D, E and K. Remember that all fats and oils are high in calories, and that oils are higher in calories than butter or margarine.

Vinegars

Choose three or four vinegars – red or white wine, cider, light malt, tarragon, sherry or balsamic vinegar, to name just a few. Each will add its own character to your recipes.

Mustards

Mustards are made from black, brown or white mustard seeds which are ground and mixed with spices. Meaux mustard is made from mixed mustard seeds and has a grainy texture with a warm, taste. Dijon mustard, made from husked and ground mustard seeds, has a sharp flavour. Its versatility in salads and with barbecues makes it ideal for the vegetarian. German mustard is mild and is best used in Scandinavian and German dishes.

Bottled sauces

Soy sauce is widely used in Eastern cookery and is made from fermented yellow soya beans mixed with wheat, salt, yeast and sugar. Light soy sauce tends to be rather salty, whereas dark soy sauce tends to be sweeter. Teriyaki sauce gives an authentic Japanese flavouring to stir-fries. Black bean and yellow bean sauces add an instant authentic Chinese flavour to stir-fries.

STORING SPICES

Your basic stock of spices should include fresh ginger and garlic, chilli powder, turmeric, paprika, cloves, cardamom, black pepper, ground coriander and ground cumin. The powdered spices will keep very well in airtight containers, while the fresh ginger and garlic will keep for 7-10 days in the refrigerator. Other useful items, to be acquired as your repertoire increases, are cumin seeds (black as well as white), onion seeds, mustard seeds, cloves, cinnamon, dried red chillies, fenugreek, vegetable ghee and garam masala (a mixture of spices that can either be bought ready-made or home-made in quantity for use whenever required).

USING SPICES

You can use spices whole, ground, roasted, fried, or mixed with yogurt to marinate meat and poultry. One spice can alter the flavour of a dish and a combination of several can produce different colours and textures. The quantities of spices given in the recipes are merely a guide. Increase or decrease them as you wish, especially in the cases of salt and chilli powder, which are a matter of taste.

Many of the recipes in this book call for ground spices, which are generally available in supermarkets as well as in Indian and Pakistani grocers. In India whole spices are ground at home, and there is no doubt that freshly ground spices do make a noticeable difference to the taste.

Some recipes require roasted spices. In India, this is done on a *thawa*, but you can use a heavy, ideally cast-iron frying-pan (skillet). No water or oil is needed: the spices are simply dry-roasted whole while the pan is shaken to stop them burning on the bottom of the pan.

Remember that long cooking over a lowish heat will improve the taste of the food as it allows the spices to be absorbed. This is why re-heating dishes the following day is no problem for most Indian food.

USEFUL ORIENTAL INGREDIENTS

Bamboo shoots

These are added for texture, as they have very little flavour. Available in cans, they are a common ingredient in Chinese cooking.

Beansprouts

These are mung bean shoots, which are very nutritious, containing many vitamins. They add crunch to a recipe and are widely available. Do not overcook them, as they wilt and do not add texture to the dish.

Black beans

These are soy beans and are very salty. They can be bought and crushed with salt and then rinsed or used in the form of a ready-made sauce for convenience.

Chinese beans

These long beans may be eaten whole and are very tender. French (green) beans may also be used.

Chinese five-spice powder

An aromatic blend of cinnamon, cloves, star anise, fennel and brown peppercorns. It is often used in marinades.

Chinese leaves

A light green leaf with a sweet flavour. It can be found readily in most supermarkets.

Hoisin sauce

A dark brown, sweet, thick sauce that is widely available. It is made from spices, soy sauce, garlic and chilli and is often served as a dipping sauce.

Lychees

These are worth buying fresh, as they are easy to prepare. Inside the inedible skin is a fragrant white fruit. Lychees are available canned and are a classic ingredient.

Mango

Choose a ripe mango for its sweet, scented flesh. If a mango is underripe when bought, leave it in a sunny place for a few days before using.

Noodles

The Chinese use several varieties of noodle. You will probably find it easier to use the readily available dried varieties, such as egg noodles, which are yellow, rice stick noodles, which are white and very fine, or transparent noodles, which are opaque when dry and turn transparent on cooking. However, cellophane or rice noodles may be used instead.

Oyster sauce

Readily available, this sauce is made from oysters, salt, seasonings and cornflour (cornstarch) and is brown in colour.

Pak choi

Also known as Chinese cabbage, this has a mild, slightly bitter flavour.

Rice vinegar

This has a mild, sweet taste that is quite delicate. It is available in some supermarkets, but if not available use cider vinegar instead.

Rice wine

This is similar to dry sherry in colour, alcohol content and smell, but it is worth buying rice wine for its distinctive flavour.

Sesame oil

This is made from roasted sesame seeds and has an intense flavour. It burns easily and is therefore added at the end of cooking for flavour, and is not used for frying.

Soy sauce

This is widely available, but it is worth buying a good grade of sauce. It is produced in both light and dark varieties – the former is used with fish and vegetables for a lighter colour and flavour, while the latter, being darker, richer, saltier and more intense, is used as a dipping sauce or with strongly flavoured meats.

Star anise

This is an eight-pointed, star-shaped pod with a strong aniseed flavour. The spice is also available ground. If a pod is added to a dish, it should be removed before serving.

Szechuan pepper

This is quite hot and spicy and should be used sparingly. It is red in colour and is readily available.

Tofu (bean curd)

This soya bean paste is available in several forms. The cake variety, which is soft and spongy and a white-grey colour, is used in this book. It is very bland, but adds texture to dishes and is perfect for absorbing all the other flavours in the dish.

Water chestnuts

These are flat and round and can usually only be purchased in cans, already peeled. They add a delicious crunch to dishes and have a sweet flavour.

Yellow beans

Again a soy bean and very salty. Use a variety that is chunky rather than smooth.

Soups & Starters

The soups and starters in this chapter combine a variety of flavours and textures from all over the world. There are thicker soups, thin clear consommés and soups to appeal to vegetarians. The range of soups include thick and creamy winter warmers and light and spicy oriental recpies. Many have been chosen because of their nutritional content and may be eaten as part of a low-fat diet. All, however, can be eaten as starters or as a light snack. With the addition of other types of starters, you will find something to suit every taste – and all are delicious.

All of these recipes are easy to prepare and appetizing. They are colourful and flavoursome, providing an excellent beginning to any dinner party or just for an everyday snack. Depending on the main course, whet your guests' appetite with a tasty Dhal Soup, Prawn Omelette or oriental Thai Chicken Noodle Soup. All of these dishes are sure to get your meal off to the right start.

Thai Chicken Noodle Soup

Serves 4–6

INGREDIENTS

1 sheet of dried egg noodles from a 250 g/9 oz pack
1 tbsp oil
4 skinless, boneless chicken thighs, diced
1 bunch spring onions (scallions), sliced

2 garlic cloves, chopped
2 cm/³/4 inch piece fresh ginger root, finely chopped
850 ml/1¹/2 pints/3³/4 cups chicken stock
200 ml/7 fl oz/scant 1 cup coconut milk

3 tsp red Thai curry paste
3 tbsp peanut butter
2 tbsp light soy sauce
1 small red (bell) pepper, chopped
60 g/2 oz/¹/2 cup frozen peas
salt and pepper

1 Put the noodles in a shallow dish and soak in boiling water following the instructions on the packet.

2 Heat the oil in a large saucepan or wok, add the chicken, and fry for 5 minutes, stirring until lightly browned. Add the white part of the spring onions (scallions), the garlic and ginger and fry for 2 minutes, stirring. Add the stock, coconut milk, curry paste, peanut butter and soy sauce. Season with salt and

pepper to taste. Bring to the boil, stirring, then simmer for 8 minutes, stirring occasionally. Add the red (bell) pepper, peas and green spring onion (scallion) tops and cook for 2 minutes.

3 Add the drained noodles and heat through. Spoon into individual bowls and serve with a spoon and fork.

VARIATION

Green Thai curry paste can be used instead of red curry paste for a less fiery flavour.

Chicken & Pasta Broth

Serves 6

INGREDIENTS

350 g/12 oz boneless chicken breasts	850 ml/1¹/₂ pints/3³/₄ cups chicken	Parmesan cheese (optional) and
2 tbsp sunflower oil	stock	crusty bread, to serve
1 medium onion, diced	2 tsp dried mixed herbs	
250 g/9 oz/1¹/₂ cups carrots, diced	125 g/4¹/₂ oz/1 cup small pasta shapes	
250 g/9 oz cauliflower florets	salt and pepper	

1 Using a sharp knife, finely dice the chicken, discarding any skin.

2 Heat the oil in a large saucepan and quickly sauté the chicken and vegetables until they are lightly coloured.

3 Stir in the stock and herbs. Bring to the boil and add the pasta shapes. Return to the boil, cover and simmer for 10 minutes, stirring occasionally to prevent the pasta shapes sticking together.

4 Season with salt and pepper to taste and sprinkle with Parmesan cheese, if using. Serve with fresh crusty bread.

COOK'S TIP

You can use any small pasta shapes for this soup – try conchigliette or ditalini or even spaghetti broken up into small pieces. To make a fun soup for children you could add animal-shaped or alphabet pasta.

VARIATION

Broccoli florets can be used to replace the cauliflower florets. Substitute 2 tablespoons chopped fresh mixed herbs for the dried mixed herbs.

Cream of Chicken Soup

Serves 4

INGREDIENTS

60 g/2 oz/4 tbsp unsalted butter
1 large onion, peeled and chopped
300 g/10½ oz cooked chicken, shredded finely

600 ml/1 pint/2½ cups chicken stock
1 tbsp chopped fresh tarragon
150 ml/¼ pint/⅔ cup double (heavy) cream

salt and pepper
fresh tarragon leaves, to garnish
deep fried croûtons, to serve

1 Melt the butter in a large saucepan and fry the onion for 3 minutes.

2 Add the chicken to the pan with 300 ml/ ½ pint/1¼ cups of the chicken stock.

3 Bring to the boil and simmer for 20 minutes. Allow to cool, then liquidize the soup.

4 Add the remainder of the stock and season with salt and pepper.

5 Add the chopped tarragon, pour the soup into a tureen or individual serving bowls and add a swirl of cream.

6 Garnish the soup with fresh tarragon and serve with deep fried croûtons.

VARIATION

To make garlic croûtons, crush 3–4 garlic cloves in a pestle and mortar and add to the oil.

VARIATION

If you can't find fresh tarragon, freeze-dried tarragon makes a good substitute. Single (light) cream can be used instead of the double (heavy) cream.

Cream of Chicken & Tomato Soup

Serves 2

INGREDIENTS

60 g/2 oz/4 tbsp unsalted butter
1 large onion, chopped
500 g/1 lb 2 oz chicken, shredded
    very finely
600 ml/1 pint/2½ cups chicken stock

6 medium tomatoes, chopped finely
pinch of bicarbonate of soda
    (baking soda)
1 tbsp caster (superfine) sugar

150 ml/1¼ pint/⅔ cup double
    (heavy) cream
salt and pepper
fresh basil leaves, to garnish
croûtons, to serve

1 Melt the butter in a large saucepan and fry the onion and shredded chicken for 5 minutes.

2 Add 300 ml/½ pint/1¼ cups chicken stock to the pan, with the tomatoes and bicarbonate of soda (baking soda).

3 Bring the soup to the boil and simmer for 20 minutes.

4 Allow the soup to cool, then blend in a food processor.

5 Return the soup to the pan, add the remaining chicken stock, season and add the sugar. Pour the soup into a tureen and add a swirl of double (heavy) cream. Serve the soup with croûtons and garnish with basil.

COOK'S TIP

For a healthier version of this soup, use single (light) cream instead of the double (heavy) cream and omit the sugar.

VARIATION

For an Italian-style soup, add 1 tbsp chopped fresh basil with the stock in step 2. Alternatively, add ½ tsp curry powder or chilli powder to make a spicier version of this soup.

Brown Lentil Soup with Pasta

Serves 4

INGREDIENTS

4 rashers streaky bacon, cut into small squares	50 g/1¾ oz/¼ cup farfalline or spaghetti broken into small pieces	1.2 litres/2 pints/5 cups hot ham or vegetable stock
1 onion, chopped		2 tbsp chopped, fresh mint
2 garlic cloves, crushed	1 x 420 g/14½ oz can brown lentils, drained	
2 sticks celery, chopped		

1 Place the bacon in a large frying pan (skillet) together with the onions, garlic and celery. Dry fry for 4–5 minutes, stirring, until the onion is tender and the bacon is just beginning to brown.

2 Add the farfalline or spaghetti pieces to the pan (skillet) and cook, stirring, for about 1 minute to coat the pasta in the oil.

3 Add the lentils and the stock and bring to the boil. Reduce the heat and leave to simmer for 12–15 minutes or until the pasta is tender.

4 Remove the pan (skillet) from the heat and stir in the chopped fresh mint.

5 Transfer the soup to warm soup bowls and serve immediately.

VARIATION

Any type of pasta can be used in this recipe, try fusilli, conchiglie or rigatoni, if you prefer.

COOK'S TIP

If you prefer to use dried lentils, add the stock before the pasta and cook for 1–1¼ hours until the lentils are tender. Add the pasta and cook for a further 12–15 minutes.

Vegetable Soup with Cannelini Beans

Serves 4

INGREDIENTS

1 small aubergine (eggplant)
2 large tomatoes
1 potato, peeled
1 carrot, peeled
1 leek
420 g/14½ oz can cannelini beans

850 ml/1½ pints/3¾ cups hot
vegetable or chicken stock
2 tsp dried basil
10 g/½ oz dried porcini mushrooms,
soaked for 10 minutes in
enough warm water to cover

50 g/1¾ oz/¼ cup vermicelli
3 tbsp pesto (see page 110 or use
shop bought)
freshly grated Parmesan cheese,
to serve (optional)

1 Slice the aubergine (eggplant) into rings about 10 mm/½ inch thick, then cut each ring into 4.

2 Cut the tomatoes and potato into small dice. Cut the carrot into sticks, about 2.5 cm/1 inch long and cut the leek into rings.

3 Place the cannelini beans and their liquid in a large saucepan. Add the aubergine (eggplant), tomatoes, potatoes, carrot and leek, stirring to mix.

4 Add the stock to the pan and bring to the boil. Reduce the heat and leave to simmer for 15 minutes.

5 Add the basil, dried mushrooms, their soaking liquid and the vermicelli and simmer for 5 minutes or until all of the vegetables are tender.

6 Remove the pan from the heat and stir in the pesto.

7 Serve with freshly grated Parmesan cheese.

COOK'S TIP

Porcini are a wild mushroom grown in southern Italy. When dried and rehydrated they have a very intense flavour, so although they are expensive to buy only a small amount are required to add flavour to soups or risottos.

Creamy Tomato Soup

Serves 4

INGREDIENTS

50 g/1¾ oz/3 tbsp butter
700 g/1 lb 9oz ripe tomatoes,
  preferably plum, roughly
  chopped

850 ml/1½ pints/3¾ hot
  vegetable stock
150 ml/ 5 fl oz/2/3 cup milk or
  single (light) cream

50 g/1¾ oz/¼ cup ground
  almonds
1 tsp sugar
2 tbsp shredded basil leaves
salt and pepper

1 Melt the butter in a large saucepan. Add the tomatoes and cook for 5 minutes until the skins start to wrinkle. Season to taste with salt and pepper.

2 Add the stock to the pan, bring to the boil, cover and simmer for 10 minutes.

3 Meanwhile, under a preheated grill (broiler), lightly toast the ground almonds until they are golden-brown. This will take only 1-2 minutes, so watch them closely.

4 Remove the soup from the heat and place in a food processor and blend the mixture to form a smooth consistency. Alternatively, mash the soup with a potato masher.

5 Pass the soup through a sieve to remove any tomato skin or pips.

6 Place the soup in the pan and return to the heat. Stir in the milk or cream, ground almonds and sugar. Warm the soup through and add the shredded basil just before serving.

7 Transfer the creamy tomato soup to warm soup bowls and serve hot.

VARIATION

Very fine breadcrumbs can be used instead of the ground almonds, if you prefer. Toast them in the same way as the almonds and add with the milk or cream in step 6.

Tuscan Onion Soup

Serves 4

INGREDIENTS

50 g/1¾ oz pancetta ham, diced
1 tbsp olive oil
4 large white onions, sliced
thinly in rings

3 garlic cloves, chopped
850 ml/1¾ pints/3¾ cups hot
chicken or ham stock
4 slices ciabatta or other

Italian bread
50 g/1¾ oz/3 tbsp butter
75 g/2¾ oz Gruyère or Cheddar
salt and pepper

1 Dry fry the pancetta in a large saucepan for 3–4 minutes until it begins to brown. Remove the pancetta from the pan and set aside until required.

2 Add the oil to the pan and cook the onions and garlic over a high heat for 4 minutes. Reduce the heat, cover and cook for 15 minutes until lightly caramelized.

3 Add the stock to the saucepan and bring to the boil. Reduce the heat and leave the mixture to simmer, covered, for about 10 minutes.

4 Toast the slices of ciabatta on both sides, under a preheated grill (broiler), for 2–3 minutes or until golden. Spread the ciabatta with butter and top with the Gruyère or Cheddar cheese. Cut the bread into bite-size pieces.

5 Add the reserved pancetta to the soup and season to taste with salt and pepper. Pour into 4 soup bowls and top with the toasted bread.

COOK'S TIP

Pancetta is similar to bacon, but it is air- and salt-cured for about 6 months. Pancetta is available from most delicatessens and some large supermarkets. If you cannot obtain pancetta use unsmoked bacon instead.

Green Soup

Serves 4

INGREDIENTS

1 tbsp olive oil	700 ml/1¼ pint/scant 3 cups	80 g/3 oz bunch watercress
1 onion, chopped	vegetable or chicken stock	125 g/4½ oz green (dwarf)
1 garlic clove, chopped	1 small cucumber or ½ large	beans, trimmed and halved
200 g/7 oz potato, peeled and	cucumber, cut into chunks	in length
cut into 2.5 cm/1 inch cubes		salt and pepper

1 Heat the oil in a large pan and fry the onion and garlic for 3–4 minutes or until softened. Add the cubed potato and fry for a further 2–3 minutes.

2 Stir in the stock, bring to the boil and leave to simmer for 5 minutes.

3 Add the cucumber to the pan and cook for a further 3 minutes or until the potatoes are tender. Test by inserting the tip of a knife into the potato cubes – it should pass through easily.

4 Add the watercress and allow to wilt. Then place the soup in a food processor and blend until smooth. Alternatively, before adding the watercress, mash the soup with a potato masher and push through a sieve, then chop the watercress finely and stir into the soup.

5 Bring a small pan of water to the boil and steam the beans for 3–4 minutes or until tender.

6 Add the beans to the soup, season and warm.

VARIATION

Try using 125 g/4½ oz mangetout (snow peas) instead of the beans, if you prefer.

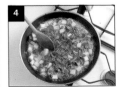

Orange, Thyme & Pumpkin Soup

Serves 4

INGREDIENTS

2 tbsp olive oil

2 medium onions, chopped

2 cloves garlic, chopped

900 g/2 lb pumpkin, peeled and
cut into 2.5 cm/1 inch chunks

1.5 litres /2¾ pints/6¼ cups
boiling vegetable or
chicken stock

finely grated rind and juice
of 1 orange

3 tbsp fresh thyme, stalks
removed

150 ml/5 fl oz/2/3 cup milk

salt and pepper

crusty bread, to serve

1 Heat the olive oil in a large saucepan. Add the onions to the pan and cook for 3–4 minutes or until softened. Add the garlic and pumpkin and cook for a further 2 minutes, stirring well.

2 Add the boiling vegetable or chicken stock, orange rind and juice and 2 tablespoons of the thyme to the pan. Leave to simmer, covered, for 20 minutes or until the pumpkin is tender.

3 Place the mixture in a food processor and

blend until smooth. Alternatively, mash the mixture with a potato masher until smooth. Season to taste with salt and pepper.

4 Return the soup to the saucepan and add the milk. Reheat the soup for 3–4 minutes or until it is piping hot but not boiling. Sprinkle with the remaining fresh thyme just before serving.

5 Divide the soup among 4 warm soup bowls and serve with lots of fresh crusty bread.

COOK'S TIP

Pumpkins are usually large vegetables. To make things a little easier, ask the greengrocer to cut a chunk off for you. Alternatively, make double the quantity and freeze the soup for up to 3 months.

Minestrone

Serves 4

INGREDIENTS

1 tbsp olive oil

100 g/3½ oz pancetta ham, diced

2 medium onions, chopped

2 cloves garlic, crushed

1 potato, peeled and cut into 10 mm/½ inch cubes

1 carrot, scraped and cut into chunks

1 leek, sliced into rings

¼ green cabbage, shredded

1 stick celery, chopped

1 x 450 g/1 lb can chopped tomatoes

1 x 210 g/7 oz can flageolet (small navy) beans, drained and rinsed

600 ml/1 pint/2½ cups hot ham or chicken stock diluted with

600 ml/1 pint/2½ cups boiling water

bouquet garni (2 bay leaves, 2 sprigs rosemary and 2 sprigs thyme, tied together)

salt and pepper

freshly grated Parmesan cheese, to serve

1 Heat the oil in a large saucepan. Add the diced pancetta, chopped onions and garlic and fry for about 5 minutes or until the onions are soft and golden.

2 Add the prepared potato, carrot, leek, cabbage and celery to the saucepan. Cook for a further 2 minutes, stirring frequently, to coat all of the vegetables in the oil.

3 Add the tomatoes, flageolet (small navy) beans, hot ham or chicken stock and bouquet garni to the pan, stirring to mix. Leave the soup to simmer, covered, for 15–20 minutes or until all of the vegetables are just tender.

4 Remove the bouquet garni, season with salt and pepper to taste and serve with plenty of freshly grated Parmesan.

VARIATION

Any combination of vegetables will work equally well in this soup.

For a special minestrone, try adding 100 g/3½ oz Parma ham (prosciutto), shredded, in step 1.

Calabrian Mushroom Soup

Serves 4

INGREDIENTS

2 tbsp olive oil	300 ml/$\frac{1}{2}$ pint/1$\frac{1}{4}$ cup milk	50 g/1$\frac{3}{4}$ oz/3 tbsp butter, melted
1 onion, chopped	850 ml1$\frac{1}{2}$ pints/3$\frac{3}{4}$ cups hot	2 garlic cloves, crushed
450g/1 lb mixed mushrooms,	vegetable stock	75 g/2$\frac{3}{4}$ oz Gruyère cheese,
such as ceps, oyster	8 slices of rustic bread or	finely grated
and button	French stick	salt and pepper

1 Heat the oil in a large frying pan (skillet) and cook the onion for 3–4 minutes or until soft and golden.

2 Wipe each mushroom with a damp cloth and cut any large mushrooms into smaller, bite-size pieces.

3 Add the mushrooms to the pan, stirring quickly to coat them in the oil.

4 Add the milk to the pan, bring to the boil, cover and leave to simmer for about 5 minutes. Gradually stir in the hot vegetable stock.

5 Under a preheated grill (broiler), toast the bread on both sides until golden.

6 Mix together the garlic and butter and spoon generously over the toast.

7 Place the toast in the bottom of a large tureen or divide it among 4 individual serving bowls and pour over the hot soup. Top with the grated Gruyère cheese and serve at once.

COOK'S TIP

Mushrooms absorb liquid, which can lessen the flavour and affect cooking properties. Wipe them with a damp cloth rather than rinsing them in water.

VARIATION

Supermarkets stock a wide variety of wild mushrooms. If you prefer, use a combination of cultivated and wild mushrooms.

Chicken & Sweetcorn Soup

Serves 4

INGREDIENTS

450 g/1 lb boned chicken
  breasts, cut into strips
1.2 litres/2 pints/5 cups
  chicken stock

150 ml/$^{1}/_{4}$ pint/$^{5}/_{8}$ cup double
  (heavy) cream
100 g/3$^{1}/_{2}$ oz/$^{3}/_{4}$ cup
  dried vermicelli
1 tbsp cornflour (cornstarch)

3 tbsp milk
175 g/6 oz sweetcorn
  (corn) kernels
salt and pepper

1 Put the chicken, stock and cream into a large saucepan and bring to the boil over a low heat. Reduce the heat slightly and simmer for about 20 minutes. Season with salt and pepper to taste.

2 Meanwhile, cook the vermicelli in lightly salted boiling water for 10-12 minutes, until just tender. Drain the pasta and keep warm.

3 Mix together the cornflour (cornstarch) and milk to make a smooth paste, then stir into the soup until thickened.

4 Add the sweetcorn (corn) and pasta to the pan and heat through.

5 Transfer the soup to a warm tureen or individual soup bowls and serve immediately.

COOK'S TIP

If you are short of time, buy ready-cooked chicken, remove any skin and cut it into slices.

VARIATION

For crab and sweetcorn soup, substitute 450 g/1 lb cooked crabmeat for the chicken breasts. Flake the crabmeat well before adding it to the saucepan and reduce the cooking time by 10 minutes. For a Chinese-style soup, substitute egg noodles for the vermicelli and use canned, creamed sweetcorn (corn).

Mussel & Potato Soup

Serves 4

INGREDIENTS

750 g/1 lb 10 oz mussels
2 tbsp olive oil
100 g/3^1/2 oz/7 tbsp unsalted
    butter
2 slices rindless, fatty bacon,
    chopped
1 onion, chopped
2 garlic cloves, crushed

60 g/2 oz/^{1}/2 cup plain
    (all purpose) flour
450 g/1 lb potatoes, thinly
    sliced
100 g/3^1/2 oz/^{3}/4 cup
    dried conchigliette
300 ml/^{1}/2 pint/1^1/4 cups
    double (heavy) cream

1 tbsp lemon juice
2 egg yolks
salt and pepper

TO GARNISH:
2 tbsp finely chopped fresh
    parsley
lemon wedges

1 Debeard the mussels and scrub them under cold water for 5 minutes. Discard any mussels that do not close immediately when sharply tapped.

2 Bring a large pan of water to the boil, add the mussels, oil and a little pepper and cook until the mussels open.

3 Drain the mussels, reserving the cooking liquid. Discard any mussels that are closed. Remove the mussels from their shells.

4 Melt the butter in a large saucepan and cook the bacon, onion and garlic for 4 minutes. Stir in the flour, then 1.2 litres/ 2 pints/5 cups of the reserved cooking liquid.

5 Add the potatoes to the pan and simmer for 5 minutes. Add the conchigliette and simmer for a further 10 minutes.

6 Add the cream and lemon juice, season to taste, then add the mussels to the pan.

7 Blend the egg yolks with 1-2 tbsp of the remaining cooking liquid, stir into the pan and cook for 4 minutes.

8 Ladle the soup into 4 warm individual soup bowls, garnish with the chopped fresh parsley and lemon wedges and serve.

Italian Fish Soup

Serves 4

INGREDIENTS

60 g/2 oz/4 tbsp butter
450 g/1 lb assorted fish fillets,
    such as red mullet and
    snapper
450 g/1 lb prepared seafood,
    such as squid and prawns
    (shrimp)
225 g/8 oz fresh crabmeat
1 large onion, sliced

25 g/1 oz/¼ cup plain
    (all purpose) flour
1.2 litres/2 pints/5 cups fish
    stock
100 g/3½ oz/¾ cup dried
    pasta shapes, such as
    ditalini or elbow macaroni
1 tbsp anchovy essence

grated rind and juice of
    1 orange
50 ml/2 fl oz/½ cup dry
    sherry
300 ml/½ pint/1¼ cups
    double (heavy) cream
salt and black pepper
crusty brown bread, to serve

1 Melt the butter in a
large saucepan and
cook the fish fillets,
seafood, crabmeat and
onion over a low heat for
6 minutes.

2 Stir the flour into the
mixture.

3 Gradually add the fish
stock and bring to the
boil, stirring constantly.
Reduce the heat and
simmer for 30 minutes.

4 Add the pasta and cook
for 10 minutes.

5 Stir in the anchovy
essence, orange rind,
orange juice, sherry and
double (heavy) cream.
Season to taste.

6 Heat the soup until
completely warmed
through. Transfer the soup
to a tureen or to warm soup
bowls and serve with crusty
brown bread.

COOK'S TIP

*The heads, tails, trimmings
and bones of most non-oily
fish can be used to make fish
stock. Simmer 900 g/2 lb
fish pieces in a pan with
150 ml/5 fl oz white wine,
1 chopped onion, 1 sliced
carrot, 1 sliced celery stick
(stalk), 4 black peppercorns,
1 bouquet garni and 1.75
litres/3 pints/7½ cups water
for 30 minutes, then strain.*

Clear Chicken & Egg Soup

Serves 4

INGREDIENTS

1 tsp salt	1 leek, sliced	1 tbsp dry sherry
1 tbsp rice wine vinegar	125 g/4¹/₂ oz broccoli florets	dash of chilli sauce
4 eggs	125 g/4¹/₂ oz/1 cup shredded	chilli powder, to garnish
850 ml/1¹/₂ pints/3³/₄ cups	cooked chicken	
chicken stock	2 open-cap mushrooms, sliced	

1 Bring a large saucepan of water to the boil and add the salt and rice wine vinegar. Reduce the heat so that it is just simmering and carefully break the eggs into the water, one at a time. Poach the eggs for 1 minute. Remove the poached eggs with a slotted spoon and set aside.

2 Bring the stock to the boil in a separate pan and add the leek, broccoli, chicken, mushrooms and sherry and season with chilli sauce to taste. Cook for 10–15 minutes.

3 Add the poached eggs to the soup and cook for a further 2 minutes. Carefully transfer the soup and poached eggs to 4 individual soup bowls. Dust with a little chilli powder to garnish and serve immediately.

COOK'S TIP

You could use 4 dried Chinese mushrooms, rehydrated according to the packet instructions, instead of the open-cap mushrooms, if you prefer.

VARIATION

You could substitute 125 g/4¹/₂ oz fresh or canned crabmeat or the same quantity of fresh or frozen cooked prawns (shrimp) for the chicken, if desired.

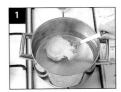

Curried Chicken & Sweetcorn (Corn) Soup

Serves 4

INGREDIENTS
---

175 g/6 oz can sweetcorn
  (corn), drained
850 ml/1 1/2 pints/3 3/4 cups
  chicken stock
350 g/12 oz cooked, lean
  chicken, cut into strips

16 baby corn cobs
1 tsp Chinese curry powder
1-cm/1/2-inch piece fresh root
  ginger (ginger root), grated

3 tbsp light soy sauce
2 tbsp chopped chives

1 Place the canned
sweetcorn (corn) in a
food processor, together
with 150 ml/1/4 pint/2/3 cup
of the chicken stock and
process until the mixture
forms a smooth purée.

2 Pass the sweetcorn
purée through a fine
sieve, pressing with the
back of a spoon to remove
any husks.

3 Pour the remaining
chicken stock into a

large pan and add the strips
of cooked chicken. Stir in
the sweetcorn (corn) purée.

4 Add the baby corn cobs
and bring the soup to
the boil. Boil the soup for
10 minutes.

5 Add the curry powder,
ginger and soy sauce
and cook for 10–15
minutes. Stir in the chives.

6 Transfer the soup to
warm bowls and serve.

COOK'S TIP

*Prepare the soup up to 24
hours in advance without
adding the chicken, let cool,
cover and store in the
refrigerator. Add the chicken
and heat the soup through
thoroughly before serving.*

Hot & Sour Soup

Serves 4

INGREDIENTS

2 tbsp cornflour (cornstarch)
4 tbsp water
2 tbsp light soy sauce
3 tbsp rice wine vinegar
$1/2$ tsp ground black pepper
1 small fresh red chilli,
    finely chopped

1 egg
2 tbsp vegetable oil
1 onion, chopped
850 ml/$1^{1}/_2$ pints/$3^{3}/_4$ cups
    chicken or beef consommé
1 open-cap mushroom, sliced

50 g/$1^{3}/_4$ oz skinless chicken
    breast, cut into very thin
    strips
1 tsp sesame oil

1 Blend the cornflour (cornstarch) with the water to form a smooth paste. Add the soy sauce, rice wine vinegar, pepper and chilli and mix together.

2 Break the egg into a separate bowl and beat well.

3 Heat the oil in a preheated wok and fry the onion for 1–2 minutes.

4 Stir in the consommé, mushroom and chicken and bring to the boil. Cook for 15 minutes or until the chicken is tender.

5 Pour the cornflour (cornstarch) mixture into the soup and cook, stirring, until it thickens.

6 As you are stirring, gradually drizzle the egg into the soup, to create threads of egg.

7 Sprinkle with the sesame oil and serve immediately.

COOK'S TIP

Make sure that the egg is poured in very slowly and that you stir continuously to create threads of egg and not large pieces.

Beef & Vegetable Noodle Soup

Serves 4

| INGREDIENTS |

225 g/8 oz lean beef
1 garlic clove, crushed
2 spring onions (scallions), chopped
3 tbsp soy sauce

1 tsp sesame oil
225 g/8 oz egg noodles
850 ml/1 1/2 pints/3 3/4 cups beef stock
3 baby corn cobs, sliced

1/2 leek, shredded
125 g/4 1/2 oz broccoli, cut into florets (flowerets)
pinch of chilli powder

1 Using a sharp knife, cut the beef into thin strips and place them in a shallow glass bowl.

2 Add the garlic, spring onions (scallions), soy sauce and sesame oil and mix together well, turning the beef to coat. Cover and leave to marinate in the refrigerator for 30 minutes.

3 Cook the noodles in a saucepan of boiling water for 3–4 minutes. Drain the noodles thoroughly and set aside until required.

4 Put the beef stock in a large saucepan and bring to the boil.

5 Add the beef, together with the marinade, the baby corn, leek and broccoli. Cover and leave to simmer over a low heat for 7–10 minutes, or until the beef and vegetables are tender and cooked through.

6 Stir in the noodles and chilli powder and cook for a further 2–3 minutes. Transfer to bowls and serve immediately.

COOK'S TIP

Vary the vegetables used, or use those to hand. If preferred, use a few drops of chilli sauce instead of chilli powder, but remember it is very hot!

Lamb & Rice Soup

Serves 4

INGREDIENTS

150 g/5¹/₂ oz lean lamb
50 g/1³/₄ oz/¹/₄ cup rice
850 ml/1¹/₂ pints/3³/₄ cups
    lamb stock

1 leek, sliced
1 garlic clove, thinly sliced
2 tsp light soy sauce
1 tsp rice wine vinegar

1 medium open-cap
    mushroom, thinly sliced
salt

1 Using a sharp knife, trim any fat from the lamb and cut the meat into thin strips. Set aside until required.

2 Bring a large pan of lightly salted water to the boil and add the rice. Bring back to the boil, stir once, reduce the heat and cook for 10–15 minutes, until tender. Drain, rinse under cold running water, drain again and set aside until required.

3 Meanwhile, put the lamb stock in a large saucepan and bring to the boil.

4 Add the lamb strips, leek, garlic, soy sauce and rice wine vinegar to the stock in the pan. Reduce the heat, cover and leave to simmer for 10 minutes, or until the lamb is tender and cooked through.

5 Add the mushroom slices and the rice to the pan and cook for a further 2–3 minutes, or until the mushroom is completely cooked through.

6 Ladle the soup into 4 individual warmed soup bowls and serve immediately.

COOK'S TIP

Use a few dried Chinese mushrooms, rehydrated according to the packet instructions and chopped, as an alternative to the open-cap mushroom. Add the Chinese mushrooms with the lamb in step 4.

Crab & Ginger Soup

Serves 4

INGREDIENTS

1 carrot, chopped
1 leek, chopped
1 bay leaf
850 ml/1¹/₂ pints/3³/₄ cups
    fish stock

2 medium-sized cooked crabs
2.5-cm/1-inch piece fresh root
    ginger (ginger root), grated
1 tsp light soy sauce

¹/₂ tsp ground star anise
salt and pepper

1 Put the carrot, leek, bay leaf and stock into a large pan and bring to the boil. Reduce the heat, cover and simmer for 10 minutes, or until the vegetables are nearly tender.

2 Meanwhile, remove all of the meat from the cooked crabs. Break off the claws, break the joints and remove the meat (you may require a fork or skewer for this). Add the crabmeat to the saucepan of fish stock.

3 Add the ginger, soy sauce and star anise to the fish stock and bring to the boil. Leave to simmer for about 10 minutes, or until the vegetables are tender and the crab is heated through. Season.

4 Ladle the soup into warmed serving bowls and garnish with crab claws. Serve at once.

COOK'S TIP

If fresh crabmeat is unavailable, use drained canned crabmeat or thawed frozen crabmeat instead.

COOK'S TIP

To prepare cooked crab, loosen the meat from the shell by banging the back of the underside with a clenched fist. Stand the crab on its edge with the shell towards you. Force the shell from the body with your thumbs. Twist off the legs and claws and remove the meat. Twist off the tail; discard. Remove and discard the gills. Cut the body in half along the centre and remove the meat. Scoop the brown meat from the shell with a spoon.

Chinese Cabbage Soup

Serves 4

INGREDIENTS

450 g/1 lb pak choi
600 ml/1 pint/2¹/₂ cups
   vegetable stock
1 tbsp rice wine vinegar

1 tbsp light soy sauce
1 tbsp caster (superfine) sugar
1 tbsp dry sherry
1 fresh red chilli, thinly sliced

1 tbsp cornflour (cornstarch)
2 tbsp water

1 Trim the stems of the pak choi and shred the leaves.

2 Heat the stock in a large saucepan. Add the pak choi and cook for 10–15 minutes.

3 Mix the rice wine vinegar, soy sauce, sugar and sherry together. Add this mixture to the stock, together with the sliced chilli. Bring to the boil, lower the heat and cook for 2–3 minutes.

4 Blend the cornflour (cornstarch) with the water to form a smooth paste. Gradually stir the cornflour (cornstarch) mixture into the soup. Cook, stirring constantly, until it thickens. Cook for a further 4–5 minutes. Ladle the soup into individual warm serving bowls and serve immediately.

VARIATION

Boil about 2 tbsp rice in lightly salted water until tender. Drain and spoon into the base of the soup bowls. Ladle the soup over the rice and serve immediately.

COOK'S TIP

Pak choi, *also known as bok choi or spoon cabbage, has long, white leaf stalks and fleshy, spoon-shaped, shiny green leaves. There are a number of varieties available, which differ mainly in size rather than flavour.*

Coconut & Crab Soup

Serves 4

INGREDIENTS

1 tbsp groundnut oil

2 tbsp Thai red curry paste

1 red (bell) pepper, deseeded and sliced

600 ml/1 pint/2½ cups coconut milk

600 ml/1 pint/2½ cups fish stock

2 tbsp fish sauce

225 g/8 oz canned or fresh white crab meat

225 g/8 oz fresh or frozen crab claws

2 tbsp chopped fresh coriander (cilantro)

3 spring onions (scallions), trimmed and sliced

1 Heat the oil in a large preheated wok.

2 Add the red curry paste and red (bell) pepper to the wok and stir-fry for 1 minute.

3 Add the coconut milk, fish stock and fish sauce to the wok and bring to the boil.

4 Add the crab meat, crab claws, coriander (cilantro) and spring onions (scallions) to the wok. Stir the mixture well and heat thoroughly for 2–3 minutes.

5 Transfer the soup to warm bowls and serve hot.

COOK'S TIP

Coconut milk adds a sweet and creamy flavour to the dish. It is available in powdered form or in tins ready to use.

COOK'S TIP

Clean the wok after each use by washing it with water, using a mild detergent if necessary, and a soft cloth or brush. Do not scrub or use any abrasive cleaner as this will scratch the surface. Dry thoroughly with paper towels or over a low heat, then wipe the surface all over with a little oil. This forms a sealing layer to protect the surface of the wok from moisture and prevents it rusting.

Chilli Fish Soup

Serves 4

INGREDIENTS

15 g/½ oz Chinese dried mushrooms
2 tbsp sunflower oil
1 onion, sliced
100 g/3½ oz/1½ cups mangetout
(snow peas)

100 g/3½ oz/1½ cups bamboo
shoots
3 tbsp sweet chilli sauce
1.2 litres/2 pints/5 cups fish or
vegetable stock

3 tbsp light soy sauce
2 tbsp fresh coriander (cilantro)
450 g/1 lb cod fillet, skinned and
cubed

1 Place the mushrooms in a large bowl. Pour over enough boiling water to cover and leave to stand for 5 minutes. Drain the mushrooms thoroughly. Using a sharp knife, roughly chop the mushrooms.

2 Heat the sunflower oil in a preheated wok. Add the onion to the wok and stir-fry for 5 minutes, or until softened.

3 Add the mangetout (snow peas), bamboo shoots, chilli sauce, stock and soy sauce to the wok and bring to the boil.

4 Add the coriander (cilantro) and cubed fish to the wok. Leave to simmer for 5 minutes or until the fish is cooked through.

5 Transfer the soup to warm bowls, garnish with extra coriander (cilantro) if wished and serve hot.

VARIATION

Cod is used in this recipe as it is a meaty white fish. For real luxury, use monkfish tail instead.

COOK'S TIP

There are many different varieties of dried mushrooms, but shiitake are best. They are not cheap, but a small amount will go a long way.

Sweet Potato & Onion Soup

Serves 4

INGREDIENTS

2 tbsp vegetable oil
900 g/2 lb sweet potatoes, diced
1 carrot, diced
2 onions, sliced
2 garlic cloves, crushed

600 ml/1 pint/2½ cups vegetable
  stock
300 ml/½ pint/1¼ cups
  unsweetened orange juice
225 ml/8 fl oz/1 cup natural yogurt

2 tbsp chopped fresh coriander
  (cilantro)
salt and pepper
TO GARNISH:
coriander (cilantro) sprigs
orange rind

1 Heat the vegetable oil in a large saucepan and add the diced sweet potatoes and carrot, sliced onions and garlic. Sauté gently for 5 minutes, stirring constantly.

2 Pour in the vegetable stock and orange juice and bring them to the boil.

3 Reduce the heat to a simmer, cover the saucepan and cook the vegetables for 20 minutes or until the sweet potato and carrot cubes are tender.

4 Transfer the mixture to a food processor or blender in batches and process for 1 minute until puréed. Return the purée to the rinsed-out saucepan.

5 Stir in the natural yogurt and chopped coriander (cilantro) and season to taste. Serve the soup garnished with coriander (cilantro) sprigs and orange rind.

COOK'S TIP

This soup can be chilled before serving, if preferred. If chilling it, stir the yogurt into the dish just before serving. Serve in chilled bowls.

Indian Potato & Pea Soup

Serves 4

INGREDIENTS

2 tbsp vegetable oil	1 tsp ground coriander	100 g/3½ oz frozen peas
225 g/8 oz floury (mealy)	1 tsp ground cumin	4 tbsp natural yogurt
potatoes, diced	900 ml/1½ pints/3¾cups	salt and pepper
1 large onion, chopped	vegetable stock	chopped fresh coriander
2 garlic cloves, crushed	1 red chilli, chopped	(cilantro), to garnish
1 tsp garam masala		

1 Heat the vegetable oil in a large saucepan and add the diced potatoes, onion and garlic. Sauté gently for about 5 minutes, stirring constantly.

2 Add the ground spices and cook for 1 minute, stirring all the time.

3 Stir in the vegetable stock and chopped red chilli and bring the mixture to the boil. Reduce the heat, cover the pan and simmer for 20 minutes until the potatoes begin to break down.

4 Add the peas and cook for a further 5 minutes. Stir in the yogurt and season to taste.

5 Pour into warmed soup bowls, garnish with chopped fresh coriander (cilantro) and serve hot with warm bread.

COOK'S TIP

Potatoes blend perfectly with spices, this soup being no exception. For an authentic Indian dish, serve this soup with warm naan bread.

VARIATION

For slightly less heat, deseed the chilli before adding it to the soup. Always wash your hands after handling chillies as they contain volatile oils that can irritate the skin and make your eyes burn if you touch your face.

Potato, Cabbage & Chorizo Soup

Serves 4

INGREDIENTS

2 tbsp olive oil	1 litre/1³/₄ pints/4¹/₂ cups pork or	50 g/1³/₄ oz chorizo sausage,
3 large potatoes, cubed	vegetable stock	sliced
2 red onions, quartered	150 g/5¹/₂ oz Savoy cabbage,	salt and pepper
1 garlic clove, crushed	shredded	paprika, to garnish

1 Heat the olive oil in a large saucepan and add the cubed potatoes, quartered red onions and garlic. Sauté gently for 5 minutes, stirring constantly.

2 Add the pork or vegetable stock and bring to the boil. Reduce the heat and cover the saucepan. Simmer the vegetables for about 20 minutes until the potatoes are tender.

3 Process the soup in a food processor or blender in 2 batches for 1 minute each. Return the puréed soup to a clean pan.

4 Add the shredded Savoy cabbage and sliced chorizo sausage to the pan and cook for a further 7 minutes. Season to taste.

5 Ladle the soup into warmed soup bowls, garnish with a sprinkling of paprika and serve.

COOK'S TIP

Chorizo sausage requires no pre-cooking. In this recipe, it is added towards the end of the cooking time so that it does not overpower the other flavours in the soup.

VARIATION

If chorizo sausage is not available, you could use any other spicy sausage or even salami in its place.

Chinese Potato & Pork Broth

Serves 4

INGREDIENTS

1 litre/1³/₄ pints/4¹/₂ cups chicken stock	4 tbsp water	3 spring onions (scallions), sliced thinly
2 large potatoes, diced	1 tbsp light soy sauce	1 red (bell) pepper, sliced
2 tbsp rice wine vinegar	1 tsp sesame oil	225 g/8 oz can bamboo shoots, drained
125 g/4¹/₂ oz pork fillet, sliced	1 carrot, cut into very thin strips	
2 tbsp cornflour (cornstarch)	1 tsp ginger root, chopped	

1 Add the chicken stock, diced potatoes and 1 tbsp of the rice wine vinegar to a saucepan and bring to the boil. Reduce the heat until the stock is just simmering.

2 In a small bowl, mix the cornflour (cornstarch) with the water. Stir the mixture into the hot stock.

3 Bring the stock back to the boil, stirring until thickened, then reduce the heat until it is just simmering again.

4 Place the pork slices in a shallow dish and season with the remaining rice wine vinegar, soy sauce and sesame oil.

5 Add the pork slices, carrot strips and chopped ginger to the stock and cook for 10 minutes. Stir in the sliced spring onions (scallions), red (bell) pepper and bamboo shoots. Cook for a further 5 minutes.

6 Pour the soup into warmed bowls and serve immediately.

COOK'S TIP

Sesame oil is very strongly flavoured and is, therefore, only used in small quantities.

VARIATION

For extra heat, add 1 chopped red chilli or 1 tsp of chilli powder to the soup in step 5.

Celery, Stilton & Walnut Soup

Serves 4

INGREDIENTS

50 g/1¾ oz/4 tbsp butter
2 shallots, chopped
3 celery sticks, chopped
1 garlic clove, crushed
2 tbsp plain (all-purpose) flour

600 ml/1 pint/2½ cups
    vegetable stock
300 ml/½ pint/1¼ cups milk
150 g/5½ oz/1½ cups blue Stilton
    cheese, crumbled, plus extra to
    garnish

2 tbsp walnut halves, roughly
    chopped
150 ml/¼ pint/⅔ cup natural
    (unsweetened) yogurt
salt and pepper
chopped celery leaves, to garnish

1 Melt the butter in a large saucepan and sauté the shallots, celery and garlic for 2–3 minutes, stirring, until softened.

2 Add the flour and cook for 30 seconds.

3 Gradually stir in the vegetable stock and milk and bring to the boil.

4 Reduce the heat to a gentle simmer and add the crumbled blue Stilton cheese and walnut halves. Cover and leave to simmer

for 20 minutes.

5 Stir in the natural (unsweetened) yogurt and heat for a further 2 minutes without boiling.

6 Season the soup, then transfer to a warm soup tureen or individual serving bowls, garnish with chopped celery leaves and extra crumbled blue Stilton cheese and serve at once.

COOK'S TIP

As well as adding protein, vitamins and useful fats to the diet, nuts add important flavour and texture to vegetarian meals.

VARIATION

Use an alternative blue cheese, such as Dolcelatte or Gorgonzola, if preferred or a strong vegetarian Cheddar cheese, grated.

Red (Bell) Pepper & Chilli Soup

Serves 4

INGREDIENTS

225 g/8 oz red (bell) peppers,
seeded and sliced
1 onion, sliced
2 garlic cloves, crushed
1 green chilli, chopped

300 ml/½ pint/1½ cups passata
(sieved tomatoes)
600 ml/1 pint/2½ cups
vegetable stock
2 tbsp chopped basil

fresh basil sprigs, to garnish

1 Put the (bell) peppers in a large saucepan with the onion, garlic and chilli. Add the passata (sieved tomatoes) and vegetable stock and bring to the boil, stirring well.

2 Reduce the heat to a simmer and cook for 20 minutes or until the (bell) peppers have softened. Drain, reserving the liquid and vegetables separately.

3 Sieve the vegetables by pressing through a sieve (strainer) with the back of a spoon.

Alternatively, blend in a food processor until smooth.

4 Return the vegetable purée to a clean saucepan with the reserved cooking liquid. Add the basil and heat through until hot. Garnish the soup with fresh basil sprigs and serve.

COOK'S TIP

Basil is a useful herb to grow at home. It can be grown easily in a window box.

VARIATION

This soup is also delicious served cold with 150 ml/¼ pint/⅔ cup of natural (unsweetened) yogurt swirled into it.

Dhal Soup

Serves 4

INGREDIENTS

25 g/1 oz/2 tbsp butter	1 tsp ground cumin	vegetable stock
2 garlic cloves, crushed	1 kg/2 lb 4 oz canned, chopped	300 ml/¹/₂ pint/1¹/₄ cups coconut milk
1 onion, chopped	tomatoes, drained	salt and pepper
¹/₂ tsp turmeric	175 g/6 oz/1 cup red lentils	chopped coriander (cilantro) and
1 tsp garam masala	2 tsp lemon juice	lemon slices, to garnish
¹/₄ tsp chilli powder	600 ml/1 pint/2¹/₂ cups	naan bread, to serve

1 Melt the butter in a large saucepan and sauté the garlic and onion for 2–3 minutes, stirring. Add the spices and cook for a further 30 seconds.

2 Stir in the tomatoes, red lentils, lemon juice, vegetable stock and coconut milk and bring to the boil.

3 Reduce the heat and simmer for 25–30 minutes until the lentils are tender and cooked.

4 Season to taste and spoon the soup into a warm tureen. Garnish and serve with warm naan bread.

COOK'S TIP

You can buy cans of coconut milk from supermarkets and delicatessens. It can also be made by grating creamed coconut, which comes in the form of a solid bar, and mixing it with water.

COOK'S TIP

Add small quantities of hot water to the pan whilst the lentils are cooking if they begin to absorb too much of the liquid.

Tuscan Bean & Vegetable Soup

Serves 4

INGREDIENTS
---

1 medium onion, chopped
1 garlic clove, finely chopped
2 celery sticks, sliced
1 large carrot, diced
400 g/14 oz can chopped
  tomatoes
150 ml/5 fl oz/²/₃ cup Italian
  dry red wine

1.2 litres/2 pints/5 cups fresh
  vegetable stock
1 tsp dried oregano
425 g/15 oz can mixed beans
  and pulses
2 medium courgettes
  (zucchini), diced
1 tbsp tomato purée (paste)

salt and pepper

TO SERVE:
low-fat pesto sauce
  crusty bread

1 Place the onion, garlic, celery and carrot in a large saucepan. Stir in the tomatoes, red wine, vegetable stock and oregano.

2 Bring the vegetable mixture to the boil, cover and leave to simmer for 15 minutes. Stir the beans and courgettes (zucchini) into the mixture, and continue to cook, uncovered, for a further 5 minutes.

3 Add the tomato purée (paste) to the mixture and season well with salt and pepper to taste. Then heat through, stirring occasionally, for 2–3 minutes, but do not allow the mixture to boil again.

4 Ladle the soup into warm bowls and top with a spoonful of low-fat pesto on each portion. Serve the soup accompanied with plenty of fresh crusty bread.

VARIATION

For a more substantial soup, add 350 g/12 oz diced lean cooked chicken or turkey with the tomato purée (paste) in step 3.

Fresh Figs with Parma Ham (Prosciutto)

Serves 4

INGREDIENTS

40 g/1½ oz rocket (arugula)

4 fresh figs

4 slices Parma ham (prosciutto)

4 tbsp olive oil

1 tbsp fresh orange juice

1 tbsp clear honey

1 small red chilli

1 Tear the rocket (arugula) into more manageable pieces and arrange on 4 serving plates.

2 Using a sharp knife, cut each of the figs into quarters and place them on top of the rocket (arugula) leaves.

3 Using a sharp knife, cut the Parma ham (prosciutto) into strips and scatter over the rocket (arugula) and figs.

4 Place the oil, orange juice and honey in a screw-top jar. Shake the jar until the mixture emulsifies and forms a thick dressing. Transfer to a bowl.

5 Using a sharp knife, dice the chilli, remembering not to touch your face before you have washed your hands (see Cook's Tip, right). Add the chopped chilli to the dressing and mix well.

6 Drizzle the dressing over the Parma ham (prosciutto), rocket (arugula) and figs, tossing to mix well. Serve at once.

COOK'S TIP

Chillies can burn the skin for several hours after chopping, so it is advisable to wear gloves when you are handling the very hot varieties.

COOK'S TIP

Parma, in the Emilia-Romagna region of Italy, is famous for its ham, prosciutto di Parma, thought to be the best in the world.

Cured Meats with Olives & Tomatoes

Serves 4

INGREDIENTS

4 plum tomatoes

1 tbsp balsamic vinegar

6 canned anchovy fillets, drained
   and rinsed

2 tbsp capers, drained and rinsed

125 g/4^1/$_2$ oz green olives, pitted

175 g/6 oz mixed, cured meats,
   sliced

8 fresh basil leaves

1 tbsp extra virgin olive oil

salt and pepper

crusty bread, to serve

1 Using a sharp knife, cut the tomatoes into evenly-sized slices. Sprinkle the tomato slices with the balsamic vinegar and a little salt and pepper to taste and set aside.

2 Chop the anchovy fillets into pieces measuring about the same length as the olives.

3 Push a piece of anchovy and a caper into each olive.

4 Arrange the sliced meat on 4 individual serving plates together with the tomatoes, filled olives and basil leaves.

5 Lightly drizzle the olive oil over the sliced meat, tomatoes and olives.

6 Serve the cured meats, olives and tomatoes with lots of fresh crusty bread.

COOK'S TIP

Fill a screw-top jar with the stuffed olives, cover with olive oil and use when required – they will keep for 1 month in the refrigerator.

COOK'S TIP

The cured meats for this recipe are up to your individual taste. They can include a selection of Parma ham (prosciutto), pancetta, bresaola (dried salt beef) and salame di Milano (pork and beef sausage).

Chick Peas with Parma Ham (Prosciutto)

Serves 4

INGREDIENTS

1 tbsp olive oil	1 small red (bell) pepper, deseeded	1 x 400g/14 oz can chickpeas,
1 medium onion, thinly sliced	and cut into thin strips	drained and rinsed
1 garlic clove, chopped	200 g/7 oz Parma ham	1 tbsp chopped parsley, to garnish
	(prosciutto), cut into chunks	crusty bread, to serve

1 Heat the oil in a large frying pan (skillet). Add the sliced onion, chopped garlic and sliced (bell) pepper and cook for 3–4 minutes or until the vegetables have softened.

2 Add the Parma ham (prosciutto) to the frying pan (skillet) and fry for 5 minutes or until the ham (prosciutto) is just beginning to brown.

3 Add the chickpeas to the frying pan (skillet) and cook, stirring, for 2–3 minutes until warmed through.

4 Sprinkle with chopped parsley and transfer to warm serving plates. Serve with lots of fresh crusty bread.

COOK'S TIP

Whenever possible, use fresh herbs when cooking. They are becoming more readily available, especially since the introduction of 'growing' herbs, small pots of herbs which you can buy from the supermarket or greengrocer. This ensures the herbs are fresh and also provides a continuous supply.

VARIATION

Try adding a small finely diced chilli in step 1 for a spicier taste, if you prefer.

Deep-Fried Seafood

Serves 4

INGREDIENTS

200 g/7 oz prepared squid	oil, for deep-frying	TO SERVE:
200 g/7 oz blue (raw) tiger prawns (shrimp), peeled	50 g/1½ oz plain (all-purpose) flour	garlic mayonnaise (see Cook's Tip)
150 g/5½ oz whitebait	1 tsp dried basil	lemon wedges
	salt and pepper	

1 Carefully rinse the squid, prawns (shrimp) and whitebait under cold running water, completely removing any dirt or grit.

2 Using a sharp knife, slice the squid into rings, leaving the tentacles whole.

3 Heat the oil in a large saucepan to 180°–190°C/350°–375°F or until a cube of bread browns in 30 seconds.

4 Place the flour in a bowl and season with the salt, pepper and basil.

5 Roll the squid, prawns (shrimp) and whitebait in the seasoned flour until coated all over. Carefully shake off any excess flour.

6 Cook the seafood in the heated oil in batches for 2–3 minutes or until crispy and golden all over. Remove all of the seafood with a perforated spoon and leave to drain thoroughly on kitchen paper.

7 Transfer the seafood to serving plates and serve with garlic mayonnaise and lemon wedges.

COOK'S TIP

To make garlic mayonnaise for serving with the deep-fried seafood, crush 2 garlic cloves, stir into 8 tablespoons of mayonnaise and season with salt and pepper and a little chopped parsley.

Bruschetta with Tomatoes

Serves 4

INGREDIENTS

300 g/10½ oz cherry tomatoes
4 sun-dried tomatoes
4 tbsp extra virgin olive oil

16 fresh basil leaves, shredded
8 slices ciabatta
2 garlic cloves, peeled

salt and pepper

1 Using a sharp knife, cut the cherry tomatoes in half.

2 Using a sharp knife, slice the sun-dried tomatoes into strips.

3 Place the cherry tomatoes and sun-dried tomatoes in a bowl. Add the olive oil and the shredded basil leaves and toss to mix well. Season to taste with a little salt and pepper.

4 Using a sharp knife, cut the garlic cloves in half. Lightly toast the ciabatta bread.

5 Rub the garlic, cut-side down, over both sides of the toasted ciabatta bread.

6 Top the ciabatta bread with the tomato mixture and serve immediately.

COOK'S TIP

Ciabatta is an Italian rustic bread which is slightly holey and quite chewy. It is very good in this recipe as it absorbs the full flavour of the garlic and extra virgin olive oil.

VARIATION

Plum tomatoes are also good in this recipe. Halve them, then cut them into wedges. Mix them with the sun-dried tomatoes in step 3.

Casserole of Beans in Tomato Sauce

Serves 4

INGREDIENTS

1 x 400g/14 oz can cannellini beans	1 stick celery	450 g/1 lb tomatoes
1 x 400g/14 oz can borlotti beans	2 garlic cloves, chopped	75 g/2¾ oz rocket (arugula)
2 tbsp olive oil	175 g/6 oz baby onions, halved	

1 Drain both cans of beans and reserve 6 tbsp of the liquid.

2 Heat the oil in a large pan. Add the celery, garlic and onions and sauté for 5 minutes or until the onions are golden.

3 Cut a cross in the base of each tomato and plunge them into a bowl of boiling water for 30 seconds until the skins split. Remove them with a perforated spoon and leave until cool enough to handle. Peel off the skin and chop the flesh. Add the tomato flesh and the reserved bean liquid to the pan and cook for 5 minutes.

4 Add the beans to the pan and cook for a further 3–4 minutes or until the beans are hot.

5 Stir in the rocket (arugula) and allow to wilt slightly before serving.

VARIATION

For a spicier tasting dish, add 1–2 teaspoons of hot pepper sauce with the beans in step 4.

COOK'S TIP

Another way to peel tomatoes is once you have cut a cross in the base, push it on to a fork and hold it over a gas flame, turning it slowly so that the skin heats evenly all over. The skin will start to bubble and split, and should then slide off easily.

Tuscan Chicken Livers on Toast

Serves 4

INGREDIENTS

2 tbsp olive oil	4 fresh sage leaves, finely chopped	salt and pepper
1 garlic clove, finely chopped	or 1 tsp dried, crumbled sage	4 slices ciabatta or other Italian
225 g/8 oz fresh or frozen	2 tbsp white wine	bread
chicken livers	2 tbsp lemon juice	wedges of lemon, to garnish

1 Heat the olive oil in a frying pan (skillet) and cook the garlic for 1 minute.

2 Rinse and roughly chop the chicken livers, using a sharp knife.

3 Add the chicken liver to the frying pan (skillet) together with the white wine and lemon juice. Cook for 3–4 minutes or until the juices from the chicken liver run clear.

4 Stir in the sage and season to taste with salt and pepper.

5 Under a preheated grill (broiler), toast the bread for 2 minutes on both sides or until golden-brown.

6 Spoon the hot chicken livers on top of the toasted bread and serve garnished with a wedge of lemon.

COOK'S TIP

Overcooked liver is dry and tasteless. Cook the chopped liver for only 3–4 minutes – it should be soft and tender.

VARIATION

Another way to make crostini is to slice a crusty loaf or a French loaf into small rounds or squares. Heat the olive oil in a frying pan (skillet) and fry the slices of bread until golden brown and crisp on both sides. Remove the crostini from the pan with a perforated spoon and leave to drain on paper towels. Top with the chicken livers.

Sesame Prawn (Shrimp) Toasts

Serves 4

INGREDIENTS

225 g/8 oz cooked, peeled
    prawns (shrimp)
1 spring onion (scallion)
$^1/_4$ tsp salt
1 tsp light soy sauce

1 tbsp cornflour (cornstarch)
1 egg white, beaten
3 thin slices white bread,
    crusts removed
4 tbsp sesame seeds

vegetable oil, for deep-frying
chopped chives, to garnish

1 Put the prawns
(shrimp) and spring
onion (scallion) in a food
processor and process until
finely minced (ground).
Alternatively, chop them
very finely. Transfer to a
bowl and stir in the salt,
soy sauce, cornflour
(cornstarch) and egg white.

2 Spread the mixture on
to one side of each slice
of bread. Spread the sesame
seeds on top of the mixture,
pressing down well.

3 Cut each slice into 4
equal triangles or strips.

4 Heat the oil for deep-
frying in a wok until
almost smoking. Carefully
place the triangles in the
oil, coated side down, and
cook for 2–3 minutes, until
golden brown. Remove
with a slotted spoon and
drain on kitchen paper
(paper towels). Serve hot.

COOK'S TIP

*Fry the triangles in two
batches, keeping the first
batch warm while you cook
the second, to prevent them
from overcooking.*

VARIATION

*If wished, you could add
$^1/_2$ tsp very finely chopped
fresh root ginger and 1 tsp
Chinese rice wine to the
prawn (shrimp) mixture at
the end of step 1.*

Chinese Omelette

Serves 4

INGREDIENTS

8 eggs
225 g/8 oz/2 cups cooked
   chicken, shredded
12 tiger prawns (jumbo
   shrimp), peeled and
   deveined

2 tbsp chopped chives
2 tsp light soy sauce
dash of chilli sauce
2 tbsp vegetable oil

1 Lightly beat the eggs in a large mixing bowl.

2 Add the shredded chicken and tiger prawns (jumbo shrimp) to the eggs, mixing well.

3 Stir in the chopped chives, soy sauce and chilli sauce, mixing well.

4 Heat the oil in a large frying pan (skillet) over a medium heat and add the egg mixture, tilting the pan to coat the base completely. Cook over a medium heat, gently stirring the omelette with a fork, until the surface is just set and the underside is a golden brown colour.

5 When the omelette is set, slide it out of the pan, with the aid of a palette knife (spatula).

6 Cut the omelette into squares or slices to serve.

VARIATION

You could add extra flavour to the omelette by stirring in 3 tbsp finely chopped fresh coriander (cilantro) or 1 tsp sesame seeds with the chives in step 3.

COOK'S TIP

Add peas or other vegetables to the omelette and serve as a main course for 2 people.

Seven-Spice Aubergines (Eggplant)

Serves 4

INGREDIENTS

450 g/1 lb aubergines (eggplants), wiped	50 g/1¾ oz/3½ tbsp cornflour (cornstarch)	1 tbsp Thai seven-spice seasoning
1 egg white	1 tsp salt	oil, for deep-frying

1 Using a sharp knife, slice the aubergines (eggplants) into thin rings.

2 Place the egg white in a small bowl and whip until light and foamy.

3 Mix together the cornflour, salt and seven-spice powder on a large plate.

4 Heat the oil for deep-frying in a large wok.

5 Dip each piece of aubergine (eggplant) into the beaten egg white then coat in the cornflour and seven-spice mixture.

6 Deep-fry the coated aubergine (eggplant) slices, in batches, for 5 minutes, or until pale golden and crispy.

7 Transfer the aubergines (eggplants) to absorbent kitchen paper and leave to drain. Transfer to serving plates and serve hot.

COOK'S TIP

The best oil to use for deep-frying is groundnut oil which has a high smoke point and mild flavour, so it will neither burn or taint the food. About 600 ml/1 pint oil is sufficient.

COOK'S TIP

Thai seven-spice seasoning can be found in the spice racks of most large supermarkets.

Crispy Seaweed

Serves 4

INGREDIENTS

1 kg/2.4 lb pak choi	1 tsp salt	50 g/1¾ oz/2½ tbsp toasted pine
groundnut oil, for deep frying (about	1 tbsp caster (superfine) sugar	kernels (nuts)
850 ml/1½ pints/3¾ cups)		

1 Rinse the pak choi leaves under cold running water, then pat dry thoroughly with absorbent kitchen paper.

2 Roll each pak choi leaf up, then slice through thinly so that the leaves are finely shredded.

3 Heat the oil in a large wok. Carefully add the shredded leaves and fry for about 30 seconds or until they shrivel up and become crispy (you may need to do this in about 4 batches).

4 Remove the crispy seaweed from the wok with a slotted spoon and leave to drain on absorbent kitchen paper.

5 Transfer the crispy seaweed to a large bowl and toss with the salt, sugar and pine kernels (nuts). Serve immediately.

COOK'S TIP

As a time-saver you can use a food processor to shred the pak choi finely. Make sure you use only the best leaves; sort through the pak choi and discard any tough, outer leaves as these will spoil the overall taste and texture of the dish.

VARIATION

Use savoy cabbage instead of the pak choi if it is unavailable, making sure the leaves are well dried before frying.

Spicy Chicken Livers with Pak Choi

Serves 4

INGREDIENTS

350 g/12 oz chicken livers

2 tbsp sunflower oil

1 red chilli, deseeded and finely
    chopped

1 tsp fresh grated ginger

2 cloves garlic, crushed

2 tbsp tomato ketchup

3 tbsp sherry

3 tbsp soy sauce

1 tsp cornflour (cornstarch)

450 g/1 lb pak choi

egg noodles, to serve

1 Using a sharp knife, trim the fat from the chicken livers and slice into small pieces.

2 Heat the oil in a large wok. Add the chicken liver pieces and stir-fry over a high heat for 2–3 minutes.

3 Add the chilli, ginger and garlic and stir-fry for about 1 minute.

4 Mix together the tomato ketchup, sherry, soy sauce and cornflour (cornstarch) in a small bowl and set aside.

5 Add the pak choi to the wok and stir-fry until it just wilts.

6 Add the reserved tomato ketchup mixture to the wok and cook, stirring to mix, until the juices start to bubble.

7 Transfer to serving bowls and serve hot with noodles.

COOK'S TIP

Fresh ginger root will keep for several weeks in a dry, cool place.

COOK'S TIP

Chicken livers are available fresh or frozen from most supermarkets.

Prawn and Mushroom Omelette

Serves 4

INGREDIENTS

3 tbsp sunflower oil
2 leeks, trimmed and sliced
350 g/12 oz raw tiger prawns
  (shrimp)

25 g/1 oz/4 tbsp cornflour
  (cornstarch)
1 tsp salt
175 g/6 oz mushrooms, sliced

175 g/6 oz/1½ cups beansprouts
6 eggs
deep-fried leeks, to garnish (optional)

1 Heat the sunflower oil in a preheated wok. Add the leeks and stir-fry for 3 minutes.

2 Rinse the prawns (shrimp) under cold running water and then pat dry with absorbent kitchen paper.

3 Mix together the cornflour (cornstarch) and salt in a large bowl.

4 Add the prawns (shrimp) to the cornflour (cornstarch) and salt mixture and toss to coat all over.

5 Add the prawns (shrimp) to the wok and stir-fry for 2 minutes, or until the prawns (shrimp) are almost cooked through.

6 Add the mushrooms and beansprouts to the wok and stir-fry for a further 2 minutes.

7 Beat the eggs with 3 tablespoons of cold water. Pour the egg mixture into the wok and cook until the egg sets, carefully turning over once. Turn the omelette out on to a clean board, divide into 4 and serve hot, garnished with deep-fried leeks (if using).

COOK'S TIP

If liked, divide the mixture into 4 once the initial cooking has taken place in step 6 and cook 4 individual omelettes.

Salt & Pepper Prawns (Shrimp)

Serves 4

INGREDIENTS

2 tsp salt	450 g/1 lb peeled raw tiger prawns	1 tsp freshly grated ginger
1 tsp black pepper	(shrimp)	3 cloves garlic, crushed
2 tsp Szechuan peppercorns	2 tbsp groundnut oil	spring onions (scallions), sliced, to
1 tsp sugar	1 red chilli, deseeded and finely	garnish
	chopped	prawn (shrimp) crackers, to serve

1 Grind the salt, black pepper and Szechuan peppercorns in a pestle and mortar. Mix the salt and pepper mixture with the sugar and set aside until required.

2 Rinse the prawns (shrimp) under cold running water and pat dry with absorbent kitchen paper.

3 Heat the oil in a preheated wok. Add the prawns (shrimp), chilli, ginger and garlic and stir-fry for 4–5 minutes, or until the prawns (shrimp) are cooked through.

4 Add the salt and pepper mixture to the wok and stir-fry for 1 minute.

5 Transfer to warm serving bowls and garnish with spring onions (scallion). Serve hot with prawn (shrimp) crackers.

COOK'S TIP

Szechuan peppercorns are also known as farchiew. These wild reddish-brown peppercorns from the Szechuan region of China add an aromatic flavour to a dish.

COOK'S TIP

Tiger prawns (shrimps) are widely available and are not only colourful and tasty, but they have a meaty texture, too. If cooked tiger prawns (shrimp) are used, add them with the salt and pepper mixture in step 4 – if the cooked prawns (shrimp) are added any earlier they will toughen up and be inedible.

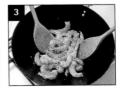

Hummus & Garlic Toasts

Serves 4

INGREDIENTS

HUMMUS:
400 g/14 oz can chickpeas
    (garbanzo beans)
juice of 1 large lemon
6 tbsp tahini (sesame seed paste)
2 tbsp olive oil

2 garlic cloves, crushed
salt and pepper
chopped fresh coriander (cilantro)
    and black olives, to garnish

TOASTS:
1 ciabatta loaf, sliced
2 garlic cloves, crushed
1 tbsp chopped fresh
    coriander (cilantro)
4 tbsp olive oil

1 To make the hummus, firstly drain the chickpeas (garbanzo beans), reserving a little of the liquid. Put the chickpeas (garbanzo beans) and liquid in a food processor and blend, gradually adding the reserved liquid and lemon juice. Blend well after each addition until smooth.

2 Stir in the tahini (sesame seed paste) and all but 1 teaspoon of the olive oil. Add the garlic, season to taste and blend again until smooth.

3 Spoon the hummus into a serving dish. Drizzle the remaining olive oil over the top, garnish with chopped coriander (cilantro) and olives. Leave to chill in the refrigerator whilst preparing the toasts.

4 Lay the slices of ciabatta on a grill (broiler) rack in a single layer.

5 Mix the garlic, coriander (cilantro) and olive oil together and drizzle over the bread slices. Cook under a hot grill (broiler) for 2–3 minutes until golden brown, turning once. Serve hot with the hummus.

COOK'S TIP

Make the hummus 1 day in advance, and chill, covered, in the refrigerator until required. Garnish and serve.

Mixed Bean Pâté

Serves 4

INGREDIENTS

400 g/14 oz can mixed beans, drained
2 tbsp olive oil
juice of 1 lemon
2 garlic cloves, crushed

1 tbsp chopped fresh coriander (cilantro)
2 spring onions (scallions), chopped
salt and pepper

shredded spring onions (scallions), to garnish

1 Rinse the beans thoroughly under cold running water and drain well.

2 Transfer the beans to a food processor or blender and process until smooth. Alternatively, place the beans in a bowl and mash with a fork or potato masher.

3 Add the olive oil, lemon juice, garlic, coriander (cilantro) and spring onions (scallions) and blend until fairly smooth. Season with salt and pepper to taste.

4 Transfer the pâté to a serving bowl and chill for at least 30 minutes. Garnish with shredded spring onions (scallions) and serve.

COOK'S TIP

Use canned beans which have no salt or sugar added and always rinse thoroughly before use.

COOK'S TIP

Serve the pâté with warm pitta bread or granary toast.

Carrot, Fennel & Potato Medley

Serves 4

INGREDIENTS

2 tbsp olive oil
1 potato, cut into thin strips
1 fennel bulb, cut into thin strips
2 carrots, grated
1 red onion, cut into thin strips
chopped chives and fennel
    fronds, to garnish

DRESSING:
3 tbsp olive oil
1 tbsp garlic wine vinegar
1 garlic clove, crushed
1 tsp Dijon mustard
2 tsp clear honey
salt and pepper

1 Heat the olive oil in a frying pan (skillet), add the potato and fennel slices and cook for 2–3 minutes until beginning to brown. Remove from the frying pan (skillet) with a slotted spoon and drain on paper towels.

2 Arrange the carrot, red onion, potato and fennel in separate piles on a serving platter.

3 Mix the dressing ingredients together and pour over the vegetables. Toss well and sprinkle with chopped chives and fennel fronds. Serve immediately or leave in the refrigerator until required.

COOK'S TIP

Fennel is an aromatic plant which has a delicate, aniseed flavour. It can be eaten raw in salads, or boiled, braised, sautéed or grilled (broiled). For this salad, if fennel is unavailable, substitute 350 g/12 oz sliced leeks.

Paprika Crisps

Serves 4

INGREDIENTS

2 large potatoes
3 tbsp olive oil

$^1/_2$ tsp paprika pepper
salt

1 Using a sharp knife, slice the potatoes very thinly so that they are almost transparent. Drain the potato slices thoroughly and pat dry with paper towels.

2 Heat the oil in a large frying pan (skillet) and add the paprika, stirring constantly, to ensure that the paprika doesn't catch and burn.

3 Add the potato slices to the frying pan (skillet) and cook them in a single layer for about 5 minutes or until the potato slices just begin to curl slightly at the edges.

4 Remove the potato slices from the pan using a perforated spoon and transfer them to paper towels to drain thoroughly.

5 Thread the potato slices on to wooden kebab (kabob) skewers.

6 Sprinkle the potato slices with a little salt and cook over a medium hot barbecue (grill) or under a medium grill (broiler) for 10 minutes, turning frequently, until the potato slices begin to crispen. Sprinkle with a little more salt, if preferred, and serve.

VARIATION
You could use curry powder or any other spice to flavour the crisps instead of the paprika, if you prefer.

Chicken Pan Bagna

Serves 6

INGREDIENTS

1 large French stick	20 g/³/₄ oz canned anchovy fillets	8 large, pitted black olives, chopped
1 garlic clove	50 g/2 oz cold roast chicken	pepper
125 ml/4 fl oz/¹/₂ cup olive oil	2 large tomatoes, sliced	

1 Using a sharp bread knife, cut the French stick in half lengthways and open out.

2 Cut the garlic clove in half and rub over the French stick.

3 Sprinkle the cut surface of the bread with the olive oil.

4 Drain the anchovies and set aside.

5 Thinly slice the chicken and arrange on top of the bread. Arrange the tomatoes and drained anchovies on top of the chicken.

6 Scatter with the chopped black olives and plenty of black pepper. Sandwich the loaf back together and wrap tightly in foil until required. Cut into slices to serve.

COOK'S TIP

Arrange a few fresh basil leaves in between the tomato slices to add a warm, spicy flavour. Use a good quality olive oil in this recipe for extra flavour.

VARIATION

You could use Italian ciabatta or olive-studded focaccia bread instead of the French stick, if you prefer. The last few years have seen a veritable interest in different breads and supermarkets now stock a wide range from home and abroad.

Salads & Snacks

As a side dish or a light meal, salads are a healthy and delicious choice. They provide a variety of nutritional benefits while being quick and easy to prepare. There are many ingredients that you can combine to create a colourful and flavoursome dish. If you are looking to create an Italian taste, Tuscan Bean Salad with Tuna is an excellent choice; alternatively, the taste of the Orient can be found in Indonesian Potato and Chicken Salad. If you require a vegetarian selection, there are many recipes to choose from, including Beetroot and Orange Rice Salad, Coconut Couscous Salad and the simple, but delicious, Mushroom Salad.

For an alternative flavour and texture other quick and tasty snacks have been added for when you want to rustle something different up. All will satisfy your hunger as well as your taste-buds. The rich variety of easy-to-make dishes includes Mexican-Style Pizzas, Tagliarini with Gorgonzola and Rosy Melon and Strawberries – something to cater for every craving and taste.

Tuscan Bean Salad with Tuna

Serves 4

INGREDIENTS

1 small white onion or 2 spring onions (scallions), finely chopped	2 medium tomatoes	1 tbsp lemon juice
2 x 400g/14 oz cans butter beans, drained	1 x 185 g/6½ oz can tuna, drained	2 tsp clear honey
	2 tbsp flat leaf parsley, chopped	1 garlic clove, crushed
	2 tbsp olive oil	

1 Place the chopped onions or spring onions (scallions) and butter beans in a bowl and mix well to combine.

2 Using a sharp knife, cut the tomatoes into wedges. Add the tomatoes to the onion and bean mixture.

3 Flake the tuna with a fork and add it to the onion and bean mixture together with the parsley.

4 In a screw-top jar, mix together the olive oil, lemon juice, honey and garlic. Shake the jar until the dressing emulsifies and thickens.

5 Pour the dressing over the bean salad. Toss the ingredients together using 2 spoons and serve.

COOK'S TIP

This salad will keep for several days in a covered container in the refrigerator. Make up the dressing just before serving and toss the ingredients together to mix well.

VARIATION

Substitute fresh salmon for the tuna if you wish to create a luxurious version of this recipe for a special occasion.

Italian Potato Salad

Serves 4

INGREDIENTS

450g/1 lb baby potatoes, unpeeled,
or larger potatoes, halved
4 tbsp natural yogurt

4 tbsp mayonnaise
8 sun-dried tomatoes

2 tbsp flat leaf parsley, chopped
salt and pepper

1 Rinse and clean the
potatoes and place
them in a large pan of water.
Bring to the boil and cook
for 8–12 minutes or until
just tender. (The cooking
time will vary according to
the size of your potatoes.)

2 Using a sharp knife,
cut the sun-dried
tomatoes into thin slices.

3 To make the dressing,
mix together the
yogurt and mayonnaise in a
bowl and season to taste
with a little salt and pepper.
Stir in the sun-dried
tomato slices and the
chopped flat leaf parsley.

4 Remove the potatoes
with a perforated spoon,
drain them thoroughly and
then set them aside to cool.
If you are using larger
potatoes, cut them into 5
cm/2 inch chunks.

5 Pour the dressing over
the potatoes and toss
to mix.

6 Leave the potato salad to
chill in the refrigerator
for about 20 minutes, then
serve as a starter or as an
accompaniment.

COOK'S TIP

*It is easier to cut the larger
potatoes once they are
cooked. Although smaller
pieces of potato will cook
more quickly, they tend
to disintegrate and
become mushy.*

Minted Fennel Salad

Serves 4

INGREDIENTS

1 bulb fennel	1 small or ½ a large cucumber	1 tbsp virgin olive oil
2 small oranges	1 tbsp chopped mint	2 eggs, hard boiled (cooked)

1 Using a sharp knife, trim the outer leaves from the fennel. Slice the fennel bulb thinly into a bowl of water and sprinkle with lemon juice (see Cook's Tip).

2 Grate the rind of the oranges over a bowl. Using a sharp knife, pare away the orange peel, then segment the orange by carefully slicing between each line of pith. Do this over the bowl in order to retain the juice.

3 Using a sharp knife, cut the cucumber into 12 mm/½ inch rounds and then cut each round into quarters.

Add the cucumber to the fennel and orange mixture together with the mint.

4 Pour the olive oil over the fennel and cucumber salad and toss well.

5 Peel and quarter the eggs and use these to decorate the top of the salad. Serve at once.

COOK'S TIP

Virgin olive oil, which has a fine aroma and flavour, is made by the cold pressing of olives. However, it may have a slightly higher acidity level than extra virgin oil.

COOK'S TIP

Fennel will discolour if it is left for any length of time without a dressing. To prevent any discoloration, place it in a bowl of water and sprinkle with lemon juice.

Mushroom Salad

Serves 4

INGREDIENTS

150 g/5½ oz firm white mushrooms	1 tbsp lemon juice	1 tbsp fresh marjoram
4 tbsp virgin olive oil	5 anchovy fillets, drained and chopped	salt and pepper

1 Gently wipe each mushroom with a damp cloth to remove any excess dirt. Slice the mushrooms thinly, using a sharp knife.

2 Mix together the olive oil and lemon juice and pour the mixture over the mushrooms. Toss together so that the mushrooms are completely coated with the lemon juice and oil.

3 Stir the chopped anchovy fillets into the mushrooms. Season the mushroom mixture with black pepper and garnish with the fresh marjoram.

4 Leave the mushroom salad to stand for 5 minutes before serving in order for all the flavours to be absorbed. Season with a little salt (see Cook's Tip, below) and then serve.

COOK'S TIP

Do not season the mushroom salad with salt until the very last minute as it will cause the mushrooms to blacken and the juices to leak. The result will not be as tasty as it should be as the full flavours won't be absorbed and it will also look very unattractive.

COOK'S TIP

If you use dried herbs rather than fresh, remember that you need only about one third of dried to fresh.

Yellow (Bell) Pepper Salad

Serves 4

INGREDIENTS

4 rashers streaky bacon, chopped	1 stick celery, finely chopped	3 tbsp olive oil
2 yellow (bell) peppers	3 plum tomatoes, cut into	1 tbsp fresh thyme
8 radishes, washed and trimmed	wedges	

1 Dry fry the chopped bacon in a frying pan (skillet) for 4–5 minutes or until crispy. Remove the bacon from the frying pan (skillet), set aside and leave to cool until required.

2 Using a sharp knife, halve and deseed the (bell) peppers. Slice them into long strips.

3 Using a sharp knife, halve the radishes and cut them into wedges.

4 Mix together the (bell) peppers, radishes, celery and tomatoes and toss the mixture in the olive oil and fresh thyme. Season to taste with a little salt and pepper.

5 Transfer the salad to serving plates and garnish with the reserved crispy bacon.

COOK'S TIP

Tomatoes are actually berries and are related to potatoes. There are many different shapes and sizes of this versatile fruit. The one most used in Italian cooking is the plum tomato which is very flavoursome.

COOK'S TIP

Pre-packaged diced bacon can be purchased from most supermarkets, which helps to save on preparation time.

122

Lentil & Tuna Salad

Serves 4

INGREDIENTS

3 tbsp virgin olive oil
1 tbsp lemon juice
1 tsp wholegrain mustard
1 garlic clove, crushed

½ tsp cumin powder
½ tsp ground coriander
1 small red onion
2 ripe tomatoes
1 x 400 g/14 oz can lentils, drained

1 x 185 g/6½ cans tuna, drained
2 tbsp fresh coriander (cilantro),
    chopped
pepper

1 Using a sharp knife, deseed the tomatoes and chop them into dice.

2 Using a sharp knife, finely chop the red onion.

3 To make the dressing, whisk together the virgin olive oil, lemon juice, mustard, garlic, cumin powder and ground coriander in a small bowl. Set aside until required.

4 Mix together the chopped onion, diced tomatoes and drained lentils in a large bowl.

5 Flake the tuna and stir it into the onion, tomato and lentil mixture.

6 Stir in the chopped coriander (cilantro).

7 Pour the dressing over the lentil and tuna salad and season with freshly ground black pepper. Serve at once.

COOK'S TIP

Lentils are a good source of protein and contain important vitamins and minerals. Buy them dried for soaking and cooking yourself, or buy canned varieties for speed and convenience.

VARIATION

Nuts would add extra flavour and texture to this salad.

Chinese Prawn (Shrimp) Salad

Serves 4

INGREDIENTS

250 g/9 oz fine egg noodles	150 g/5½ oz/1½ cups beansprouts	350 g/12 oz peeled cooked prawns
3 tbsp sunflower oil	1 ripe mango, sliced	(shrimp)
1 tbsp sesame oil	6 spring onions (scallions), sliced	2 tbsp light soy sauce
1 tbsp sesame seeds	75 g/2¾ oz radish, sliced	1 tbsp sherry

1 Place the egg noodles in a large bowl and pour over enough boiling water to cover. Leave to stand for 10 minutes.

2 Drain the noodles thoroughly and pat away any moisture with absorbent kitchen paper.

3 Heat the sunflower oil in a large wok. Add the noodles and stir-fry for 5 minutes, tossing frequently.

4 Remove the wok from the heat and add the sesame oil, sesame seeds and beansprouts, tossing to mix well.

5 In a separate bowl, mix together the sliced mango, spring onions (scallions), radish, prawns (shrimp), light soy sauce and sherry.

6 Toss the prawn (shrimp) mixture with the noodles or alternatively, arrange the noodles around the edge of a serving plate and pile the prawn (shrimp) mixture into the centre. Serve immediately.

VARIATION

If fresh mango is unavailable, use canned mango slices, rinsed and drained, instead.

Old English Spicy Chicken Salad

Serves 4

INGREDIENTS

250 g/9 oz young spinach leaves
3 sticks (stalks) celery, sliced thinly
½ cucumber
2 spring onions (scallions)
3 tbsp chopped fresh parsley
350g/12 oz boneless, roast chicken,
    sliced thinly

DRESSING:
2.5 cm/1 inch piece fresh ginger root,
    grated finely
3 tbsp olive oil
1 tbsp white wine vinegar
1 tbsp clear honey

½ tsp ground cinnamon
salt and pepper
smoked almonds, to garnish
    (optional)

1 Thoroughly wash the spinach leaves, then pat dry with paper towels.

2 Using a sharp knife, thinly slice the celery, cucumber and spring onions (scallions). Toss in a large bowl with the spinach leaves and parsley.

3 Transfer to serving plates and arrange the chicken on top of the salad.

4 In a screw-topped jar, combine all the dressing ingredients and shake well to mix.

5 Season the dressing with salt and pepper to taste, then pour over the salad. Sprinkle with a few smoked almonds, if using.

VARIATION

Substitute lamb's lettuce (corn salad) for the spinach, if you prefer.

VARIATION

Fresh young spinach leaves go particularly well with fruit – try adding a few fresh raspberries or nectarine slices to make an even more refreshing salad.

Potato, Mixed Bean & Apple Salad

Serves 4

INGREDIENTS

225 g/8 oz new potatoes, scrubbed and quartered

225 g/8 oz mixed canned beans, such as red kidney beans, flageolet and borlotti beans, drained and rinsed

1 red dessert apple, diced and tossed in 1 tbsp lemon juice

1 small yellow (bell) pepper, diced

1 shallot, sliced

½ head fennel, sliced

oak leaf lettuce leaves

DRESSING:

1 tbsp red wine vinegar

2 tbsp olive oil

½ tbsp American mustard

1 garlic clove, crushed

2 tsp chopped fresh thyme

1 Cook the quartered potatoes in a saucepan of boiling water for 15 minutes until tender. Drain and transfer to a mixing bowl.

2 Add the mixed beans to the potatoes with the diced apple and yellow (bell) pepper, and the sliced shallots and fennel. Mix well, taking care not to break up the cooked potatoes.

3 In a bowl, whisk all the dressing ingredients together, then pour it over the potato salad.

4 Line a plate or salad bowl with the oak leaf and spoon the potato mixture into the centre. Serve immediately.

COOK'S TIP

Canned beans are used here for convenience, but dried beans may be used instead. Soak for 8 hours or overnight, drain and place in a saucepan. Cover with water, bring to the boil and boil for 10 minutes, then simmer until tender.

VARIATION

Use Dijon or wholegrain mustard in place of American mustard for a different flavour.

Potato, Radish & Cucumber Salad

Serves 4

INGREDIENTS

450 g/1 lb new potatoes, scrubbed and halved	1 bunch radishes, sliced thinly	2 tbsp olive oil
½ cucumber, sliced thinly	DRESSING:	1 tbsp white wine vinegar
2 tsp salt	1 tbsp Dijon mustard	2 tbsp mixed chopped herbs

1 Cook the potatoes in a saucepan of boiling water for 10-15 minutes or until tender. Drain and leave to cool.

2 Meanwhile spread out the cucumber slices on a plate and sprinkle with the salt. Leave to stand for 30 minutes, then rinse under cold running water and pat dry with paper towels.

3 Arrange the cucumber and radish slices on a serving plate in a decorative pattern and pile the cooked potatoes in the centre of the slices.

4 In a bowl, mix the dressing ingredients together. Pour the dressing over the salad, tossing well to coat all of the salad ingredients. Leave to chill in the refrigerator before serving.

VARIATION

Dijon mustard has a mild clean taste which is perfect for this salad as it does not overpower the other flavours. If unavailable, use another mild mustard – English mustard is too strong for this salad.

COOK'S TIP

The cucumber adds not only colour but a real freshness to the salad. It is salted and left to stand to remove the excess water which would make the salad soggy. Wash the cucumber well to remove all of the salt, before adding to the salad.

Sweet Potato & Nut Salad

Serves 4

INGREDIENTS

450 g/1 lb sweet potatoes, diced
2 celery sticks, sliced
125 g/4¹/₂ oz celeriac, grated
2 spring onions (scallions), sliced
50 g/1³/₄ oz pecan nuts, chopped

2 heads chicory (endive),
    separated
1 tsp lemon juice
thyme sprigs, to garnish

DRESSING:
4 tbsp vegetable oil
1 tbsp garlic wine vinegar
1 tsp soft light brown sugar
2 tsp chopped fresh thyme

1 Cook the sweet potatoes in a saucepan of boiling water for 5 minutes until tender. Drain thoroughly and leave to cool.

2 When cooled, stir in the celery, celeriac, spring onions (scallions) and pecan nuts.

3 Line a salad plate with the chicory (endive) leaves and sprinkle with lemon juice.

4 Spoon the potato mixture into the centre of the leaves.

5 In a small bowl, whisk the dressing ingredients together.

6 Pour the dressing over the salad and serve at once, garnished with thyme sprigs.

COOK'S TIP

Sweet potatoes do not store as well as ordinary potatoes. It is best to store them in a cool, dark place (not the refrigerator) and use within 1 week of purchase.

VARIATION

For variety, replace the garlic wine vinegar in the dressing with a different flavoured oil, such as chilli or herb.

Potato, Rocket (Arugula) & Apple Salad

Serves 4

INGREDIENTS

2 large potatoes, unpeeled and sliced	150 g/5½ oz rocket (arugula) leaves	1 tsp clear honey
2 green dessert apples, diced	salt and pepper	1 tsp fennel seeds
1 tsp lemon juice		
25 g/1 oz walnut pieces	DRESSING:	
125 g/4½ oz goat's cheese, cubed	2 tbsp olive oil	
	1 tbsp red wine vinegar	

1 Cook the potatoes in a pan of boiling water for 15 minutes until tender. Drain and leave to cool. Transfer the cooled potatoes to a serving bowl.

2 Toss the diced apples in the lemon juice, drain and stir into the cold potatoes.

3 Add the walnut pieces, cheese cubes and rocket (arugula) leaves, then toss the salad to mix.

4 In a small bowl, whisk the dressing ingredients together and pour the dressing over the salad. Serve immediately.

VARIATION

Use smoked or blue cheese instead of goat's cheese, if you prefer. In addition, if rocket (arugula) is unavailable use baby spinach instead.

COOK'S TIP

Serve this salad immediately to prevent the apple from discolouring. Alternatively, prepare all of the other ingredients in advance and add the apple at the last minute.

Potato & Mixed Vegetable Salad with Lemon Mayonnaise

Serves 4

INGREDIENTS

450 g/1 lb waxy new potatoes, scrubbed
1 carrot, cut into matchsticks
225 g/8 oz cauliflower florets
225 g/8 oz baby sweetcorn cobs, halved lenghtways
175 g/6 oz French (green) beans

175 g/6 oz ham, diced
50 g/1³/₄ oz mushrooms, sliced
salt and pepper

DRESSING:
2 tbsp chopped fresh parsley
150 ml/¹/₄ pint/²/₃ cup

mayonnaise

150 ml/¹/₄ pint/²/₃ cup natural yogurt
4 tsp lemon juice
rind of 1 lemon
2 tsp fennel seeds

1 Cook the potatoes in a pan of boiling water for 15 minutes or until tender. Drain and leave to cool. When the potatoes are cold, slice them thinly.

2 Meanwhile, cook the carrot matchsticks, cauliflower florets, baby sweetcorn cobs and French (green) beans in a pan of boiling water for 5 minutes. Drain well and leave to cool.

3 Reserve 1 tsp of the chopped parsley for the garnish. In a bowl, mix the remaining dressing ingredients together.

4 Arrange the vegetables on a salad platter and top with the ham strips and sliced mushrooms.

5 Spoon the dressing over the the salad and garnish with the reserved parsley. Serve at once.

COOK'S TIP

For a really quick salad, use a frozen packet of mixed vegetables, thawed, instead of fresh vegetables.

Indonesian Potato & Chicken Salad

Serves 4

INGREDIENTS

4 large waxy potatoes, diced

300 g/10½ oz fresh pineapple, diced

2 carrots, grated

175 g/6 oz beansprouts

1 bunch spring onions (scallions), sliced

1 large courgette (zucchini), cut into matchsticks

3 celery sticks, cut into matchsticks

175 g/6 oz unsalted peanuts

2 cooked chicken breast fillets, about 125 g/4½ oz each, sliced

DRESSING:

6 tbsp crunchy peanut butter

6 tbsp olive oil

2 tbsp light soy sauce

1 red chilli, chopped

2 tsp sesame oil

4 tsp lime juice

1 Cook the diced potatoes in a saucepan of boiling water for 10 minutes or until tender. Drain and leave to cool.

2 Transfer the cooled potatoes to a salad bowl.

3 Add the pineapple, carrots, beansprouts, spring onions (scallions), courgette (zucchini), celery, peanuts and sliced chicken to the potatoes. Toss well to mix all the salad ingredients together.

4 To make the dressing, put the peanut butter in a small bowl and gradually whisk in the olive oil and light soy sauce.

5 Stir in the chopped red chilli, sesame oil and lime juice. Mix until well combined.

6 Pour the spicy dressing over the salad and toss lightly to coat all of the ingredients. Serve the salad immediately, garnished with the lime wedges.

COOK'S TIP

Unsweetened canned pineapple may be used in place of the fresh pineapple for convenience. If only sweetened canned pineapple is available, drain it and rinse under cold running water before using.

Grilled (Broiled) New Potato Salad

Serves 4

INGREDIENTS

650 g/1¹/₂ lb new potatoes, scrubbed	4 rashers smoked bacon	DRESSING:
3 tbsp olive oil	salt and pepper	4 tbsp mayonnaise
2 tbsp chopped fresh thyme	parsley sprig, to garnish	1 tbsp garlic wine vinegar
1 tsp paprika		2 garlic cloves, crushed
		1 tbsp chopped fresh parsley

1 Cook the new potatoes in a saucepan of boiling water for 10 minutes. Drain thoroughly.

2 Mix the olive oil, chopped thyme and paprika together and pour the mixture over the warm potatoes.

3 Place the bacon rashers under a preheated medium grill (broiler) and cook for 5 minutes, turning once until crisp. When cooked, roughly chop the bacon and keep warm.

4 Transfer the potatoes to the grill (broiler) pan and cook for 10 minutes, turning once.

5 Mix the dressing ingredients in a small serving bowl. Transfer the potatoes and bacon to a large serving bowl. Season with salt and pepper and mix together.

6 Spoon over the dressing, garnish with a parsley sprig and serve immediately for a warm salad. Alternatively, leave to cool and serve chilled.

VARIATION

Add spicy sausage to the salad in place of bacon – you do not need to cook it under the grill (broiler) before adding to the salad.

Potato & Italian Sausage Salad

Serves 4

INGREDIENTS

450 g/1 lb waxy potatoes
1 raddichio or lollo rosso lettuce
1 green (bell) pepper, sliced
175 g/6 oz Italian sausage, sliced
1 red onion, halved and sliced

125 g/4½ oz sun-dried
  tomatoes, sliced
2 tbsp shredded fresh basil

DRESSING:
1 tbsp balsamic vinegar
1 tsp tomato purée (paste)
2 tbsp olive oil
salt and pepper

1 Cook the potatoes in a saucepan of boiling water for 20 minutes or until cooked through. Drain and leave to cool.

2 Line a large serving platter with the radicchio or lollo rosso lettuce leaves.

3 Slice the cooled potatoes and arrange them in layers on the lettuce-lined serving platter together with the sliced green (bell) pepper, sliced Italian sausage, red onion, sun-dried tomatoes and shredded fresh basil.

4 In a small bowl, whisk the balsamic vinegar, tomato purée (paste) and olive oil together and season to taste with salt and pepper. Pour the dressing over the potato salad and serve immediately.

COOK'S TIP

You can use either packets of sun-dried tomatoes or jars of sun-dried tomatoes in oil. If using tomatoes packed in oil, simply rinse the oil from the tomatoes and pat them dry on paper towels before using.

VARIATION

Any sliced Italian sausage or salami can be used in this salad. Italy is home of the salami and there are numerous varieties to choose from – those from the south tend to be more highly spiced than those from the north of the country.

Root Vegetable Salad

Serves 4

INGREDIENTS

350 g/12 oz carrots
225 g/8 oz mooli (white radish)
115 g/4 oz radishes
350 g/12 oz celeriac
1 tbsp orange juice
2 sticks celery with leaves,
    washed and trimmed

100 g/3^1/$_2$ oz assorted salad
    leaves
25 g/1 oz chopped walnuts

DRESSING:
1 tbsp walnut oil
1 tbsp white wine vinegar

1 tsp wholegrain mustard
^{1}/$_2$ tsp finely grated orange
    rind
1 tsp celery seeds
salt and pepper

1 Using a sharp knife, peel and coarsely grate or very finely shred the carrots, mooli (white radish) and radishes. Set aside in separate bowls.

2 Using a sharp knife, peel and coarsely grate or finely shred the celeriac and mix with the orange juice.

3 Remove the celery leaves and reserve them for garnishing. Finely chop the celery sticks.

4 Divide the salad leaves among 4 serving plates and arrange the vegetables in small piles on top. Set aside while you make the dressing.

5 To make the dressing, mix the walnut oil, wine vinegar, mustard, orange rind, celery seeds and season with salt and pepper to taste. Drizzle a little over each salad. Shred the reserved celery leaves and sprinkle over the salad with the chopped walnuts.

COOK'S TIP

Also known as Chinese white radish and daikon, mooli resembles a large white parsnip. It has crisp, slightly pungent flesh, which can be eaten raw or cooked. It is a useful ingredient in stir-fries. Fresh mooli tend to have a stronger flavour than shop-bought ones.

Beetroot & Orange Rice Salad

Serves 4

INGREDIENTS

225 g/8 oz/1¹/₃ cups long-grain and wild rices (see Cook's Tip, below)
4 large oranges
450 g/1 lb cooked beetroot, peeled
2 heads of chicory
salt and pepper

fresh snipped chives, to garnish

DRESSING:
4 tbsp low-fat natural fromage frais (unsweetened yogurt)
1 garlic clove, crushed

1 tbsp wholegrain mustard
¹/₂ tsp finely grated orange rind
2 tsp clear honey

1 Cook the rices according to the instructions on the packet. Drain and set aside to cool.

2 Slice the top and bottom off each orange and remove the skin and pith. Holding the orange over a bowl to catch the juice, slice between each segment. Place the segments in a separate bowl. Cover the juice and leave to chill in the refrigerator until required.

3 Drain the beetroot if necessary and dice into cubes. Mix with the orange segments, cover and leave to chill.

4 When the rice has cooled, mix in the reserved orange juice and season with salt and pepper.

5 Line 4 serving bowls or plates with the chicory leaves. Spoon over the rice and top with the beetroot and orange segments.

6 Mix all the dressing ingredients together and spoon over the salad, or serve separately in a bowl, if preferred. Garnish with fresh snipped chives.

COOK'S TIP

Look out for boxes of ready-mixed long-grain and wild rices. Alternatively, cook 175 g/6 oz/1 cup white rice and 60 g/2 oz/¹/₄ cup wild rice separately.

Red Hot Slaw

Serves 4

INGREDIENTS

1/2 small red cabbage	TO GARNISH:	3 tbsp low-fat natural
1 large carrot	red chilli strips	(unsweetened) yogurt
2 red-skinned apples	carrot strips	1 garlic clove, crushed
1 tbsp lemon juice		1 tsp paprika
1 medium red onion	DRESSING:	1–2 tsp chilli powder
100 g/3 1/2 oz reduced-fat	3 tbsp reduced-calorie	pinch cayenne pepper
Cheddar cheese, grated	mayonnaise	(optional)
		salt and pepper

1 Cut the red cabbage in half and remove the central core. Finely shred the leaves and place in a large bowl. Peel and coarsely grate or finely shred the carrot and mix into the cabbage.

2 Core the apples and dice, leaving on the skins. Place in another bowl and toss in the lemon juice to prevent the apple browning. Mix the apple into the cabbage and carrot.

3 Peel and finely shred or grate the onion. Stir into the other vegetables along with the cheese and mix together.

4 To make the dressing, mix together the mayonnaise, yogurt, garlic and paprika in a small bowl. Add chilli powder according to taste, and the cayenne pepper, if using – remember this will add more spice to the dressing. Season well.

5 Toss the dressing into the vegetables and mix well. Cover and leave to chill in the refrigerator for 1 hour to allow the flavours to develop. Serve garnished with strips of red chilli and carrot.

Pasta Niçoise Salad

Serves 4

INGREDIENTS

225 g/8 oz farfalle (bows)
175 g/6 oz French (green)
   beans, topped and tailed
350 g/12 oz fresh tuna steaks
115 g/4 oz baby plum
   tomatoes, halved
8 anchovy fillets, drained on
   absorbent kitchen paper

2 tbsp capers in brine, drained
25 g/1 oz pitted black olives in
   brine, drained
fresh basil leaves, to garnish
salt and pepper

DRESSING:
1 tbsp olive oil
1 garlic clove, crushed
1 tbsp lemon juice
1/2 tsp finely grated lemon
   rind
1 tbsp shredded fresh basil
   leaves

1 Cook the pasta in lightly salted boiling water according to the instructions on the packet until just cooked. Drain well, set aside and keep warm.

2 Bring a small saucepan of lightly salted water to the boil and cook the French (green) beans for 5–6 minutes until just tender. Drain well and toss into the pasta. Set aside and keep warm.

3 Preheat the grill (broiler) to medium. Rinse and pat the tuna steaks dry on absorbent kitchen paper. Season on both sides with black pepper. Place the tuna steaks on the grill (broiler) rack and cook for 4–5 minutes on each side until cooked through.

4 Drain the tuna on absorbent kitchen paper and flake into bite-sized pieces. Toss the tuna into the pasta along with the tomatoes, anchovies, capers and olives. Set aside and keep warm.

5 Meanwhile, prepare the dressing. Mix all the ingredients together and season with salt and pepper to taste. Pour the dressing over the pasta mixture and mix carefully. Transfer to a warmed serving bowl and serve sprinkled with fresh basil leaves.

Coconut Couscous Salad

Serves 4

INGREDIENTS

350 g/12 oz precooked
couscous
175 g/6 oz no-need-to-soak
dried apricots
1 small bunch fresh chives
2 tbsp unsweetened
desiccated (shredded)
coconut

1 tsp ground cinnamon
salt and pepper
shredded mint leaves, to garnish

DRESSING:
1 tbsp olive oil
2 tbsp unsweetened orange
juice

$^1/_2$ tsp finely grated orange
rind
1 tsp wholegrain mustard
1 tsp clear honey
2 tbsp chopped fresh mint
leaves

1 Soak the couscous according to the instructions on the packet.

2 Bring a large saucepan of water to the boil. Transfer the couscous to a steamer or large sieve (strainer) lined with muslin (cheesecloth) and place over the pan of water. Cover and steam according to the instructions on the packet. Remove from the heat, place in a heatproof bowl and set aside to cool.

3 Meanwhile, slice the apricots into thin strips and place in a small bowl. Using scissors, snip the chives over the apricots.

4 When the couscous is cool, mix in the apricots, chives, coconut and cinnamon. Season well.

5 To make the dressing, mix all the ingredients together and season. Pour over the couscous and mix until well combined. Cover

and leave to chill for 1 hour to allow the flavours to develop. Serve garnished with mint leaves.

COOK'S TIP

To serve this salad hot, when the couscous has been steamed, mix in the apricots, chives, coconut, cinnamon and seasoning along with 1 tbsp olive oil. Transfer to a warmed serving bowl and serve.

Rosy Melon & Strawberries

Serves 4

INGREDIENTS

1/4 honeydew melon 1/2 Charentais or Cantaloupe melon	150 ml/5 fl oz/2/3 cup rosé wine 2–3 tsp rose water	175 g/6 oz small strawberries, washed and hulled rose petals, to garnish

1 Scoop out the seeds from both melons with a spoon. Then carefully remove the skin, taking care not to remove too much flesh.

2 Cut the melon flesh into thin strips and place in a bowl. Pour over the wine and sufficient rose water to taste. Mix together gently, cover and leave to chill in the refrigerator for at least 2 hours.

3 Halve the strawberries and carefully mix into the melon. Allow the melon and strawberries to stand at room temperature for about 15 minutes for the flavours to develop – if the melon is too cold, there will be little flavour.

4 Arrange on individual serving plates and serve sprinkled with a few rose petals, if wished.

COOK'S TIP

Rose water is a distillation of rose petals. It is generally available from large pharmacies and leading supermarkets as well as from more specialist food suppliers.

VARIATION

It does not matter whether the rosé wine is sweet or dry – although sweet wine contains more calories. Experiment with different types of melon. Varieties such as 'Sweet Dream' have whitish-green flesh, while Charentais melons, which have orange flesh, are fragrant and go better with a dry wine. If you wish, soak the strawberries in the wine with the melon, but always allow the fruit to return to room temperature before serving.

Spaghetti with Anchovy & Pesto Sauce

Serves 4

INGREDIENTS

90 ml/3 fl oz olive oil
2 garlic cloves, crushed
60 g/2 oz can anchovy fillets,
    drained

450 g/1 lb dried spaghetti
60 g/2 oz Pesto Sauce
2 tbsp finely chopped fresh
    oregano

90 g/3 oz/1 cup grated
    Parmesan cheese, plus
    extra for serving (optional)
salt and pepper
2 fresh oregano sprigs, to
    garnish

1 Heat 1 tbsp of the oil in a small saucepan. Add the garlic and fry for 3 minutes.

2 Add the anchovies and cook, stirring, until the anchovies have disintegrated.

3 Bring a large saucepan of lightly salted water to the boil. Add the spaghetti and the remaining olive oil and cook until just tender, but still firm to the bite.

4 Add the Pesto Sauce and chopped fresh oregano to the anchovy mixture and then season with black pepper to taste.

5 Drain the spaghetti, using a slotted spoon, and transfer to a warm serving dish. Pour the Pesto Sauce over the spaghetti and then sprinkle over the grated Parmesan cheese. Garnish with oregano sprigs and serve with extra cheese, if using.

VARIATION

For a vegetarian version of this recipe, substitute drained sun-dried tomatoes for the anchovy fillets.

COOK'S TIP

If you find canned anchovies much too salty, soak them in a saucer of cold milk for 5 minutes, drain and pat dry with kitchen paper (kitchen towels) before using.

Chargrilled Mediterranean Vegetable Kebabs (Kabobs)

Makes 8

INGREDIENTS

1 large red (bell) pepper
1 large green (bell) pepper
1 large orange (bell) pepper
1 large courgette (zucchini)
4 baby aubergines (eggplants)
2 medium red onions

2 tbsp lemon juice
1 tbsp olive oil
1 garlic clove, crushed
1 tbsp chopped, fresh
   rosemary or
   1 tsp dried rosemary

salt and pepper

TO SERVE:
cracked wheat, cooked
tomato and olive relish

1 Halve and deseed the (bell) peppers and cut into even sized pieces, about 2.5 cm/1 inch wide. Trim the courgettes (zucchini), cut in half lengthwise and slice into 2.5 cm/1 inch pieces. Place the (bell) peppers and courgettes (zucchini) into a large bowl and set aside.

2 Trim the aubergines (eggplants) and quarter them lengthwise. Peel the onions, then cut each one into 8 even-sized wedges. Add the aubergine (eggplants) and onions to the bowl containing the (bell) peppers and courgettes (zucchini).

3 In a small bowl, mix together the lemon juice, olive oil, garlic, rosemary and seasoning. Pour the mixture over the vegetables and stir to coat.

4 Preheat the grill (broiler) to medium. Thread the vegetables on to 8 skewers. Arrange the kebabs (kabobs) on the rack and cook for 10–12 minutes, turning frequently until the vegetables are lightly charred and just softened.

5 Drain the vegetable kebabs (kabobs) and serve on a bed of cracked wheat accompanied with a tomato and olive relish, if wished.

Mexican-Style Pizzas

Serves 4

INGREDIENTS

4 x ready-made individual
    pizza bases
1 tbsp olive oil
200 g/7 oz can chopped
    tomatoes with garlic and
    herbs
2 tbsp tomato purée (paste)

200 g/7 oz can kidney beans,
    drained and rinsed
115 g/4 oz sweetcorn kernels,
    thawed if frozen
1–2 tsp chilli sauce
1 large red onion, shredded

100 g/3 1/2 oz reduced-fat
    Cheddar cheese, grated
1 large green chilli, sliced into
    rings
salt and pepper

1 Preheat the oven to 220°C/425°F/Gas Mark 7. Arrange the pizza bases on a baking sheet (cookie sheet) and brush them lightly with the oil.

2 In a bowl, mix together the chopped tomatoes, tomato purée (paste), kidney beans and sweetcorn, and add chilli sauce to taste. Season with salt and pepper.

3 Spread the tomato and kidney bean mixture evenly over each pizza base to cover. Top each pizza with shredded onion and sprinkle with some grated cheese and a few slices of green chilli to taste. Bake in the oven for about 20 minutes until the vegetables are tender, the cheese has melted and the base is crisp and golden.

4 Remove the pizzas from the baking sheet (cookie sheet) and transfer to serving plates. Serve immediately.

COOK'S TIP

For a low-fat Mexican-style salad to serve with this pizza, arrange sliced tomatoes, fresh coriander (cilantro) leaves and a few slices of a small, ripe avocado. Sprinkle with fresh lime juice and coarse sea salt. Avocados have quite a high oil content, so eat in moderation.

Tagliarini with Gorgonzola

Serves 4

INGREDIENTS

25 g/1 oz/2 tbsp butter
225 g/8 oz Gorgonzola cheese,
   roughly crumbled
150 ml/¹/4 pint/⁵/8 cup double
   (heavy) cream

30 ml/2 tbsp dry white wine
1 tsp cornflour (cornstarch)
4 fresh sage sprigs, finely
   chopped
400 g/14 oz dried tagliarini

2 tbsp olive oil
salt and white pepper
fresh herb sprigs, to garnish

1 Melt the butter in a heavy-based saucepan. Stir in 175 g/6 oz of the Gorgonzola and melt, over a low heat, for 2 minutes.

2 Add the cream, wine and cornflour (cornstarch) and beat with a whisk until fully incorporated.

3 Stir in the sage and season to taste. Bring to the boil over a low heat, whisking constantly, until the sauce thickens. Remove from the heat and set aside.

4 Bring a large saucepan of lightly salted water to the boil. Add the tagliarini and 1 tbsp of the olive oil. Cook the pasta for 12–14 minutes or until just tender, drain thoroughly and toss in the remaining olive oil. Transfer the pasta to a serving dish and keep warm.

5 Reheat the sauce over a low heat, whisking constantly. Spoon the Gorgonzola sauce over the tagliarini, sprinkle over the remaining cheese, garnish and serve.

COOK'S TIP

Gorgonzola is one of the world's oldest veined cheeses and, arguably, its finest. When buying, always check that it is creamy yellow with delicate green veining. Avoid hard or discoloured cheese. It should have a rich, piquant aroma, not a bitter smell. If you find Gorgonzola too strong or rich, you could substitute Danish blue.

Spaghetti with Ricotta Cheese

Serves 4

INGREDIENTS

350 g/12 oz dried spaghetti
3 tbsp olive oil
40 g/^{1}/$_2$ oz/3 tbsp butter
2 tbsp chopped fresh flat leaf
    parsley
125 g/4^1/$_2$ oz/1 cup freshly
    ground almonds

125 g/4^1/$_2$ oz/^{1}/$_2$ cup ricotta
    cheese
pinch of grated nutmeg
pinch of ground cinnamon
150 ml/^{1}/$_4$ pint/^{5}/$_8$ cup crème
    fraîche (unsweetened
    yogurt)

125 ml/4 fl oz hot chicken
    stock
1 tbsp pine nuts (kernels)
salt and pepper
fresh flat leaf parsley sprigs,
    to garnish

1 Bring a large pan of lightly salted water to the boil. Add the spaghetti and 1 tbsp of the oil and cook until tender, but still firm to the bite.

2 Drain the pasta, return to the pan and toss with the butter and chopped parsley. Set aside and keep warm.

3 To make the sauce, mix together the ground almonds, ricotta cheese, nutmeg, cinnamon and crème fraîche (unsweetened yogurt) over a low heat to form a thick paste. Stir in the remaining oil, then gradually stir in the hot chicken stock, until smooth. Season to taste.

4 Transfer the spaghetti to a warm serving dish, pour over the sauce and toss together well (see Cook's Tip, right). Sprinkle over the pine nuts (kernels), garnish with the flat leaf parsley sprigs and serve warm.

COOK'S TIP

Use two large forks to toss spaghetti or other long pasta, so that it is thoroughly coated with the sauce. Special spaghetti forks are available from some cookware departments and kitchen shops. Holding one fork in each hand, gently ease the prongs under the pasta on each side and lift them towards the centre. Continue until the pasta is completely coated.

Vegetable Spaghetti with Lemon Dressing

Serves 4

INGREDIENTS

225 g/8 oz celeriac
2 medium carrots
2 medium leeks
1 small red (bell) pepper
1 small yellow (bell) pepper
2 garlic cloves
1 tsp celery seeds

1 tbsp lemon juice
300 g/10¹/₂ oz spaghetti
celery leaves, chopped, to
    garnish

LEMON DRESSING:
1 tsp finely grated lemon rind

1 tbsp lemon juice
4 tbsp low-fat natural
    fromage frais
    (unsweetened yogurt)
salt and pepper
2 tbsp snipped fresh chives

1 Peel the celeriac and carrots, cut into thin matchsticks and place in a bowl. Slice the leeks, rinse to flush out any trapped dirt, then shred finely. Halve, deseed and slice the (bell) peppers. Peel and thinly slice the garlic. Add these vegetables to the celeriac and the carrots.

2 Toss the vegetables with the celery seeds and lemon juice.

3 Bring a large pan of water to the boil and cook the spaghetti according to the instructions on the packet. Drain well and keep warm.

4 Bring another large saucepan of water to the boil, put the vegetables in a steamer or sieve (strainer) and place over the boiling water. Cover and steam for 6–7 minutes or until just tender.

5 When the spaghetti and vegetables are cooked, mix the ingredients for the lemon dressing together.

6 Transfer the spaghetti and vegetables to a warm serving bowl and mix with the dressing. Garnish with chopped celery leaves and serve.

Stir-Fried Tofu (Bean Curd) with Peanut & Chilli Sauce

Serves 4

INGREDIENTS

450 g/1 lb tofu (bean curd), cubed	SAUCE:	150 ml/¼ pint/²⁄₃ cup coconut milk
oil, for frying	6 tbsp crunchy peanut butter	1 tbsp tomato purée
	1 tbsp sweet chilli sauce	25 g/1 oz/¼ cup chopped salted peanuts

1 Pat away any moisture from the tofu (bean curd), using absorbent kitchen paper.

2 Heat the oil in a large wok until very hot. Cook the tofu (bean curd), in batches, for about 5 minutes, or until golden and crispy. Remove the tofu (bean curd) with a slotted spoon, transfer to absorbent kitchen paper and leave to drain.

3 To make the sauce, mix together the crunchy peanut butter, sweet chilli sauce, coconut milk, tomato purée and chopped peanuts in a bowl. Add a little boiling water if necessary to achieve a smooth consistency.

4 Transfer the crispy fried tofu (bean curd) to serving plates and serve with the peanut and chilli sauce.

COOK'S TIP

Cook the peanut and chilli sauce in a saucepan over a gentle heat before serving, if you prefer.

COOK'S TIP

Make sure that all of the moisture has been absorbed from the tofu (bean curd) before frying, otherwise it will not crispen.

Pasta Provençale

Serves 4

INGREDIENTS

225 g/8 oz penne (quills)

1 tbsp olive oil

25 g/1 oz pitted black olives, drained and chopped

25 g/1 oz dry-pack sun-dried tomatoes, soaked, drained and chopped

400 g/14 oz can artichoke hearts, drained and halved

115 g/4 oz baby courgettes (zucchini), trimmed and sliced

115 g/4 oz baby plum tomatoes, halved

100 g/3 1/2 oz assorted baby salad leaves

salt and pepper

shredded basil leaves, to garnish

DRESSING:

4 tbsp passata (sieved tomatoes)

2 tbsp low-fat natural fromage frais (unsweetened yogurt)

1 tbsp unsweetened orange juice

1 small bunch fresh basil, shredded

1 Cook the penne (quills) according to the instructions on the packet. Do not overcook the pasta – it should still have 'bite'. Drain well and return to the pan. Stir in the olive oil, salt and pepper, olives and sun-dried tomatoes. Leave to cool.

2 Gently mix the artichokes, courgettes (zucchini) and plum tomatoes into the cooked pasta. Arrange the salad leaves in a serving bowl.

3 To make the dressing, mix all the ingredients together and toss into the vegetables and pasta.

4 Spoon the mixture on top of the salad leaves and garnish with shredded basil leaves.

VARIATION

For a non-vegetarian version, stir 225 g/8 oz canned tuna in brine, drained and flaked, into the pasta together with the vegetables. Other pasta shapes can be included – look out for farfalle (bows) and rotelle (spoked wheels).

Garlic Mushrooms on Toast

Serves 4

INGREDIENTS

75 g/2¾ oz/6 tbsp vegetarian margarine	350 g/12 oz/4 cups mixed mushrooms, such as open-cap, button, oyster and shiitake, sliced	8 slices French bread
2 garlic cloves, crushed		1 tbsp chopped parsley
		salt and pepper

1 Melt the margarine in a frying pan (skillet). Add the crushed garlic and cook for 30 seconds, stirring.

2 Add the mushrooms and cook for 5 minutes, turning occasionally.

3 Toast the French bread slices under a preheated medium grill (broiler) for 2–3 minutes, turning once.

4 Transfer the toasts to a serving plate.

5 Toss the parsley into the mushrooms, mixing well, and season well with salt and pepper to taste.

6 Spoon the mushroom mixture over the bread and serve immediately.

COOK'S TIP

Add seasonings, such as curry powder or chilli powder, to the mushrooms for extra flavour, if liked.

COOK'S TIP

Store mushrooms for 24–36 hours in the refrigerator, in paper bags, as they sweat in plastic. Wild mushrooms should be washed but other varieties can simply be wiped with paper towels.

Potato, (Bell) Pepper & Mushroom Hash

Serves 4

INGREDIENTS

675 g/1½ lb potatoes, cubed
1 tbsp olive oil
2 garlic cloves, crushed
1 green (bell) pepper, cubed
1 yellow (bell) pepper, cubed
3 tomatoes, diced

75 g/2¾ oz/1 cup button
    mushrooms, halved
1 tbsp vegetarian Worcester
    sauce
2 tbsp chopped basil
salt and pepper

fresh basil sprigs, to garnish
warm, crusty bread, to serve

1 Cook the potatoes in a saucepan of boiling salted water for 7–8 minutes. Drain well and reserve.

2 Heat the oil in a large, heavy-based frying pan (skillet) and cook the potatoes for 8–10 minutes, stirring until browned.

3 Add the garlic and (bell) peppers and cook for 2–3 minutes.

4 Stir in the tomatoes and mushrooms and cook, stirring, for 5–6 minutes.

5 Stir in the vegetarian Worcester sauce and basil and season well. Garnish and serve with crusty bread.

VARIATION

This dish can also be eaten cold as a salad.

COOK'S TIP

Most brands of Worcester sauce contain anchovies so make sure you choose a vegetarian variety.

Scrambled Tofu (Bean Curd) on Toasted Rolls

Serves 4

INGREDIENTS

75 g/2¾ oz/6 tbsp
   vegetarian margarine
450 g/1 lb marinated,
   firm tofu (bean curd)

1 red onion, chopped
1 red (bell) pepper, chopped
4 ciabatta rolls
2 tbsp chopped mixed herbs

salt and pepper
fresh herbs, to garnish

1 Melt the margarine in a frying pan (skillet) and crumble the tofu (bean curd) into the pan.

2 Add the onion and (bell) pepper and cook for 3–4 minutes, stirring occasionally.

3 Meanwhile, slice the ciabatta rolls in half and toast under a hot grill (broiler) for about 2–3 minutes, turning once. Remove the toasts and transfer to a serving plate.

4 Add the herbs to the tofu (bean curd) mixture, combine and season.

5 Spoon the tofu (bean curd) mixture on to the toast and garnish with fresh herbs. Serve at once.

COOK'S TIP

Marinated tofu (bean curd) adds extra flavour to this dish. Smoked tofu (bean curd) could be used instead.

COOK'S TIP

Rub the cut surface of a garlic clove over the toasted ciabatta rolls for extra flavour.

Mixed Bean Pan-Fry

Serves 4

INGREDIENTS

350 g/12 oz/4 cups mixed green
  beans, such as French (green)
  and broad (fava) beans
2 tbsp vegetable oil
2 garlic cloves, crushed

1 red onion, halved and sliced
225 g/8 oz firm marinated
  tofu (bean curd), diced
1 tbsp lemon juice
½ tsp turmeric

1 tsp ground mixed spice
150 ml/ ¼ pint/⅔ cup
  vegetable stock
2 tsp sesame seeds

1 Trim and chop the
French (green) beans
and set aside until required.

2 Heat the oil in a frying
pan (skillet) and sauté
the garlic and onion for 2
minutes, stirring well.

3 Add the tofu (bean
curd) and cook for
2–3 minutes until just
beginning to brown.

4 Add the French
(green) beans and
broad (fava) beans. Stir in
the lemon juice, turmeric,

mixed spice and vegetable
stock and bring to the boil.

5 Reduce the heat and
simmer for 5–7 minutes
or until the beans are tender.
Sprinkle with sesame seeds
and serve immediately.

VARIATION

*Add lime juice instead of
lemon, for an alternative
citrus flavour.*

VARIATION

*Use smoked tofu (bean
curd) instead of marinated
tofu (bean curd) for an
alternative flavour.*

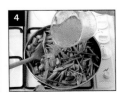

Vegetable Pasta Nests

Serves 4

INGREDIENTS

175 g/6 oz spaghetti

1 aubergine (eggplant), halved and sliced

1 courgette (zucchini), diced

1 red (bell) pepper, seeded and

chopped diagonally

6 tbsp olive oil

2 garlic cloves, crushed

50 g/1¾ oz/4 tbsp butter or vegetarian margarine, melted

15 g/½ oz/1 tbsp dry white breadcrumbs

salt and pepper

fresh parsley sprigs, to garnish

1 Bring a large saucepan of water to the boil and cook the spaghetti until 'al dente' or according to the instructions on the packet. Drain well and set aside until required.

2 Place the aubergine (eggplant), courgette (zucchini) and (bell) pepper on a baking tray (cookie sheet).

3 Mix the oil and garlic together and pour over the vegetables, tossing to coat.

4 Cook under a preheated hot grill (broiler) for about 10 minutes, turning, until tender and lightly charred. Set aside and keep warm.

5 Divide the spaghetti among 4 lightly greased Yorkshire pudding tins (pans). Using a fork, curl the spaghetti to form nests.

6 Brush the pasta nests with melted butter or margarine and sprinkle with the breadcrumbs. Bake in a preheated oven,

at 200°C/400°F/ Gas Mark 6, for 15 minutes or until lightly golden. Remove the pasta nests from the tins (pans) and transfer to serving plates. Divide the grilled (broiled) vegetables between the pasta nests, season and garnish.

COOK'S TIP

'Al dente' means 'to the bite' and describes cooked pasta that is not too soft, but still has a bite to it.

Refried Beans with Tortillas

Serves 4

INGREDIENTS

BEANS:

2 tbsp olive oil

1 onion, finely chopped

3 garlic cloves, crushed

1 green chilli, chopped

400 g/14 oz can red kidney
    beans, drained

400 g/14 oz can pinto
    beans, drained

2 tbsp chopped coriander
    (cilantro)

150 ml/¼ pint/⅔ cup
    vegetable stock

8 wheat tortillas

25 g/1 oz/ ¼ cup vegetarian
    Cheddar cheese, grated

salt and pepper

RELISH:

4 spring onions (scallions),
    chopped

1 red onion, chopped

1 green chilli, chopped

1 tbsp garlic wine vinegar

1 tsp caster (superfine) sugar

1 tomato, chopped

1 Heat the oil for the beans in a large frying pan (skillet). Add the onion and sauté for 3–5 minutes. Add the garlic and chilli and cook for 1 minute.

2 Mash the beans with a potato masher and stir into the pan with the coriander (cilantro).

3 Stir in the stock and cook the beans, stirring, for 5 minutes until soft and pulpy.

4 Place the tortillas on a baking tray (cookie sheet) and heat through in a warm oven for 1–2 minutes.

5 Mix the relish ingredients together.

6 Spoon the beans into a serving dish and top with the cheese. Season well. Roll the tortillas and serve with the relish and beans.

COOK'S TIP

Add a little more liquid to the beans when they are cooking if they begin to catch on the bottom of the frying pan (skillet).

Cabbage & Walnut Stir-Fry

Serves 4

INGREDIENTS

350 g/12 oz white cabbage	8 spring onions (scallions),	100 g/3½ oz walnut halves
350 g/12 oz red cabbage	trimmed	2 tsp Dijon mustard
4 tbsp peanut oil	225 g/8 oz firm tofu (bean curd),	2 tsp poppy seeds
1 tbsp walnut oil	cubed	salt and pepper
2 garlic cloves, crushed	2 tbsp lemon juice	

1 Using a sharp knife, shred the white and red cabbages thinly and set aside until required.

2 Heat the peanut and walnut oils in a preheated wok. Add the garlic, cabbage, spring onions (scallions) and tofu (bean curd) and cook for 5 minutes, stirring.

3 Add the lemon juice, walnuts and mustard, season with salt and pepper and cook for a further 5 minutes or until the cabbage is tender.

4 Transfer the stir-fry to a warm serving bowl, sprinkle with poppy seeds and serve.

COOK'S TIP

As well as adding protein, vitamins and useful fats to the diet, nuts and seeds add flavour and texture to vegetarian meals. Keep a good supply of them in your store-cupboard as they can be used in a great variety of dishes – salads, bakes, stir-fries to name but a few.

VARIATION

Sesame seeds could be used instead of the poppy seeds and drizzle 1 teaspoon of sesame oil over the dish just before serving, if you wish.

Marinated Grilled (Broiled) Fennel

Serves 4

INGREDIENTS

2 fennel bulbs	MARINADE:	1 tbsp chopped thyme
1 red (bell) pepper, cut into large cubes	2 tbsp lime juice	fennel fronds, to garnish
	4 tbsp olive oil	crisp salad, to serve
1 lime, cut into eight wedges	2 garlic cloves, crushed	
	1 tsp wholegrain mustard	

1 Cut each of the fennel bulbs into eight pieces and place in a shallow dish. Mix in the (bell) peppers.

2 To make the marinade, combine the lime juice, oil, garlic, mustard and thyme. Pour the marinade over the fennel and (bell) peppers and leave to marinate for 1 hour.

3 Thread the fennel and (bell) peppers on to wooden skewers with the lime wedges. Preheat a grill (broiler) to medium and grill (broil) the kebabs

(kabobs) for 10 minutes, turning and basting with the marinade.

4 Transfer to serving plates, garnish with fennel fronds and serve with a crisp salad.

VARIATION

Substitute 2 tbsp orange juice for the lime juice and add 1 tbsp honey, if you prefer.

COOK'S TIP

Soak the skewers in water for 20 minutes before using to prevent them from burning during cooking.

Ciabatta Rolls

Serves 4

INGREDIENTS

4 ciabatta rolls	FILLING:	1 bunch watercress
2 tbsp olive oil	1 red (bell) pepper	100 g/3¹/₂ oz/8 tbsp cream
1 garlic clove crushed	1 green (bell) pepper	cheese
	1 yellow (bell) pepper	
	4 radishes, sliced	

1 Slice the ciabatta rolls in half. Heat the olive oil and crushed garlic in a saucepan. Pour the garlic and oil mixture over the cut surfaces of the rolls and leave to stand.

2 Halve the (bell) peppers and place, skin side uppermost, on a grill (broiler) rack. Cook under a hot grill (broiler) for 8–10 minutes until just beginning to char. Remove the (bell) peppers from the grill (broiler), peel and slice thinly.

3 Arrange the radish slices on one half of each roll with a few watercress leaves. Spoon the cream cheese on top. Pile the (bell) peppers on top of the cream cheese and top with the other half of the roll. Serve.

COOK'S TIP

To peel (bell) peppers, wrap them in foil after grilling (broiling). This traps the steam, loosening the skins and making them easier to peel.

COOK'S TIP

Allow the (bell) peppers to cool slightly before filling the roll otherwise the cheese will melt.

Tagliatelle with Courgette (Zucchini) Sauce

Serves 4

INGREDIENTS

650 g/1 lb 7 oz courgettes (zucchini)
6 tbsp olive oil
3 garlic cloves, crushed
3 tbsp chopped basil
2 red chillies, sliced

juice of 1 large lemon
5 tbsp single (light) cream
4 tbsp grated Parmesan cheese
225 g/8 oz tagliatelle
salt and pepper

1 Using a vegetable peeler, slice the courgettes (zucchini) into thin ribbons.

2 Heat the oil in a frying pan (skillet) and sauté the garlic for 30 seconds.

3 Add the courgettes (zucchini) and cook over a gentle heat, stirring, for 5–7 minutes.

4 Stir in the basil, chillies, lemon juice, single (light) cream and grated Parmesan cheese and season with salt and pepper to taste.

5 Meanwhile, cook the tagliatelle in a large pan of lightly salted boiling water for 10 minutes until 'al dente'. Drain the pasta thoroughly and put in a warm serving bowl.

6 Pile the courgette (zucchini) mixture on top of the pasta. Serve.

VARIATION

Lime juice and zest could be used instead of the lemon as an alternative.

Olive, (Bell) Pepper & Cherry Tomato Pasta

Serves 4

INGREDIENTS

225 g/8 oz/2 cups penne

2 tbsp olive oil

2 tbsp butter

2 garlic cloves, crushed

1 green (bell) pepper,
    thinly sliced

1 yellow (bell) pepper,
    thinly sliced

16 cherry tomatoes, halved

1 tbsp chopped oregano

125 ml/4 fl oz/½ cup dry
    white wine

2 tbsp quartered, pitted
    black olives

75 g/2¾ oz rocket (arugula)

salt and pepper

fresh oregano sprigs, to garnish

1 Cook the pasta in a saucepan of boiling salted water for 8–10 minutes or until 'al dente'. Drain thoroughly.

2 Heat the oil and butter in a pan until the butter melts. Sauté the garlic for 30 seconds. Add the (bell) peppers and cook for 3–4 minutes, stirring.

3 Stir in the cherry tomatoes, oregano, wine and olives and cook for 3–4 minutes. Season well with salt and pepper and stir in the rocket until just wilted.

4 Transfer the pasta to a serving dish, spoon over the sauce and mix well. Garnish and serve.

COOK'S TIP

Ensure that the saucepan is large enough to prevent the pasta from sticking together during cooking.

Spinach & Pine Kernel (Nut) Pasta

Serves 4

INGREDIENTS

225 g/8 oz pasta shapes
    or spaghetti
125 ml/4 fl oz/½ cup olive oil
2 garlic cloves, crushed
1 onion, quartered
    and sliced

3 large flat mushrooms, sliced
225 g/8 oz spinach
2 tbsp pine kernels (nuts)
85 ml/3 fl oz/6 tbsp dry
    white wine
salt and pepper

Parmesan shavings,
    to garnish

1 Cook the pasta in a saucepan of boiling salted water for 8–10 minutes or until 'al dente'. Drain well.

2 Meanwhile, heat the oil in a large saucepan and sauté the garlic and onion for 1 minute.

3 Add the sliced mushrooms and cook for 2 minutes, stirring occasionally.

4 Add the spinach and cook for 4–5 minutes or until the spinach has wilted.

5 Stir in the pine kernels (nuts) and wine, season well and cook for 1 minute.

6 Transfer the pasta to a warm serving bowl and toss the sauce into it, mixing well. Garnish with shavings of Parmesan cheese and serve.

COOK'S TIP

Freshly grate a little nutmeg over the dish for extra flavour as it is particularly good with spinach.

Tofu (Bean Curd) & Vegetable Stir-Fry

Serves 4

INGREDIENTS

175 g/6 oz/1¼ cups potatoes, cubed	2 courgettes (zucchini), diced	2 tbsp chopped basil
1 tbsp olive oil	8 canned artichoke hearts, halved	salt and pepper
1 red onion, sliced	150 ml/¼ pint/⅔ cup passata (sieved tomatoes)	
225 g/8 oz firm tofu (bean curd), diced	1 tsp caster (superfine) sugar	

1 Cook the potatoes in a saucepan of boiling water for 10 minutes. Drain thoroughly and set aside until required.

2 Heat the oil in a large frying pan (skillet) and sauté the red onion for 2 minutes until the onion has softened, stirring.

3 Stir in the tofu (bean curd) and courgettes (zucchini) and cook for 3–4 minutes until they begin to brown slightly. Add the potatoes, stirring to mix.

4 Stir in the artichoke hearts, passata (sieved tomatoes), sugar and basil, season with salt and pepper and cook for a further 5 minutes, stirring well. Transfer the stir-fry to serving dishes and serve immediately.

COOK'S TIP

Canned artichoke hearts should be drained thoroughly and rinsed before use because they often have salt added.

VARIATION

Aubergines (eggplants) could be used instead of the courgettes (zucchini), if preferred.

Meat & Poultry

The variety of ways in which meat and poultry can be cooked are included to create a sumptuous selection of dishes. Barbeques, stir-fries, roasts and casseroles are combined to offer a wealth of textures and flavours. Classic and traditional recipes feature alongside more exotic dishes taken from all around the world, incorporating exciting new ingredients alongside family favourites.

For the poultry-lover there are pasta dishes, risottos and bakes, incorporating a variety of healthy and colourful ingredients. For those who enjoy Asian cuisine, choose from Chilli Chicken, Honey-Glazed Duck, Pork Fry with Vegetables and Lamb with Mushroom Sauce. All of these recipes are mouth-watering and quick and easy to prepare.

The dishes in this chapter range from easy, economic mid-week suppers to sophisticated and elegant main courses for special occasions. All of the recipes are extremely wholesome, offering a comprehensive range of tastes. Those on a low-fat diet should choose lean cuts of meat and look out for low-fat mince to enjoy the dishes featured here.

Chicken & Spinach Salad

Serves 4

INGREDIENTS

4 boneless, skinless chicken
    breasts, 150 g/5^1/$_2$ oz each
450 ml/16 fl oz/2 cups fresh
    chicken stock
1 bay leaf
225 g/8 oz fresh young
    spinach leaves

1 small red onion, shredded
115 g/4 oz fresh raspberries
salt and freshly ground
    pink peppercorns
fresh toasted croûtons, to
    garnish

DRESSING:
4 tbsp low-fat natural
    (unsweetened) yogurt
1 tbsp raspberry vinegar
2 tsp clear honey

1 Place the chicken breasts in a frying pan (skillet). Pour over the fresh chicken stock and add the bay leaf. Bring to the boil, cover and simmer for 15–20 minutes, turning half-way through, until the chicken is cooked through. Leave the chicken to cool in the liquid.

2 Arrange the spinach leaves on 4 serving plates and top with the onion. Cover and leave to chill.

3 Drain the cooked chicken and pat dry on absorbent kitchen paper. Slice the chicken breasts thinly and arrange, fanned out, over the spinach and onion. Sprinkle with the raspberries.

4 To make the dressing, mix all the ingredients together in a small bowl.

5 Drizzle a spoonful of dressing over each chicken breast and season with salt and ground pink

peppercorns to taste. Serve with freshly toasted croûtons.

VARIATION

This recipe is delicious with smoked chicken, but it will be more expensive and richer, so use slightly less. It would make an impressive starter for a dinner party.

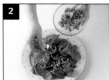

Harlequin Chicken

Serves 4

INGREDIENTS

10 skinless, boneless chicken thighs	1 tbsp sunflower oil	wholemeal (whole wheat) bread and
1 medium onion	400 g/14 oz can chopped tomatoes	a green salad, to serve
1 each medium red, green and	2 tbsp chopped fresh parsley	
yellow (bell) peppers	pepper	

1 Using a sharp knife, cut the chicken thighs into bite-size pieces.

2 Peel and thinly slice the onion. Halve and deseed the (bell) peppers and cut into small diamond shapes.

3 Heat the oil in a shallow frying pan (skillet). Add the chicken and onion and fry quickly until golden.

4 Add the (bell) peppers, cook for 2–3 minutes, then stir in the tomatoes and parsley and season with pepper.

5 Cover tightly and simmer for about 15 minutes, until the chicken and vegetables are tender. Serve hot with wholemeal (whole wheat) bread and a green salad.

COOK'S TIP

You can use dried parsley instead of fresh but remember that you only need about one half of dried to fresh.

COOK'S TIP

If you are making this dish for small children, the chicken can be finely chopped or minced (ground) first.

Steamed Chicken &
Spring Vegetable Parcels

Serves 4

INGREDIENTS

4 boneless, skinless chicken breasts	250 g/9 oz/1 cup young carrots	1 tsp light soy sauce
1 tsp ground lemon grass	250 g/9 oz/1¾ cups young	250 g/9 oz/¾ cup spinach leaves
2 spring onions (scallions), chopped	courgettes (zucchini)	2 tsp sesame oil
finely	2 sticks (stalks) celery	salt and pepper

1 With a sharp knife, make a slit through one side of each chicken breast, to open out a large pocket. Sprinkle the inside of the pocket with lemon grass, salt and pepper. Tuck the spring onions (scallions) into the pockets.

2 Trim the carrots, courgettes and celery then cut into small matchsticks. Plunge them into a pan of boiling water for 1 minute, drain and toss in the soy sauce.

3 Pack the vegetables into the pockets in each chicken breast and fold over firmly to enclose. Reserve any remaining vegetables. Wash the spinach leaves thoroughly, then drain and pat dry with paper towels. Wrap the chicken breasts firmly in the spinach leaves to enclose completely. If the leaves are too firm to wrap the chicken easily, steam them for a few seconds until they are softened and flexible.

4 Place the wrapped chicken in a steamer and steam over rapidly boiling water for 20–25 minutes until cooked.

5 Stir-fry any leftover vegetable sticks and spinach for 1–2 minutes in the sesame oil and serve with the chicken.

Chicken with Two (Bell) Pepper Sauce

Serves 4

INGREDIENTS

2 tbsp olive oil
2 medium onions, chopped finely
2 garlic cloves, crushed
2 red (bell) peppers, chopped
good pinch cayenne pepper

2 tsp tomato purée (paste)
2 yellow (bell) peppers, chopped
pinch of dried basil
4 skinless, boneless chicken breasts
150 ml/¼ pint/⅔ cup dry white wine

150 ml/¼ pint/⅔ cup chicken stock
bouquet garni
salt and pepper
fresh herbs, to garnish

1 Heat 1 tablespoon of oil in each of two medium-sized saucepans. Place half the chopped onions, 1 of the garlic cloves, the red (bell) peppers, the cayenne pepper and the tomato purée (paste) in one of the saucepans. Place the remaining onion, garlic, yellow (bell) peppers and basil in the other pan.

2 Cover each pan and cook over a very low heat for 1 hour until the (bell) peppers are soft. If either mixture becomes dry,

add a little water. Work each mixture separately in a food processor, then sieve separately.

3 Return the separate mixtures to the pans and season. The two sauces can be gently re-heated while the chicken is cooking.

4 Put the chicken breasts into a frying pan (skillet) and add the wine and stock. Add the bouquet garni and bring the liquid to simmer. Cook the chicken for about 20 minutes until tender.

5 To serve, pour a serving of each sauce on to four serving plates, slice the chicken breasts and arrange on the plates. Garnish with fresh herbs.

COOK'S TIP

Make your own bouquet garni by tying together sprigs of your favourite herbs with string, or wrap up dried herbs in a piece of muslin. A popular combination is thyme, parsley and bay.

Chicken Risotto alla Milanese

Serves 4

INGREDIENTS

125 g/4¹/₂ oz/¹/₂ cup butter
900 g/2 lb chicken meat, sliced thinly
1 large onion, chopped
500 g/1 lb 2 oz/2¹/₂ cups risotto rice

600 ml/1 pint/2¹/₂ cups chicken stock
150 ml/¹/₄ pint/²/₃ cup white wine
1 tsp crumbled saffron
salt and pepper

60 g/2 oz/¹/₂ cup grated Parmesan
cheese, to serve

1 Heat 60 g/2 oz/4 tbsp of butter in a deep frying pan (skillet), and fry the chicken and onion until golden brown.

2 Add the rice, stir well, and cook for 15 minutes.

3 Heat the stock until boiling and gradually add to the rice. Add the white wine, saffron, salt and pepper to taste and mix well. Simmer gently for 20 minutes, stirring occasionally, and adding more stock if the risotto becomes too dry.

4 Leave to stand for a few minutes and just before serving add a little more stock and simmer for a further 10 minutes. Serve the risotto, sprinkled with the grated Parmesan cheese and the remaining butter.

COOK'S TIP

A risotto should have moist but separate grains. Stock should be added a little at a time and only when the last addition has been completely absorbed.

VARIATION

The possibilities for risotto are endless – try adding the following just at the end of cooking time: cashew nuts and sweetcorn, lightly sautéed courgettes (zucchini) and basil, or artichokes and oyster mushrooms.

Elizabethan Chicken

Serves 4

INGREDIENTS

15 g/½ oz/1 tbsp butter
1 tbsp sunflower oil
4 skinless, boneless chicken breasts
4 shallots, finely chopped
150 ml/¼ pint/⅔ cup chicken stock

1 tbsp cider vinegar
175 g/6 oz/1 cup halved seedless
   grapes
120 ml/4 floz/½ cup double (heavy)
   cream

1 tsp freshly grated nutmeg
cornflour (cornstarch), to thicken,
   (optional)
salt and pepper

1 Heat the butter and sunflower oil in a wide, flameproof casserole or pan and quickly fry the chicken breasts until golden brown, turning once. Remove the chicken breasts and keep warm while you are cooking the shallots.

2 Add the chopped shallots to the pan and fry gently until softened and lightly browned. Return the chicken breasts to the pan.

3 Add the chicken stock and cider vinegar to the pan, bring to the boil then cover and simmer gently for 10–12 minutes, stirring occasionally.

4 Transfer the chicken to a serving dish. Add the grapes, cream and nutmeg to the pan. Heat through, seasoning with salt and pepper to taste. Add a little cornflour (cornstarch) to thicken the sauce, if desired. Pour the sauce over the chicken and serve.

VARIATION

If desired, add a little dry white wine or vermouth to the sauce in step 3.

212

Speedy Peanut Pan-Fry

Serves 4

INGREDIENTS

300 g/10½ oz/2 cups courgettes (zucchini)

250 g/9 oz/1⅓ cups baby sweetcorn (baby corn)

300 g/10½ oz/3¾ cups button mushrooms

250 g/9 oz/3 cups thread egg noodles

2 tbsp corn oil

1 tbsp sesame oil

8 boneless chicken thighs or 4 breasts, sliced thinly

350 g/12 oz/1½ cups bean sprouts

4 tbsp smooth peanut butter

2 tbsp soy sauce

2 tbsp lime or lemon juice

60 g/2 oz/½ cup roasted peanuts

pepper

coriander (cilantro), to garnish

1 Using a sharp knife, trim and thinly slice the courgettes (zucchini), baby sweetcorn (baby corn) and button mushrooms.

2 Bring a large pan of lightly salted boiling water to the boil and cook the noodles for 3–4 minutes. Meanwhile, heat the corn oil and sesame oil in a large frying pan (skillet) or wok and fry the chicken over a fairly high heat for 1 minute.

3 Add the sliced courgettes (zucchini), corn (baby corn) and button mushrooms and stir-fry for 5 minutes.

4 Add the bean sprouts, peanut butter, soy sauce, lime or lemon juice and pepper, then cook for a further 2 minutes.

5 Drain the noodles, transfer to a serving dish and scatter with the peanuts. Serve with the stir-fried chicken and vegetables, garnished with a sprig of fresh coriander (cilantro).

COOK'S TIP

Try serving this stir-fry with rice sticks. These are broad, pale, translucent ribbon noodles made from ground rice.

Parma-Wrapped Chicken Cushions

Serves 4

INGREDIENTS

125 g/4¹/₂ oz/¹/₂ cup frozen spinach, defrosted	4 Parma ham (prosciutto) slices	1 tbsp plain (all-purpose) flour
125 g/4¹/₂ oz/¹/₂ cup ricotta cheese	25 g/1 oz/2 tbsp butter	150 ml/¹/₄ pint/²/₃ cup dry white or red wine
pinch grated nutmeg	1 tbsp olive oil	300 ml/¹/₂ pint/1¹/₄ cups chicken stock
4 skinless, boneless chicken breasts, each weighing 175 g/6 oz	12 small onions or shallots	salt and pepper
	125 g/4¹/₂ oz/1¹/₂ cups button mushrooms, sliced	

1 Put the spinach into a sieve (strainer) and press out the water with a spoon. Mix with the ricotta and nutmeg and season with salt and pepper to taste.

2 Using a sharp knife, slit each chicken breast through the side and enlarge each cut to form a pocket. Fill with the spinach mixture, reshape the chicken breasts, wrap each breast tightly in a slice of ham and secure with cocktail sticks. Cover and chill in the refrigerator.

3 Heat the butter and oil in a frying pan (skillet) and brown the chicken breasts for 2 minutes on each side. Transfer the chicken to a large, shallow ovenproof dish and keep warm until required.

4 Fry the onions and mushrooms for 2–3 minutes until lightly browned. Stir in the plain (all-purpose) flour then gradually add the wine and stock. Bring to the boil, stirring constantly. Season and spoon the mixture around the chicken.

5 Cook the chicken uncovered in a preheated oven, 200°C/400°F/Gas Mark 6, for 20 minutes. Turn the breasts over and cook for a further 10 minutes. Remove the cocktail sticks and serve with the sauce, together with carrot purée and green beans, if wished.

Poached Breast of Chicken with Whiskey Sauce

Serves 6

INGREDIENTS

25 g/1 oz/2 tbsp butter	600 ml/1 pint/2¹/₂ cups chicken stock	2 tbsp freshly grated horseradish
60 g/2 oz/¹/₂ cup shredded leeks	6 chicken breasts	1 tsp honey, warmed
60 g/2 oz/¹/₃ cup diced carrot	50 ml/2 fl oz/¹/₄ cup whiskey	1 tsp chopped fresh parsley
60 g/2 oz/¹/₄ cup diced celery	200 ml/7 fl oz/1 scant cup crème	salt and pepper
4 shallots, sliced	fraîche	sprig of fresh parsley, to garnish

1 Melt the butter in a large saucepan and add the leeks, carrot, celery and shallots. Cook for 3 minutes, add half the chicken stock and cook for about 8 minutes.

2 Add the remaining chicken stock, bring to the boil, add the chicken breasts and cook for 10 minutes.

3 Remove the chicken and thinly slice. Place on a large, hot serving dish and keep warm until required.

4 In another saucepan, heat the whisky until reduced by half. Strain the chicken stock through a fine sieve, add to the pan and reduce the liquid by half.

5 Add the crème fraîche, the horseradish and the honey. Heat gently and add the chopped parsley and salt and pepper to taste. Stir until well blended.

6 Pour a little of the whiskey sauce around the chicken and pour the remaining sauce into a sauceboat to serve.

7 Serve with a vegetable patty made from the leftover vegetables, mashed potato and fresh vegetables. Garnish with the parsley sprig.

Devilled Chicken

Serves 2–3

INGREDIENTS

25 g/1 oz/¼ cup plain (all-purpose) flour
1 tbsp cayenne pepper
1 tsp paprika
350 g/12 oz skinless, boneless chicken, diced

25 g/1 oz/2 tbsp butter
1 onion, chopped finely
450 ml/16 fl oz/2 cups milk, warmed
4 tbsp apple purée

125 g/4½ oz/¾ cup green (white) grapes
150 ml/¼ pint/⅔ cup soured cream
sprinkle of paprika, to garnish

1 Mix the flour, cayenne pepper and paprika together and use to coat the chicken.

2 Shake off any excess flour. Melt the butter in a saucepan and gently fry the chicken with the onion for 4 minutes.

3 Stir in the flour and spice mixture. Add the milk slowly, stirring until the sauce thickens.

4 Simmer until the sauce is smooth.

5 Add the apple purée and grapes and simmer gently for 20 minutes.

6 Transfer the chicken and devilled sauce to a serving dish and top with soured cream and a sprinkle of paprika.

COOK'S TIP

Add more paprika if desired – as it is quite a mild spice, you can add plenty without it being too overpowering.

VARIATION

For a healthier alternative to soured cream, use natural (unsweetened) yogurt.

Italian Chicken Spirals

Serves 4

INGREDIENTS

4 skinless, boneless, chicken breasts
25 g/1 oz/1 cup fresh basil leaves
15 g/½ oz/2 tbsp hazelnuts
1 garlic clove, crushed

250 g/9 oz/2 cups wholemeal
    (whole wheat) pasta spirals
2 sun-dried tomatoes or fresh
    tomatoes
1 tbsp lemon juice

1 tbsp olive oil
1 tbsp capers
60 g/2 oz/½ cup black olives
salt and pepper

1 Beat the chicken breasts with a rolling pin to flatten evenly.

2 Place the basil and hazelnuts in a food processor and process until finely chopped. Mix with the garlic, salt and pepper.

3 Spread the basil mixture over the chicken breasts and roll up from one short end to enclose the filling. Wrap the chicken roll tightly in foil so that they hold their shape, then seal the ends well.

4 Bring a large pan of lightly salted water to the boil and cook the pasta until tender, but still firm to the bite.

5 Place the chicken parcels in a steamer basket or colander set over the pan, cover tightly, and steam for 10 minutes. Dice the tomatoes.

6 Drain the pasta and return to the pan with the lemon juice, olive oil, tomatoes, capers and olives. Heat through.

7 Pierce the chicken with a skewer to make sure that the juices run clear and not pink, then slice the chicken, arrange over the pasta and serve.

VARIATION

Sun-dried tomatoes have a wonderful, rich flavour, but if you can't find them use fresh tomatoes.

Garlic Chicken Cushions

Serves 4

INGREDIENTS

4 part-boned chicken breasts	1 tbsp olive oil	10 stuffed olives, sliced
125 g/4¹/₂ oz/¹/₂ cup frozen spinach, defrosted	1 onion, chopped	salt and pepper
150 g/5¹/₂ oz/¹/₂ cup ricotta cheese	1 red (bell) pepper, sliced	pasta, to serve
2 garlic cloves, crushed	400 g/14 oz can chopped tomatoes	
	6 tbsp wine or chicken stock	

1 Make a slit between the skin and meat on one side of each chicken breast. Lift the skin to form a pocket, being careful to leave the skin attached to the other side.

2 Put the spinach into a sieve and press out the water with a spoon. Mix with the ricotta, half the garlic and seasoning.

3 Spoon the spinach mixture under the skin of each chicken breast then secure the edge of the skin with cocktail sticks.

4 Heat the oil in a frying pan (skillet), add the onion and fry for a minute, stirring. Add the remaining garlic and red (bell) pepper and cook for 2 minutes. Stir in the tomatoes, wine or stock, olives and seasoning. Set the sauce aside and chill the chicken if preparing in advance.

5 Bring the sauce to the boil, pour into a shallow ovenproof dish and arrange the chicken breasts on the top in a single layer.

6 Cook, uncovered in a preheated oven, 200°C/400°F/ Gas Mark 6, for 35 minutes until the chicken is golden and cooked through. Test by making a slit in one of the chicken breasts with a skewer to make sure the juices run clear and not pink. Spoon a little of the sauce over the chicken breasts then transfer to serving plates. Serve with pasta.

Chicken Strips & Dips

Serves 2

INGREDIENTS

2 boneless chicken breasts	PEANUT DIP:	TOMATO DIP:
15 g/¹⁄₂ oz/2 tbsp plain (all-purpose) flour	3 tbsp smooth or crunchy peanut butter	5 tbsp creamy fromage frais
1 tbsp sunflower oil	4 tbsp natural (unsweetened) yogurt	1 medium tomato
	1 tsp grated orange rind	2 tsp tomato purée (paste)
	orange juice (optional)	1 tsp chopped fresh chives

1 Using a sharp knife, slice the chicken into fairly thin strips and toss in the flour to coat.

2 Heat the oil in a non-stick pan and fry the chicken until golden and thoroughly cooked. Remove the chicken strips from the pan and drain well on absorbent paper towels.

3 To make the peanut dip, mix together all the ingredients in a bowl (if desired, add a little orange juice to thin the consistency).

4 To make the tomato dip, chop the tomato and mix with the remaining ingredients.

5 Serve the chicken strips with the dips and a selection of vegetable sticks for dipping.

VARIATION

For a lower-fat alternative, poach the strips of chicken in a small amount of boiling chicken stock for 6–8 minutes.

VARIATION

For a refreshing guacamole dip, combine 1 mashed avocado, 2 finely chopped spring onions (scallions), 1 chopped tomato, 1 crushed garlic clove and a squeeze of lemon juice. Remember to add the lemon juice immediately after the avocado has been mashed to prevent discolouration.

Chicken Lady Jayne

Serves 4

INGREDIENTS

4 chicken breasts or suprêmes, each
about 125 g/4½ oz

4 tbsp corn oil

8 shallots, sliced

rind and juice of 1 lemon

2 tsp Worcestershire sauce

4 tbsp chicken stock

1 tbsp chopped fresh parsley

3 tbsp coffee liqueur

3 tbsp brandy, warmed

1 Place the chicken breasts or suprêmes on a chopping board, cover with cling film (plastic wrap) and pound them until flattened with a wooden meat mallet or a rolling pin.

2 Heat the oil in a large frying pan (skillet) and fry the chicken for 3 minutes on each side. Add the shallots and cook for a further 3 minutes.

3 Sprinkle with lemon juice and lemon rind and add the Worcestershire sauce and chicken stock. Cook for 2 minutes, then sprinkle with the chopped fresh parsley.

4 Add the coffee liqueur and the brandy and flame the chicken by lighting the spirit with a taper or long match. Cook until the flame is extinguished and serve.

COOK'S TIP

A suprême is a chicken fillet that sometimes has part of the wing bone remaining. Chicken breasts can be used instead.

COOK'S TIP

Flattening the suprêmes means that they take less time to cook.

Golden Glazed Chicken

Serves 6

INGREDIENTS

6 boneless chicken breasts	2 tbsp clear honey	3 tbsp chopped mint
1 tsp turmeric	2 tbsp sunflower oil	salt and pepper
1 tbsp wholegrain mustard	350 g/12 oz/1½ cups long grain rice	mint sprigs, to garnish
300 ml/½ pint/1¼ cups orange juice	1 orange	

1 With a sharp knife, mark the surface of the chicken breasts in a diamond pattern. Mix together the turmeric, mustard, orange juice and honey and pour over the chicken. Chill until required.

2 Lift the chicken from the marinade and pat dry on paper towels.

3 Heat the oil in a wide pan, add the chicken and sauté until golden, turning once. Drain off any excess oil. Pour over the marinade, cover and simmer for 10–15 minutes until the chicken is tender.

4 Boil the rice in lightly salted water until tender and drain well. Finely grate the rind from the orange and stir into the rice with the mint.

5 Using a sharp knife, remove the peel and white pith from the orange and cut the flesh into segments.

6 Serve the chicken with the orange and mint rice, garnished with orange segments and mint sprigs.

VARIATION

To make a slightly sharper sauce, use small grapefruit instead of the oranges.

Mediterranean Chicken Parcels

Serves 6

INGREDIENTS

1 tbsp olive oil	500 g/1 lb 2 oz/3½ cups courgettes	1 small bunch fresh basil or oregano
6 skinless chicken breast fillets	(zucchini), sliced	pepper
250 g/9 oz/2 cups Mozzarella cheese	6 large tomatoes, sliced	rice or pasta, to serve

1 Cut six pieces of foil each about 25 cm/10 inches square. Brush the foil squares lightly with oil and set aside until required.

2 With a sharp knife, slash each chicken breast at intervals, then slice the Mozzarella cheese and place between the cuts in the chicken.

3 Divide the courgettes (zucchini) and tomatoes between the pieces of foil and sprinkle with black pepper. Tear or roughly chop the basil or oregano and scatter over the vegetables in each parcel.

4 Place the chicken on top of each pile of vegetables then wrap in the foil to enclose the chicken and vegetables, tucking in the ends.

5 Place on a baking tray (cookie sheet) and bake in a preheated oven, 200°C/400°F/Gas Mark 6, for about 30 minutes.

6 To serve, unwrap each foil parcel and serve with rice or pasta.

COOK'S TIP

To aid cooking, place the vegetables and chicken on the shiny side of the foil so that once the parcel is wrapped up the dull surface of the foil is facing outwards. This ensures that the heat is absorbed into the parcel and not reflected away from it.

Chicken, Corn & Mangetout (Snow Pea) Sauté

Serves 4

INGREDIENTS

4 skinless, boneless chicken breasts	2 tbsp sunflower oil	1 tbsp sunflower seeds
250 g/9 oz/1⅓ cups baby sweetcorn (baby corn)	1 tbsp sherry vinegar	pepper
250 g/9 oz mangetout (snow peas)	1 tbsp honey	rice or egg noodles, to serve
	1 tbsp light soy sauce	

1 Using a sharp knife, slice the chicken breasts into long, thin strips. Cut the baby sweetcorn (baby corn) in half lengthways and top and tail the mangetout (snow peas). Set the vegetables aside until required.

2 Heat the sunflower oil in a wok or a wide frying pan (skillet) and fry the chicken over a fairly high heat, stirring constantly, for 1 minute.

3 Add the baby sweetcorn (baby corn) and mangetout (snow peas) and stir over a moderate heat for 5–8 minutes, until evenly cooked.

4 Mix together the sherry vinegar, honey and soy sauce and stir into the pan with the sunflower seeds. Season with pepper to taste. Cook, stirring constantly, for 1 minute. Serve the sauté hot with rice or Chinese egg noodles.

COOK'S TIP

Rice vinegar or balsamic vinegar makes a good substitute for the sherry vinegar.

Savoury Chicken Sausages

Serves 4–6

INGREDIENTS

175 g/6 oz/3 cups fresh breadcrumbs
250 g/9 oz cooked chicken, minced
   (ground)
1 small leek, chopped finely

pinch each of mixed herbs and
   mustard powder
2 eggs, separated
4 tbsp milk

crisp breadcrumbs for coating
25 g/1 oz/2 tbsp beef dripping
salt and pepper

1 In a large clean bowl, combine the breadcrumbs, minced (ground) chicken, leek, mixed herbs and mustard powder, and season with salt and pepper. Mix together until thoroughly incorporated.

2 Add 1 whole egg and an egg yolk with a little milk to bind the mixture.

3 Divide the mixture into 6 or 8 and shape into thick or thin sausages.

4 Whisk the remaining egg white until frothy. Coat the sausages first in the egg white and then in the crisp breadcrumbs.

5 Heat the dripping and fry the sausages for 6 minutes until golden brown. Serve.

COOK'S TIP

Make your own minced (ground) chicken by working lean cuts of chicken in a food processor.

VARIATION

If you want to lower the saturated fat content of this recipe, use a little oil for frying instead of the dripping.

Golden Chicken Risotto

Serves 4

INGREDIENTS

2 tbsp sunflower oil

15 g/^{1}/$_2$ oz/1 tbsp butter or margarine

1 medium leek, thinly sliced

1 large yellow (bell) pepper, diced

3 skinless, boneless chicken breasts, diced

350 g/12 oz round grain (arborio) rice

few strands saffron

1.5 litres/2^3/$_4$ pints/6^1/$_4$ cups chicken stock

200 g/7 oz can baby sweetcorn (baby corn)

60 g/2 oz/^{1}/$_2$ cup toasted unsalted peanuts

60 g/2 oz/^{1}/$_2$ cup grated Parmesan cheese

salt and pepper

1 Heat the oil and butter or margarine in a large saucepan. Fry the leek and (bell) pepper for 1 minute then stir in the chicken and cook, stirring until golden brown.

2 Stir in the rice and cook for 2–3 minutes.

3 Stir in the saffron strands, and salt and pepper to taste. Add the stock, a little at a time, cover and cook over a low heat, stirring occasionally, for about 20 minutes, until the rice is tender and most of the liquid is absorbed. Do not let the risotto dry out – add more stock if necessary.

4 Stir in the baby sweetcorn (baby corn), peanuts and Parmesan cheese, then adjust the seasoning to taste. Serve hot.

COOK'S TIP

Risottos can be frozen, before adding the Parmesan cheese, for up to 1 month, but remember to reheat this risotto thoroughly as it contains chicken.

Quick Chicken Bake

Serves 4

INGREDIENTS

500 g/1 lb 2 oz minced (ground)
    chicken
1 large onion, chopped finely
2 carrots, diced finely
25 g/1 oz/2 tbsp plain (all-purpose)
    flour

1 tbsp tomato purée (paste)
pinch of fresh thyme
900 g/2 lb potatoes, creamed with
    butter and milk and highly
    seasoned

300 ml/1½ pint/1¼ cups chicken
    stock
90 g/3 oz/¾ cup grated Lancashire
    cheese
salt and pepper
peas, to serve

1 Dry-fry the minced (ground) chicken, onion and carrots in a non-stick saucepan for 5 minutes, stirring frequently.

2 Sprinkle the chicken with the flour and simmer for a further 2 minutes.

3 Gradually blend in the tomato purée (paste) and stock then simmer for 15 minutes. Season and add the thyme.

4 Transfer the chicken and vegetable mixture to an ovenproof casserole and allow to cool.

5 Spoon the mashed potato over the chicken mixture and sprinkle with the Lancashire cheese. Bake in a preheated oven, 200°C/400°F/Gas Mark 6, for 20 minutes, or until the cheese is bubbling and golden, then serve with the peas.

VARIATION

Instead of Lancashire cheese, you could sprinkle Cotswold cheese over the top. This is a tasty blend of Double Gloucester, onion and chives, and is ideal for melting as a topping. Alternatively, you could use a mixture of cheeses, depending on whatever you have available.

Tom's Toad in the Hole

Serves 4–6

INGREDIENTS

125 g/4½ oz/1 cup plain
(all-purpose) flour
pinch of salt

1 egg, beaten
200 ml/7 fl oz/1 scant cup milk
75 ml/3 fl oz/⅓ cup water

2 tbsp beef dripping(s)
250 g/9 oz chicken breasts
250 g/9 oz Cumberland sausage

1 Mix the flour and salt in a bowl, make a well in the centre and add the beaten egg.

2 Add half the milk, and using a wooden spoon, work in the flour slowly.

3 Beat the mixture until smooth, then add the remaining milk and water.

4 Beat again until the mixture is smooth. Let the mixture stand for at least 1 hour.

5 Add the dripping(s) to individual baking tins (pans) or to one large baking tin (pan). Cut up the chicken and sausage so that you get a generous piece in each individual tin (pan) or several scattered around the large tin (pan).

6 Heat in a preheated oven, 220°C/425°F/ Gas Mark 7, for 5 minutes until very hot. Remove the tins (pans) from the oven and pour in the batter, leaving space for the mixture to expand.

7 Return to the oven to cook for 35 minutes, until risen and golden brown. Do not open the oven door for at least 30 minutes.

8 Serve while hot, with chicken or onion gravy, or on its own.

VARIATION

Use skinless, boneless chicken legs instead of chicken breast in the recipe. Cut up as directed. Instead of Cumberland sausage, use your favourite variety of sausage.

Neapolitan Pork Steaks

Serves 4

INGREDIENTS
---

2 tbsp olive oil
1 garlic clove, chopped
1 large onion, sliced
1 x 400 g/14 oz can tomatoes

2 tsp yeast extract
4 pork loin steaks, each about
125 g/4½ oz
75 g/2¾ oz black olives, pitted

2 tbsp fresh basil, shredded
freshly grated Parmesan cheese,
to serve

---

1 Heat the oil in a large frying pan (skillet). Add the onions and garlic and cook, stirring, for 3–4 minutes or until they just begin to soften.

2 Add the tomatoes and yeast extract to the frying pan (skillet) and leave to simmer for about 5 minutes or until the sauce starts to thicken.

3 Cook the pork steaks, under a preheated grill (broiler), for 5 minutes on both sides, until the the meat is golden and cooked through. Set the pork steaks aside and keep warm.

4 Add the olives and fresh shredded basil to the sauce in the frying pan (skillet) and stir quickly to combine.

5 Transfer the steaks to warm serving plates. Top the steaks with the sauce, sprinkle with freshly grated Parmesan cheese and serve immediately.

COOK'S TIP

Parmesan is a mature and exceptionally hard cheese produced in Italy. You only need to add a little as it has a very strong flavour.

COOK'S TIP

There are many types of canned tomato available – for example plum tomatoes, or tomatoes chopped in water, or chopped sieved tomatoes (passata). The chopped variety are often canned with added flavours such as garlic, basil, onion, chilli and mixed herbs, and are a good storecupboard standby.

Escalopes with Italian Sausage & Capers

Serves 4

INGREDIENTS

1 tbsp olive oil	finely grated rind and juice	4 turkey or veal escalopes, each
6 canned anchovy fillets, drained	of 1 orange	about 125 g/4½ oz
1 tbsp capers, drained	75 g/2¾ oz Italian sausage, diced	salt and pepper
1 tbsp fresh rosemary, stalks	3 tomatoes, skinned and chopped	crusty bread or cooked polenta,
removed		to serve

1 Heat the oil in a large frying pan (skillet). Add the anchovies, capers, fresh rosemary, orange rind and juice, Italian sausage and tomatoes to the pan and cook for 5–6 minutes, stirring occasionally.

2 Meanwhile, place the turkey or veal escalopes between sheets of greaseproof paper. Pound the meat with a meat mallet or the end of a rolling pin to flatten it.

3 Add the meat to the mixture in the frying pan (skillet). Season to taste with salt and pepper, cover and cook for 3–5 minutes on each side, slightly longer if the meat is thicker.

4 Transfer to serving plates and serve with fresh crusty bread or cooked polenta.

VARIATION

Try using 4-minute steaks, slightly flattened, instead of the turkey or veal. Cook them for 4–5 minutes on top of the sauce in the pan.

COOK'S TIP

Polenta is typical of northern Italian cuisine. It is often fried or toasted and used to mop up the juices of the main course.

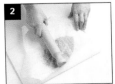

Creamed Strips of Sirloin with Rigatoni

Serves 4

INGREDIENTS

75 g/3 oz/6 tbsp butter
450 g/1 lb sirloin steak,
  trimmed and cut into thin
  strips
175 g/6 oz button
  mushrooms, sliced
1 tsp mustard

pinch of freshly grated root
  ginger
2 tbsp dry sherry
150 ml/¹/4 pint/⁵/8 cup double
  (heavy) cream
salt and pepper
4 slices hot toast, cut into
  triangles, to serve

PASTA:
450 g/1 lb dried rigatoni
2 tbsp olive oil
2 fresh basil sprigs
115 g/4 oz/8 tbsp butter

1 Melt the butter in a frying pan (skillet) and fry the steak over a low heat for 6 minutes. Transfer to an ovenproof dish and keep warm.

2 Add the mushrooms to the remaining juices in the frying pan (skillet) and cook for 2–3 minutes. Add the mustard, ginger, salt and pepper. Cook for 2 minutes, then add the

sherry and cream. Cook for 3 minutes, then pour the cream sauce over the steak.

3 Bake the steak and cream mixture in a preheated oven at 90°C/375°F/Gas 5 for 10 minutes.

4 Bring a pan of lightly salted water to the boil. Add the rigatoni, olive oil and 1 basil sprig and boil

for 10 minutes. Drain and transfer to a warm serving plate. Toss the pasta with the butter and garnish with the remaining basil sprig.

5 Serve the steak with the pasta and triangles of warm toast.

Egg Noodles with Beef

Serves 4

INGREDIENTS
---

285 g/10 oz egg noodles
3 tbsp walnut oil
2.5 cm/1 inch piece fresh root
   ginger, cut into thin strips
5 spring onions (scallions),
   finely shredded
2 garlic cloves, finely chopped

1 red (bell) pepper, cored,
   seeded and thinly sliced
100 g/3^1/2 oz button
   mushrooms, thinly sliced
340 g/12 oz fillet steak, cut
   into thin strips
1 tbsp cornflour (cornstarch)
5 tbsp dry sherry

3 tbsp soy sauce
1 tsp soft brown sugar
225 g/8 oz/1 cup beansprouts
1 tbsp sesame oil
salt and pepper
spring onion (scallion) strips,
   to garnish

---

1 Bring a large saucepan of water to the boil. Add the noodles and cook according to the instructions on the packet. Drain and set aside.

2 Heat the walnut oil in a preheated wok. Add the ginger, spring onions (scallions) and garlic and stir-fry for 45 seconds. Add the (bell) pepper, mushrooms and steak and stir-fry for 4 minutes. Season to taste.

3 Mix together the cornflour (cornstarch), sherry and soy sauce in a small jug to form a paste, and pour into the wok. Sprinkle over the brown sugar and stir-fry all of the ingredients for 2 minutes.

4 Add the beansprouts, drained noodles and sesame oil to the wok, stir and toss together for 1 minute. Garnish with strips of spring onion (scallion) and serve.

COOK'S TIP

If you do not have a wok, you could prepare this dish in a frying pan (skillet). However, a wok is preferable, as the round base ensures an even distribution of heat and it is easier to keep stirring and tossing the contents when stir-frying.

Stir-Fried Pork with Pasta & Vegetables

Serves 4

INGREDIENTS

3 tbsp sesame oil
350 g/12 oz pork fillet
(tenderloin), cut into thin
strips
450 g/1 lb dried taglioni
1 tbsp olive oil
8 shallots, sliced
2 garlic cloves, finely chopped

2.5 cm/1 inch piece fresh root
ginger, grated
1 fresh green chilli, finely
chopped
1 red (bell) pepper, cored,
seeded and thinly sliced
1 green (bell) pepper, cored,
seeded and thinly sliced

3 courgettes (zucchini), thinly
sliced
2 tbsp ground almonds
1 tsp ground cinnamon
1 tbsp oyster sauce
60 g/2 oz creamed coconut
(see Cook's Tip, below),
grated
salt and pepper

1 Heat the sesame oil in a preheated wok. Season the pork and stir-fry for 5 minutes.

2 Bring a pan of salted water to the boil. Add the taglioni and olive oil and cook for 12 minutes. Set aside and keep warm.

3 Add the shallots, garlic, ginger and chilli to the wok and stir-fry for 2 minutes. Add the (bell) peppers and courgettes and stir-fry for 1 minute.

4 Add the ground almonds, cinnamon, oyster sauce and coconut cream to the wok and stir-fry for 1 minute.

5 Drain the taglioni and transfer to a serving dish. Top with the stir-fry and serve immediately.

COOK'S TIP

Creamed coconut is available from Chinese and Asian food stores and some large supermarkets. It is sold in compressed blocks and adds a concentrated coconut flavour to the dish.

Orecchioni with Pork in Cream Sauce, Garnished with Quail Eggs

Serves 4

INGREDIENTS

450 g/1 lb pork fillet
(tenderloin), thinly sliced
4 tbsp olive oil
225 g/8 oz button
mushrooms, sliced

200 ml/7 fl oz/^{7}/8 cup Italian
Red Wine Sauce (see page
52)
1 tbsp lemon juice
pinch of saffron

350 g/12 oz/3 cups dried
orecchioni
4 tbsp double (heavy) cream
12 quail eggs (see Cook's Tip,
below)
salt

1 Pound the slices of pork until wafer thin, then cut into strips.

2 Heat the olive oil in a frying pan (skillet) and stir-fry the pork for 5 minutes, then stir-fry the mushrooms for 2 minutes.

3 Pour over the Italian Red Wine Sauce and simmer for 20 minutes.

4 Meanwhile, bring a large saucepan of

lightly salted water to the boil. Add the lemon juice, saffron and orecchioni and cook for 12 minutes, until tender but still firm to the bite. Drain the pasta and keep warm.

5 Stir the cream into the pan with the pork and heat gently for 3 minutes.

6 Boil the quail eggs for 3 minutes, cool them in cold water and remove the shells.

7 Transfer the pasta to a warm serving plate, top with the pork and the sauce and garnish with the eggs. Serve immediately.

COOK'S TIP

In this recipe, the quail eggs are soft-boiled (soft-cooked). As they are very difficult to shell when warm, they should be thoroughly cooled first. Otherwise, they will break up unattractively.

Sliced Breast of Duckling with Linguine

Serves 4

INGREDIENTS

4 x 275 g/10$^1/_2$ oz boned
   breasts of duckling
25 g/1 oz/2 tbsp butter
50 g/2 oz/3$^3/_8$ cups finely
   chopped carrots
50 g/2 oz/4 tbsp finely
   chopped shallots
1 tbsp lemon juice

150 ml/$^1/_4$ pint/$^5/_8$ cup meat
   stock
4 tbsp clear honey
115 g/4 oz/$^3/_4$ cup fresh or
   thawed frozen raspberries
25 g/1 oz/$^1/_4$ cup plain (all
   purpose) flour
1 tbsp Worcestershire sauce

400 g/14 oz fresh linguine
1 tbsp olive oil
salt and pepper

TO GARNISH:
fresh raspberries
fresh sprig of flat-leaf parsley

1 Trim and score the
duck breasts and
season well. Melt the
butter in a frying pan
(skillet) and fry the duck
breasts until lightly
coloured.

2 Add the carrots,
shallots, lemon juice
and half the meat stock and
simmer for 1 minute. Stir
in half the honey and half
the raspberries. Stir in half

the flour and cook for
3 minutes. Add the pepper
and Worcestershire sauce.

3 Stir in the remaining
stock and cook for
1 minute. Stir in the
remaining honey,
raspberries and flour. Cook
for a further 3 minutes.

4 Remove the duck from
the pan, but continue
simmering the sauce.

5 Bring a large pan of
salted water to the
boil. Add the linguine and
olive oil and cook until
tender. Drain and divide
between 4 plates.

6 Slice the duck breast
lengthways into
5 mm/¼ inch thick pieces.
Pour a little sauce over the
pasta and arrange the sliced
duck in a fan shape on top.
Garnish and serve.

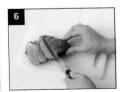

Chilli Chicken

Serves 4

INGREDIENTS

350 g/12 oz skinless, boneless
lean chicken
$^1/_2$ tsp salt
1 egg white, lightly beaten
2 tbsp cornflour (cornstarch)
4 tbsp vegetable oil
2 garlic cloves, crushed

1-cm/$^1/_2$-inch piece fresh root
ginger, grated
1 red (bell) pepper, seeded and
diced
1 green (bell) pepper, seeded
and diced
2 fresh red chillies, chopped

2 tbsp light soy sauce
1 tbsp dry sherry or Chinese
rice wine
1 tbsp wine vinegar

1 Cut the chicken into cubes and place in a mixing bowl. Add the salt, egg white, cornflour (cornstarch) and 1 tbsp of the oil. Turn the chicken in the mixture to coat well.

2 Heat the remaining oil in a preheated wok. Add the garlic and ginger and stir-fry for 30 seconds.

3 Add the chicken pieces to the wok and stir-fry for 2–3 minutes, or until browned.

4 Stir in the (bell) peppers, chillies, soy sauce, sherry or Chinese rice wine and wine vinegar and cook for 2–3 minutes, until the chicken is cooked through. Transfer to a serving dish and serve.

VARIATION

This recipe works well if you use 350 g/12 oz lean steak, cut into thin strips or 450 g/ 1 lb raw prawns (shrimp) instead of the chicken.

COOK'S TIP

When preparing chillies, wear rubber gloves to prevent the juices from burning and irritating your hands. Be careful not to touch your face, especially your lips or eyes, until you have washed your hands.

258

Lemon Chicken

Serves 4

INGREDIENTS

vegetable oil, for deep-frying
650 g/1 1/2 lb skinless, boneless
    chicken, cut into strips
lemon slices and shredded
    spring onions (scallions),
    to garnish

SAUCE:
1 tbsp cornflour (cornstarch)
6 tbsp cold water
3 tbsp fresh lemon juice
2 tbsp sweet sherry
1/2 tsp caster (superfine) sugar

1 Heat the oil in a wok until almost smoking. Reduce the heat and stir-fry the chicken strips for 3–4 minutes, until cooked through. Remove the chicken with a slotted spoon, set aside and keep warm. Drain the oil from the wok.

2 To make the sauce, mix the cornflour with 2 tablespoons of the water to form a paste.

3 Pour the lemon juice and remaining water into the mixture in the wok. Add the sherry and sugar and bring to the boil, stirring until the sugar has completely dissolved.

4 Stir in the cornflour mixture and return to the boil. Reduce the heat and simmer, stirring constantly, for 2-3 minutes, until the sauce is thickened and clear.

5 Transfer the chicken to a warm serving plate and pour the sauce over the top. Garnish with the lemon slices and shredded spring onions (scallions) and serve immediately.

COOK'S TIP

If you would prefer to use chicken portions rather than strips, cook them in the oil, covered, over a low heat for about 30 minutes, or until cooked through.

Chicken Chop Suey

Serves 4

INGREDIENTS

4 tbsp light soy sauce	2 garlic cloves, crushed	shredded leek, to garnish
2 tsp light brown sugar	350 g/12 oz beansprouts	
500 g/1¼ lb skinless, boneless chicken breasts	3 tsp sesame oil	
	1 tbsp cornflour (cornstarch)	
3 tbsp vegetable oil	3 tbsp water	
2 onions, quartered	425 ml/¾ pint/2 cups chicken stock	

1 Mix the soy sauce and sugar together, stirring until the sugar has dissolved.

2 Trim any fat from the chicken and cut the meat into thin strips. Place the chicken strips in a shallow glass dish and spoon the soy mixture over them, turning to coat. Leave to marinate in the refrigerator for 20 minutes.

3 Heat the oil in a preheated wok. Add the chicken and stir-fry for 2–3 minutes, until golden brown.

4 Add the onions and garlic and cook for a further 2 minutes. Add the beansprouts, cook for a further 4–5 minutes, then add the sesame oil.

5 Blend the cornflour (cornstarch) with the water to form a smooth paste. Pour the stock into the wok, together with the cornflour (cornstarch) paste and bring to the boil, stirring constantly until the sauce is thickened and clear. Transfer to a warm serving dish, garnish with shredded leek and serve immediately.

VARIATION

This recipe may be made with strips of lean steak, pork or with mixed vegetables. Change the type of stock accordingly.

Spicy Peanut Chicken

Serves 4

INGREDIENTS

300 g/10^1/2 oz skinless,
   boneless chicken breast
2 tbsp peanut oil
125 g/4^1/2 oz/1 cup shelled
   peanuts
1 fresh red chilli, sliced
1 green (bell) pepper, seeded
   and cut into strips

1 tsp sesame oil
fried rice, to serve

SAUCE:
150 ml/^{1}/4 pint/^{2}/3 cup
   chicken stock
1 tbsp Chinese rice wine or
   dry sherry

1 tbsp light soy sauce
1^1/2 tsp light brown sugar
2 garlic cloves, crushed
1 tsp grated fresh root ginger
1 tsp rice wine vinegar

1 Trim any fat from the chicken and cut the meat into 2.5-cm/ 1-inch cubes. Set aside.

2 Heat the peanut oil in a preheated wok. Add the peanuts and stir-fry for 1 minute. Remove the peanuts with a slotted spoon and set aside.

3 Add the chicken to the wok and cook for 1–2 minutes. Stir in the chilli and (bell) pepper and cook

for 1 minute. Remove from the wok with a slotted spoon.

4 Put half of the peanuts in a food processor and process until almost smooth. Alternatively, place them in a plastic bag and crush with a rolling pin.

5 To make the sauce, add the chicken stock, Chinese rice wine or dry sherry, soy sauce, sugar, garlic, ginger and rice wine vinegar to the wok.

6 Heat the sauce without boiling and stir in the peanut purée, remaining peanuts, chicken, chilli and (bell) pepper. Sprinkle with the sesame oil, stir and cook for 1 minute. Serve hot.

COOK'S TIP

If necessary, process the peanuts with a little of the stock in step 4 to form a softer paste.

Chinese Chicken Salad

Serves 4

INGREDIENTS

225 g/8 oz skinless, boneless
chicken breasts
2 tsp light soy sauce
1 tsp sesame oil
1 tsp sesame seeds
2 tbsp vegetable oil
125 g/4 1/2 oz beansprouts

1 red (bell) pepper, seeded and
thinly sliced
1 carrot, cut into matchsticks
3 baby corn cobs, sliced
snipped chives and carrot
matchsticks, to garnish

SAUCE:
2 tsp rice wine vinegar
1 tbsp light soy sauce
dash of chilli oil

1 Place the chicken in a shallow glass dish.

2 Mix together the soy sauce and sesame oil and pour over the chicken. Sprinkle with sesame seeds and leave to stand for 20 minutes.

3 Remove the chicken from the marinade and cut the meat into slices.

4 Heat the oil in a preheated wok. Add the chicken and fry for 4-5 minutes, until cooked through and golden brown on both sides. Remove the chicken from the wok with a slotted spoon, set aside and leave to cool.

5 Add the beansprouts, (bell) pepper, carrot and baby corn cobs to the wok and stir-fry for 2–3 minutes. Remove from the wok with a slotted spoon, set aside and leave to cool.

6 To make the sauce, mix the rice wine vinegar, light soy sauce and chilli oil together.

7 Arrange the chicken and vegetables on a serving plate. Spoon the sauce over the salad, garnish and serve.

COOK'S TIP

If you have time, make the sauce and leave to stand for 30 minutes for the flavours to fully develop.

Honey-Glazed Duck

Serves 4

INGREDIENTS

1 tsp dark soy sauce	2 tsp cornflour (cornstarch)	TO GARNISH:
2 tbsp clear honey	2 tsp water	celery leaves
1 tsp garlic vinegar	2 large boneless duck breasts,	cucumber wedges
2 garlic cloves, crushed	about 225g/8 oz each	snipped chives
1 tsp ground star anise		

1 Mix the soy sauce, clear honey, garlic vinegar, garlic and star anise. Blend the cornflour (cornstarch) with the water to form a smooth paste and stir it into the mixture.

2 Place the duck breasts in a shallow ovenproof dish. Brush with the soy marinade, turning to coat them completely. Cover and leave to marinate in the refrigerator for at least 2 hours, or overnight.

3 Remove the duck from the marinade and cook in a preheated oven, at 220°C/425°F/Gas Mark 7, for 20–25 minutes, basting frequently with the glaze.

4 Remove the duck from the oven and transfer to a preheated grill (broiler). Grill (broil) for about 3–4 minutes to caramelize the top.

5 Remove the duck from the grill (broiler) pan and cut into thin slices. Arrange the duck slices in a warm serving dish, garnish with celery leaves, cucumber wedges and snipped chives and serve immediately.

COOK'S TIP

If the duck begins to burn slightly while it is cooking in the oven, cover with foil. Check that the duck breasts are cooked through by inserting the point of a sharp knife into the thickest part of the flesh – the juices should run clear.

Pork Fry with Vegetables

Serves 4

INGREDIENTS

350 g/12 oz lean pork
   fillet (tenderloin)
2 tbsp vegetable oil
2 garlic cloves, crushed
1-cm/½-inch piece fresh root
   ginger, cut into slivers
1 carrot, cut into thin strips

1 red (bell) pepper, seeded and
   diced
1 fennel bulb, sliced
25 g/1 oz water chestnuts,
   halved
75 g/2 ¾ oz beansprouts
2 tbsp Chinese rice wine

300 ml/½ pint/1¼ cups pork
   or chicken stock
pinch of dark brown sugar
1 tsp cornflour (cornstarch)
2 tsp water

1 Cut the pork into thin slices. Heat the oil in a preheated wok. Add the garlic, ginger and pork and stir-fry for 1–2 minutes, until the meat is sealed.

2 Add the carrot, (bell) pepper, fennel and water chestnuts to the wok and stir-fry for 2-3 minutes.

3 Add the beansprouts and stir-fry for 1 minute. Remove the pork and vegetables from the wok and keep warm.

4 Add the Chinese rice wine, pork or chicken stock and sugar to the wok. Blend the cornflour (cornstarch) to a smooth paste with the water and stir it into the sauce. Bring to the boil, stirring, until thickened and clear.

5 Return the meat and vegetables to the wok and cook for 1–2 minutes, until heated through and coated with the sauce. Transfer to a warm serving dish and serve immediately.

COOK'S TIP

Use dry sherry instead of the Chinese rice wine if you have difficulty obtaining it.

Beef & Broccoli Stir-Fry

Serves 4

INGREDIENTS

225 g/8 oz lean steak, trimmed
2 garlic cloves, crushed
dash of chilli oil
1-cm/¹/₂-inch piece fresh root
  ginger, grated

¹/₂ tsp Chinese five-spice
  powder
2 tbsp dark soy sauce
2 tbsp vegetable oil
150 g/5 oz broccoli florets
1 tbsp light soy sauce

150 ml/¹/₄ pint/²/₃ cup beef
  stock
2 tsp cornflour (cornstarch)
4 tsp water
carrot strips, to garnish

1 Cut the steak into thin strips and place in a shallow glass dish. Mix together the garlic, chilli oil, ginger, Chinese five-spice powder and soy sauce in a small bowl and pour over the beef, tossing to coat the strips. Leave to marinate in the refrigerator.

2 Heat 1 tbsp of the vegetable oil in a wok. Add the broccoli and stir-fry over a medium heat for 4–5 minutes. Remove from the wok with a slotted spoon and set aside.

3 Heat the remaining oil in the wok. Add the steak together with the marinade, and stir-fry for 2-3 minutes, until the steak is browned and sealed.

4 Return the broccoli to the wok and stir in the soy sauce and stock.

5 Blend the cornflour (cornstarch) with the water to form a smooth paste and stir it into the wok. Bring to the boil, stirring, until thickened and clear. Cook for 1 minute.

6 Transfer the beef and broccoli stir-fry to a warm serving dish, arrange the carrot strips in a lattice on top and serve.

COOK'S TIP

Leave the steak to marinate for several hours for a fuller flavour. Cover and leave to marinate in the refrigerator if preparing in advance.

Spicy Beef

Serves 4

INGREDIENTS
---

225 g/8 oz fillet steak
2 garlic cloves, crushed
1 tsp powdered star anise
1 tbsp dark soy sauce
spring onion (scallion) tassels,
    to garnish

SAUCE:
2 tbsp vegetable oil
1 bunch spring onions
    (scallions), halved
    lengthways
1 tbsp dark soy sauce

1 tbsp dry sherry
1/4 tsp chilli sauce
150 ml/1/4 pint/2/3 cup water
2 tsp cornflour (cornstarch)
4 tsp water

1 Cut the steak into thin strips and place in a shallow dish.

2 Mix together the garlic, star anise and dark soy sauce in a bowl and pour over the steak strips, turning them to coat thoroughly. Cover and leave to marinate in the refrigerator for at least 1 hour.

3 To make the sauce, heat the oil in a preheated wok. Reduce the heat, add the halved spring onions (scallions) and stir-fry for 1-2 minutes. Remove from the wok with a slotted spoon and set aside.

4 Add the beef to the wok, together with the marinade, and stir-fry for 3–4 minutes. Return the halved spring onions (scallions) to the wok and add the soy sauce, sherry, chilli sauce and two thirds of the water.

5 Blend the cornflour (cornstarch) with the remaining water and stir into the wok. Bring to the boil, stirring until the sauce thickens and clears.

6 Transfer to a warm serving dish, garnish with spring onion (scallion) tassels and serve immediately.

COOK'S TIP

Omit the chilli sauce for a milder dish.

274

Beef & Beans

Serves 4

INGREDIENTS

450 g/1 lb rump or fillet steak, cut into 2.5-cm/1-inch pieces

MARINADE:
2 tsp cornflour (cornstarch)
2 tbsp dark soy sauce
2 tsp peanut oil

SAUCE:
2 tbsp vegetable oil
3 garlic cloves, crushed
1 small onion, cut into 8
225 g/8 oz thin green beans, halved
25 g/1 oz/1/4 cup unsalted cashews
25 g/1 oz canned bamboo shoots, drained and rinsed

2 tsp dark soy sauce
2 tsp Chinese rice wine or dry sherry
125 ml/4 fl oz/1/2 cup beef stock
2 tsp cornflour (cornstarch)
4 tsp water
salt and pepper

1 To make the marinade, mix together the cornflour (cornstarch), soy sauce and peanut oil.

2 Place the steak in a shallow glass bowl. Pour the marinade over the steak, turn to coat, cover and marinate in the refrigerator for 30 minutes.

3 To make the sauce, heat the oil in a preheated wok. Add the garlic, onion, beans, cashews and bamboo shoots and stir-fry for 2–3 minutes.

4 Remove the steak from the marinade, drain, add to the wok and stir-fry for 3–4 minutes.

5 Mix the soy sauce, Chinese rice wine or sherry and beef stock together. Blend the cornflour (cornstarch) with the water and add to the soy sauce mixture, mixing to combine.

6 Stir the mixture into the wok and bring the sauce to the boil, stirring until thickened and clear. Reduce the heat and leave to simmer for 2–3 minutes. Season to taste and serve immediately.

Lamb with Mushroom Sauce

Serves 4

INGREDIENTS

350 g/12 oz lean boneless
  lamb, such as fillet or loin
2 tbsp vegetable oil
3 garlic cloves, crushed
1 leek, sliced

1 tsp cornflour (cornstarch)
4 tbsp light soy sauce
3 tbsp Chinese rice wine or
  dry sherry
3 tbsp water

$^1/_2$ tsp chilli sauce
175 g/6 oz large mushrooms,
  sliced
$^1/_2$ tsp sesame oil
fresh red chillies, to garnish

1 Cut the lamb into thin strips.

2 Heat the oil in a preheated wok. Add the lamb strips, garlic and leek and stir-fry for about 2–3 minutes.

3 Mix together the cornflour (cornstarch), soy sauce, Chinese rice wine or dry sherry, water and chilli sauce in a bowl and set aside.

4 Add the mushrooms to the wok and stir-fry for 1 minute.

5 Stir in the sauce and cook for 2–3 minutes, or until the lamb is cooked through and tender. Sprinkle the sesame oil over the top and transfer to a warm serving dish. Garnish with red chillies and serve immediately.

COOK'S TIP

Use rehydrated dried Chinese mushrooms obtainable from specialist shops or Chinese supermarkets for a really authentic flavour.

VARIATION

The lamb can be replaced with lean steak or pork fillet (tenderloin) in this classic recipe from Beijing. You could also use 2–3 spring onions (scallions), 1 shallot or 1 small onion instead of the leek, if you prefer.

Sesame Lamb Stir-Fry

Serves 4

INGREDIENTS

450 g/1 lb boneless lean lamb	2 garlic cloves, crushed	1 tbsp dark soy sauce
2 tbsp peanut oil	3 fl oz/85 ml/$^1/_3$ cup lamb or	4$^1/_2$ tsp sesame seeds
2 leeks, sliced	vegetable stock	
1 carrot, cut into matchsticks	2 tsp light brown sugar	

1 Cut the lamb into thin strips. Heat the peanut oil in a preheated wok. Add the lamb and stir-fry for 2–3 minutes. Remove the lamb from the wok with a slotted spoon and set aside.

2 Add the leek, carrot and garlic to the wok and stir-fry in the remaining oil for 1–2 minutes. Remove from the wok with a slotted spoon and set aside. Drain any oil from the wok.

3 Place the stock, sugar and soy sauce in the wok and add the lamb.

Cook, stirring constantly to coat the lamb, for 2–3 minutes. Sprinkle the sesame seeds over the top, turning the lamb to coat.

4 Spoon the leek mixture on to a warm serving dish and top with the lamb. Serve immediately.

COOK'S TIP

Be careful not to burn the sugar in the wok when heating and coating the meat, otherwise the flavour of the dish will be spoiled.

VARIATION

This recipe would be equally delicious made with strips of skinless chicken or turkey breast or with prawns (shrimp). The cooking times remain the same.

Grilled Minced Lamb

Serves 4

INGREDIENTS

5 tbsp oil
2 onions, sliced
450 g/1 lb minced lamb
2 tbsp yogurt
1 tsp chilli powder
1 tsp fresh ginger root, finely
    chopped

1 tsp fresh garlic, crushed
1 tsp salt
1¹/₂ tsp garam masala
¹/₂ tsp ground allspice
2 fresh green chillies
fresh coriander (cilantro)
    leaves

salad leaves, to serve

TO GARNISH:
fresh coriander (cilantro)
    leaves, chopped
1 lemon, cut into wedges

1 Heat the oil in a saucepan. Add the sliced onions and fry until golden brown.

2 Place the minced lamb in a large bowl. Add the yogurt, chilli powder, ginger, garlic, salt, garam masala, ground allspice and mix to combine.

3 Add the lamb mixture to the fried onions and stir-fry for 10-15 minutes. Remove the mixture from the heat and set aside.

4 Meanwhile, place the green chillies and half of the coriander (cilantro) leaves in a processor and grind. Alternatively, finely chop the green chillies and coriander (cilantro) with a sharp knife. Set aside until required.

5 Put the minced lamb mixture in a food processor and grind. Alternatively, place in a large bowl and mash with a fork. Mix the lamb mixture with the chillies and

coriander (cilantro) and blend well.

6 Transfer the mixture to a shallow heatproof dish. Cook under a preheated medium-hot grill (broiler) for 10-15 minutes, moving the mixture about with a fork. Watch it carefully to prevent it from burning.

7 Garnish with coriander (cilantro) leaves and lemon wedges, and serve with salad leaves.

Minced Lamb with Peas

Serves 4

INGREDIENTS

6 tbsp oil	2 tomatoes, chopped	1 tsp chilli powder
1 medium onion, sliced	1 tsp salt	450 g/1 lb lean minced lamb
3 green chillies	1 tsp fresh ginger root, finely	100 g/3¹/₂ oz peas
fresh coriander (cilantro)	chopped	
leaves	1 tsp fresh garlic, crushed	

1 Heat the oil in a medium-sized saucepan. Add the onion slices and fry until golden brown, stirring.

2 Add two of the green chillies, half of the fresh coriander (cilantro) leaves and the chopped tomatoes to the pan and reduce the heat to a gentle simmer.

3 Add the salt, ginger, garlic and chilli powder to the mixture in the pan and stir everything well to combine.

4 Add the minced lamb to the pan and stir-fry the mixture for 7-10 minutes, until the meat turns brown.

5 Add the peas to the mixture in the pan and cook for a further 3-4 minutes, stirring occasionally.

6 Transfer the lamb and pea mixture to warm serving plates and garnish with the remaining chopped green chilli and the fresh coriander (cilantro) leaves.

COOK'S TIP

The flavour of garlic can be changed according to how it is prepared. For instance, a whole garlic clove added to a dish will give it the flavour but not the 'bite' of garlic; a halved clove will add a little bite while a finely chopped garlic clove will release most of the flavour and a crushed clove will release all of the flavour.

Lean Lamb Cooked in Spinach

Serves 2-4

INGREDIENTS
---

300 ml/^{1}/$_2$ pint/1^1/$_4$ cups oil
2 medium onions, sliced
^{1}/$_4$ bunch fresh coriander
   (cilantro)
3 green chillies, chopped
1^1/$_2$ tsp fresh ginger root,
   finely chopped
1^1/$_2$ tsp fresh garlic, crushed
1 tsp chilli powder

^{1}/$_2$ tsp turmeric
450 g/1 lb lean lamb, with or
   without the bone
1 tsp salt
1 kg/2 lb 4 oz fresh spinach,
   trimmed, washed and
   chopped or 425g/
   15 oz can spinach

700 ml/1^1/$_4$ pints/3^1/$_4$ cups
   water

TO GARNISH:
fresh red chillies, finely
   chopped

1 Heat the oil in a saucepan and fry the onions until they turn a pale colour.

2 Add the fresh coriander (cilantro) and 2 of the chopped green chillies to the pan and stir-fry for 3-5 minutes.

3 Reduce the heat and add the ginger, garlic, chilli powder and turmeric to the pan, stirring to mix.

4 Add the lamb to the pan and stir-fry for a further 5 minutes. Add the salt and the fresh or canned spinach and cook, stirring occasionally with a wooden spoon, for a further 3-5 minutes.

5 Add the water, stirring, and cook over a low heat, covered, for about 45 minutes. Remove the lid and check the meat. If it is not tender, turn the meat

over, increase the heat and cook, uncovered, until the surplus water has been absorbed. Stir-fry the mixture for a further 5-7 minutes.

6 Transfer the lamb and spinach mixture to a serving dish and garnish with finely chopped red chillies. Serve hot.

Stuffed Tomatoes

Serves 4-6

INGREDIENTS

6 large, firm tomatoes	1 tsp fresh ginger root, finely	450 g/1 lb minced lamb
50 g/1³/₄ oz/4 tbsp unsalted	chopped	1 green chilli
butter	1 tsp fresh garlic, crushed	fresh coriander (cilantro)
5 tbsp oil	1 tsp pepper	leaves
1 medium onion, finely	1 tsp salt	salad leaves and lemon
chopped	½ tsp garam masala	wedges, to serve

1 Preheat the oven to 180°C/ 350°F/Gas Mark 4. Rinse the tomatoes, cut off the tops and scoop out the flesh.

2 Grease a heatproof dish with 50 g/1¹/₄ oz/ 4 tbsp butter. Place the tomatoes in the dish.

3 Heat the oil in a pan and fry the onion until golden brown.

4 Lower the heat and add the ginger, garlic, pepper, salt and garam masala. Stir-fry the mixture for 3-5 minutes.

5 Add the minced lamb to the saucepan and fry for 10-15 minutes.

6 Add the green chilli and fresh coriander (cilantro) leaves and continue stir-frying the mixture for 3-5 minutes.

7 Spoon the lamb mixture into the tomatoes and replace the tops. Cook the tomatoes in the oven for 15-20 minutes.

8 Transfer the tomatoes to serving plates and serve hot.

VARIATION

You could use the same recipe to stuff red or green (bell) peppers, if you prefer.

Fried Kidneys

Serves 4

INGREDIENTS

450 g/1 lb lamb's kidneys
2 tsp turmeric
2¹/₂ tsp salt
150 ml/¹/₄ pint/²/₃ cup water

1 green (bell) pepper, sliced
1 tsp fresh ginger root, finely
  chopped
1 tsp fresh garlic, crushed

1 tsp chilli powder
3 tbsp oil
1 small onion, finely chopped
coriander (cilantro) leaves, to
  garnish

1 Using a sharp knife, remove the very fine skin surrounding each kidney. Cut each kidney into 4-6 pieces.

2 Place the kidney pieces in a bowl with the turmeric and 2 teaspoons of salt. Pour in the water, mix with a spoon to combine the ingredients and leave to marinate for about 1 hour. Drain the kidney pieces thoroughly and discard the marinade, then rinse them under cold running water until the water runs completely clear.

3 Place the kidneys in a small saucepan together with the green (bell) pepper. Pour in enough water to cover and cook over a medium heat, leaving the lid of the pan slightly ajar so that the steam can escape, until all of the water has evaporated.

4 Add the ginger, garlic, chilli powder and remaining salt to the kidney mixture and blend until well combined.

5 Add the oil, onion and the coriander (cilantro)

to the pan, and stir-fry for 7-10 minutes.

6 Transfer the kidneys to a serving plate, garnish and serve hot.

COOK'S TIP

Many people are resistant to the idea of cooking or eating kidneys because they often have rather a strong smell – even when cooked. However, if you wash and soak them in water, you can largely avoid this problem.

Stir-Fried Ginger Chicken

Serves 4

INGREDIENTS

2 tbsp sunflower oil
1 onion, sliced
175 g/6 oz carrots, cut into thin
    sticks
1 clove garlic, crushed

350 g/12 oz boneless skinless chicken
    breasts
2 tbsp fresh ginger, peeled and grated
1 tsp ground ginger
4 tbsp sweet sherry

1 tbsp tomato purée
1 tbsp demerara sugar
100 ml/3½ fl oz/⅓ cup orange juice
1 tsp cornflour (cornstarch)
1 orange, peeled and segmented
fresh snipped chives, to garnish

1 Heat the oil in a large preheated wok. Add the onion, carrots and garlic and stir-fry over a high heat for 3 minutes or until the vegetables begin to soften.

2 Using a sharp knife, slice the chicken into thin strips. Add the chicken to the wok together with the fresh ginger and ground ginger. Stir-fry for a further 10 minutes, or until the chicken is well cooked through and golden in colour.

3 Mix together the sherry, tomato purée, sugar, orange juice and cornflour (cornstarch) in a bowl. Stir the mixture into the wok and heat through until the mixture bubbles and the juices start to thicken.

4 Add the orange segments and carefully toss to mix.

5 Transfer the stir-fried chicken to warm serving bowls and garnish with freshly snipped chives. Serve immediately.

COOK'S TIP

Make sure that you do not continue cooking the dish once the orange segments have been added in step 4, otherwise they will break up.

Chicken, Spring Green & Yellow Bean Stir-Fry

Serves 4

INGREDIENTS

2 tbsp sunflower oil

450 g/1 lb skinless, boneless chicken breasts

2 cloves garlic, crushed

1 green (bell) pepper

100 g/3½ oz/1½ cups mangetout (snow peas)

6 spring onions (scallions), sliced, plus extra to garnish

225 g/8 oz spring greens or cabbage, shredded

160 g/5¾ oz jar yellow bean sauce

50 g/1¾ oz/3 tbsp roasted cashew nuts

1 Heat the sunflower oil in a large preheated wok.

2 Using a sharp knife, slice the chicken into thin strips.

3 Add the chicken to the wok together with the garlic. Stir-fry for about 5 minutes or until the chicken is sealed on all sides and beginning to turn golden.

4 Using a sharp knife, deseed the green (bell) pepper and cut into thin strips.

5 Add the mangetout (snow peas), spring onions (scallions), green (bell) pepper strips and spring greens or cabbage to the wok. Stir-fry for a further 5 minutes or until the vegetables are just tender.

6 Stir in the yellow bean sauce and heat through for about 2 minutes or until the mixture starts to bubble.

7 Scatter with the roasted cashew nuts.

8 Transfer the chicken, spring green and yellow bean stir-fry to warm serving plates and garnish with extra spring onions (scallions), if desired. Serve the stir-fry immediately.

COOK'S TIP

Do not add salted cashew nuts to this dish otherwise, combined with the slightly salty sauce, the dish will be very salty indeed.

Chicken, (Bell) Pepper & Orange Stir-Fry

Serves 4

INGREDIENTS

3 tbsp sunflower oil	1 red (bell) pepper, deseeded and sliced	finely grated rind and juice of 1 orange
350 g/12 oz boneless chicken thighs,	75 g/2¾ oz/1¼ cups mangetout	1 tsp cornflour (cornstarch)
skinned and cut into thin strips	(snow peas)	2 oranges
1 onion, sliced	4 tbsp light soy sauce	100 g/3½ oz/1 cup beansprouts
1 clove garlic, crushed	4 tbsp sherry	cooked rice or noodles, to serve
	1 tbsp tomato purée	

1 Heat the sunflower oil in a large preheated wok.

2 Add the strips of chicken to the wok and stir-fry for 2–3 minutes or until sealed on all sides.

3 Add the sliced onion, garlic, (bell) pepper and mangetout (snow peas) to the wok. Stir-fry the mixture for a further 5 minutes, or until the vegetables are just becoming tender and the chicken is completely cooked through.

4 Mix together the soy sauce, sherry, tomato purée, orange rind and juice and the cornflour (cornstarch) in a measuring jug.

5 Add the mixture to the wok and cook, stirring, until the juices start to thicken.

6 Using a sharp knife, peel and segment the oranges.

7 Add the orange segments and bean-sprouts to the mixture in the wok and heat through for a further 2 minutes.

8 Transfer the stir-fry to serving plates and serve at once with cooked rice or noodles.

COOK'S TIP

Beansprouts are sprouting mung beans and are a regular ingredient in Chinese cooking. They require very little cooking and may even be eaten raw, if wished.

Duck with Baby Corn Cobs & Pineapple

Serves 4

INGREDIENTS

4 duck breasts
1 tsp Chinese five spice powder
1 tbsp cornflour (cornstarch)
1 tbsp chilli oil

225 g/8 oz baby onions, peeled
2 cloves garlic, crushed
100 g/3½ oz/1 cup baby corn cobs
175 g/6 oz/1¼ cups canned
    pineapple chunks

6 spring onions (scallions), sliced
100 g/3½ oz/1 cup beansprouts
2 tbsp plum sauce

1 Remove any skin from the duck breasts. Cut the duck breasts into thin slices.

2 Mix together the five spice powder and the cornflour (cornstarch) in a large bowl.

3 Toss the duck in the five spice powder and cornflour (cornstarch) mixture until well coated.

4 Heat the oil in a preheated wok. Stir-fry the duck for 10 minutes, or until just beginning to crispen around the edges.

5 Remove the duck from the wok and set aside until required.

6 Add the onions and garlic to the wok and stir-fry for 5 minutes, or until the onions have softened.

7 Add the baby corn cobs to the wok and stir-fry for a further 5 minutes.

8 Add the pineapple, spring onions (scallions) and beansprouts and stir-fry for 3–4 minutes. Stir in the plum sauce.

9 Return the cooked duck to the wok and toss until well mixed. Transfer to warm serving dishes and serve hot.

COOK'S TIP

Buy pineapple chunks in natural juice rather than syrup for a fresher flavour. If you can only obtain pineapple in syrup, rinse it in cold water and drain thoroughly before using.

Stir-Fried Turkey with Cranberry Glaze

Serves 2–3

INGREDIENTS

1 turkey breast	50 g/1¾ oz/½ cup fresh or frozen	4 tbsp cranberry sauce
2 tbsp sunflower oil	cranberries	3 tbsp light soy sauce
15 g/½ oz/2 tbsp stem ginger	100 g/3½ oz/¼ cup canned	salt and pepper
	chestnuts	

1 Remove any skin from the turkey breast. Using a sharp knife, thinly slice the turkey breast.

2 Heat the oil in a large preheated wok.

3 Add the turkey to the wok and stir-fry for 5 minutes, or until cooked through.

4 Using a sharp knife, finely chop the stem ginger.

5 Add the ginger and the cranberries to the wok and stir-fry for 2–3 minutes

or until the cranberries have softened.

6 Add the chestnuts, cranberry sauce and soy sauce, season to taste with salt and pepper and allow to bubble for 2–3 minutes.

7 Transfer to serving dishes and serve at once.

COOK'S TIP

If you wish, use a turkey escalope instead of the breast for really tender, lean meat.

COOK'S TIP

It is very important that the wok is very hot before you stir-fry. Test by holding your hand flat about 7.5 cm/3 inches above the base of the interior – you should be able to feel the heat radiating from it.

Stir-Fried Beef & Vegetables with Sherry & Soy Sauce

Serves 4

INGREDIENTS

2 tbsp sunflower oil	1 small head Chinese leaves,	SAUCE:
350 g/12 oz fillet of beef, sliced	shredded	3 tbsp medium sherry
1 red onion, sliced	150 g/5½ oz/1½ cups beansprouts	3 tbsp light soy sauce
175 g/6 oz courgettes (zucchini),	225 g/8 oz can bamboo shoots,	1 tsp ground ginger
sliced diagonally	drained	1 clove garlic, crushed
175 g/6 oz carrots, thinly sliced	150 g/5½ oz/1½ cup cashew nuts,	1 tsp cornflour (cornstarch)
1 red (bell) pepper, deseeded and sliced	toasted	1 tbsp tomato purée

1 Heat the sunflower oil in a preheated wok.

2 Add the beef and onion to the wok and stir-fry for 4–5 minutes or until the onion begins to soften and the meat is just browning.

3 Using a sharp knife, trim the courgette (zucchini) and slice diagonally.

4 Add the carrots, (bell) pepper, and courgettes (zucchini) and stir-fry for 5 minutes.

5 Toss in the Chinese leaves, beansprouts and bamboo shoots and heat through for 2–3 minutes, or until the leaves are just beginning to wilt.

6 Scatter the cashews nuts over the stir-fry.

7 To make the sauce, mix together the sherry, soy sauce, ground ginger, garlic, cornflour (cornstarch) and tomato purée. Pour the sauce over the stir-fry and toss until well combined. Allow the sauce to bubble for 2–3 minutes or until the juices start to thicken.

8 Transfer to warm serving dishes and serve at once.

Beef with Green Peas & Black Bean Sauce

Serves 4

INGREDIENTS

450 g/1 lb rump steak	2 cloves garlic, crushed	160 g/5³/₄ oz jar black bean sauce
2 tbsp sunflower oil	150 g/5¹/₂ oz/1 cup fresh or frozen	150 g/5¹/₂ oz Chinese leaves,
1 onion	peas	shredded

1 Using a sharp knife, trim away any fat from the beef. Cut the beef into thin slices.

2 Heat the sunflower oil in a large preheated wok.

3 Add the beef to the wok and stir-fry for 2 minutes.

4 Using a sharp knife, peel and slice the onion.

5 Add the onion, garlic and peas to the wok and stir-fry for a further 5 minutes.

6 Add the black bean sauce and Chinese leaves to the mixture in the wok and heat through for a further 2 minutes or until the Chinese leaves have wilted.

7 Transfer to warm serving bowls and serve immediately.

COOK'S TIP

Buy a chunky black bean sauce if you can for the best texture and flavour.

COOK'S TIP

Chinese leaves are now widely available. They look like a pale, elongated head of lettuce with light green, tightly packed crinkly leaves.

Pork Fillet Stir-Fry with Crunchy Satay Sauce

Serves 4

INGREDIENTS

150 g/5½ oz carrots	1 yellow (bell) pepper, deseeded and	SATAY SAUCE:
2 tbsp sunflower oil	sliced	6 tbsp crunchy peanut butter
350 g/12 oz pork neck fillet, thinly	150 g/5½ oz/2⅓ cups mangetout	6 tbsp coconut milk
sliced	(snow peas)	1 tsp chilli flakes
1 onion, sliced	75 g/3 oz/1½ cups fine asparagus	1 clove garlic, crushed
2 cloves garlic, crushed	chopped salted peanuts, to serve	1 tsp tomato purée

1 Using a sharp knife, slice the carrots into thin sticks.

2 Heat the oil in a large wok. Add the pork, onion and garlic and stir-fry for 5 minutes or until the lamb is cooked through.

3 Add the carrots, (bell) pepper, mangetout (snow peas) and asparagus to the wok and stir-fry for 5 minutes.

4 To make the satay sauce, place the peanut butter, coconut milk, chilli flakes, garlic and tomato purée in a small pan and heat gently, stirring, until well combined.

5 Transfer the stir-fry to warm serving plates. Spoon the satay sauce over the stir-fry and scatter with chopped peanuts. Serve immediately.

COOK'S TIP

Cook the sauce just before serving as it tends to thicken very quickly and will not be spoonable if you cook it too far in advance.

Spicy Pork Balls

Serves 4

INGREDIENTS

450 g/1 lb pork mince
2 shallots, finely chopped
2 cloves garlic, crushed
1 tsp cumin seeds
½ tsp chilli powder

25 g/1 oz/½ cup wholemeal
   breadcrumbs
1 egg, beaten
2 tbsp sunflower oil
400 g/14 oz can chopped tomatoes,
   flavoured with chilli

2 tbsp soy sauce
200 g/7 oz can water chestnuts,
   drained
3 tbsp chopped fresh coriander
   (cilantro)

1 Place the pork mince in a large mixing bowl. Add the shallots, garlic, cumin seeds, chilli powder, breadcrumbs and beaten egg and mix together well.

2 Take small pieces of the mixture and form into balls between the palms of your hands.

3 Heat the sunflower oil in a large preheated wok. Add the pork balls to the wok and stir-fry, in batches, over a high heat for about 5 minutes or until sealed on all sides.

4 Add the tomatoes, soy sauce and water chestnuts and bring to the boil. Return the pork balls to the wok, reduce the heat and leave to simmer for 15 minutes.

5 Scatter with chopped fresh coriander (cilantro) and serve hot.

COOK'S TIP

Add a few teaspoons of chilli sauce to a tin of chopped tomatoes, if you can't find the flavoured variety.

COOK'S TIP

Coriander (cilantro) is also known as Chinese parsley, but has a much stronger flavour and should be used with care. Parsley is not a viable alternative; use basil if coriander (cilantro) is not available.

Twice-Cooked Pork with (Bell) Peppers

Serves 4

INGREDIENTS

15 g/½ oz Chinese dried mushrooms	1 red (bell) pepper, deseeded and	1 yellow (bell) pepper, deseeded and
450g/1 lb pork leg steaks	diced	diced
2 tbsp vegetable oil	1 green (bell) pepper, deseeded and	4 tbsp oyster sauce
1 onion, sliced	diced	

1 Place the mushrooms in a large bowl. Pour over enough boiling water to cover and leave to stand for 20 minutes.

2 Using a sharp knife, trim any excess fat from the pork steaks. Cut the pork into thin strips.

3 Bring a large saucepan of water to the boil. Add the pork to the boiling water and cook for 5 minutes.

4 Remove the pork from the pan with a slotted spoon and leave to drain thoroughly.

5 Heat the oil in a large preheated wok. Add the pork to the wok and stir-fry for about 5 minutes.

6 Remove the mushrooms from the water and leave to drain thoroughly. Roughly chop the mushrooms.

7 Add the mushrooms, onion and the (bell) peppers to the wok and stir-fry for 5 minutes.

8 Stir in the oyster sauce and cook for 2–3 minutes. Transfer to serving bowls and serve immediately.

VARIATION

Use open-cap mushrooms, sliced, instead of Chinese mushrooms, if you prefer.

Spring Onion (Scallion) & Lamb Stir-Fry with Oyster Sauce

Serves 4

INGREDIENTS

450 g/1 lb lamb leg steaks	2 cloves garlic, crushed	6 tbsp oyster sauce
1 tsp ground Szechuan peppercorns	8 spring onions (scallions), sliced	175 g/6 oz Chinese leaves
1 tbsp groundnut oil	2 tbsp dark soy sauce	prawn (shrimp) crackers, to serve

1 Using a sharp knife, remove any excess fat from the lamb. Slice the lamb thinly.

2 Sprinkle the ground Szechuan peppercorns over the meat and toss together until well combined.

3 Heat the oil in a preheated wok. Add the lamb and stir-fry for 5 minutes.

4 Mix the garlic, spring onions (scallions) and soy sauce, add to the wok and stir-fry for 2 minutes.

5 Add the oyster sauce and Chinese leaves and stir-fry for a further 2 minutes, or until the leaves have wilted and the juices are bubbling.

6 Transfer the stir-fry to warm serving bowls and serve hot.

COOK'S TIP

Oyster sauce is made from oysters which are cooked in brine and soy sauce. Sold in bottles, it will keep in the refrigerator for months.

COOK'S TIP

Prawn (shrimp) crackers consist of compressed slivers of prawn (shrimp) and flour paste. They expand when deep-fried.

Stir-Fried Lamb with Orange

Serves 4

INGREDIENTS

450 g/1 lb minced lamb
2 cloves garlic, crushed
1 tsp cumin seeds
1 tsp ground coriander

1 red onion, sliced
finely grated zest and juice of
   1 orange
2 tbsp soy sauce

1 orange, peeled and segmented
salt and pepper
snipped fresh chives, to garnish

1 Add the minced lamb to a preheated wok. Dry fry the minced lamb for 5 minutes, or until the mince is evenly browned. Drain away any excess fat from the wok.

2 Add the garlic, cumin seeds, coriander and red onion to the wok and stir-fry for a further 5 minutes.

3 Stir in the finely grated orange zest and juice and the soy sauce, cover, reduce the heat and leave to simmer, stirring occasionally, for 15 minutes.

4 Remove the lid, raise the heat, add the orange segments and salt and pepper to taste and heat through for a further 2–3 minutes.

5 Transfer to warm serving plates and garnish with chives.

VARIATION

Use lime or lemon juice and zest instead of the orange, if you prefer.

COOK'S TIP

If you wish to serve wine with your meal, try light, dry white wines and lighter Burgundy-style red wines as they blend well with Oriental food.

Shish Kebabs (Kabobs)

Makes 4

INGREDIENTS

450 g/1 lb lean lamb	4 tbsp olive oil	TO SERVE:
1 red onion, cut into wedges	grated rind and juice of	4 pitta breads
1 green (bell) pepper, deseeded	$^1/_2$ lemon	few crisp lettuce leaves,
	1 clove garlic, crushed	shredded
MARINADE:	$^1/_2$ tsp dried oregano	2 tomatoes, sliced
1 onion	$^1/_2$tsp dried thyme	chilli sauce (optional)

1 Cut the lamb into large, evenly-sized chunks.

2 To make the marinade, grate the onion or chop it very finely in a food processor. Remove the juice by squeezing the onion between two plates set over a small bowl.

3 Combine the onion juice with the remaining marinade ingredients in a non-metallic dish and add the meat. Toss the meat in the marinade, cover and leave to marinate in the refrigerator for at least 2 hours or overnight.

4 Divide the onion wedges into 2. Cut the (bell) peppers into chunks.

5 Remove the meat from the marinade, reserving the liquid for basting. Thread the meat on to skewers, alternating with the onion and (bell) peppers. Barbecue (grill) for 8–10 minutes, turning and basting frequently.

6 Split open the pitta breads and fill with a little lettuce, and the meat and vegetables. Top with tomatoes and chilli sauce.

VARIATION

These kebabs (kabobs) are delicious served with saffron-flavoured rice. For easy saffron rice, simply use saffron stock cubes when cooking the rice.

Lamb Cutlets with Rosemary

Serves 4

INGREDIENTS
---

8 lamb cutlets
5 tbsp olive oil
2 tbsp lemon juice
1 clove garlic, crushed
1/2 tsp lemon pepper
salt
8 sprigs rosemary

jacket potatoes, to serve

SALAD:
4 tomatoes, sliced
4 spring onions (scallions),
    sliced diagonally

DRESSING:
2 tbsp olive oil
1 tbsp lemon juice
1 clove garlic, chopped
1/4 tsp fresh rosemary,
    chopped finely

---

1 Trim the lamb chops by cutting away the flesh with a sharp knife to expose the tips of the bones.

2 Place the oil, lemon juice, garlic, lemon pepper and salt in a shallow, non-metallic dish and whisk with a fork to combine.

3 Lay the sprigs of rosemary in the dish and place the lamb on top. Leave to marinate for at least 1 hour, turning the lamb cutlets once.

4 Remove the chops from the marinade and wrap a little kitchen foil around the bones to stop them from burning.

5 Place the sprigs of rosemary on the rack and place the lamb on top. Barbecue (grill) for 10–15 minutes, turning once.

6 Meanwhile make the salad and dressing. Arrange the tomatoes on a serving dish and scatter the spring onions (scallions)

on top. Place all the ingredients for the dressing in a screw-top jar, shake well and pour over the salad. Serve with the barbecued (grilled) lamb cutlets and jacket potatoes.

Sweet Lamb Fillet

Serves 4

INGREDIENTS

2 fillets of neck of lamb, each
    225 g/8 oz
1 tbsp olive oil
1/2 onion, chopped finely
1 clove garlic, crushed
2.5 cm/1 inch piece root
    (fresh) ginger, grated

5 tbsp apple juice
3 tbsp smooth apple sauce
1 tbsp light muscovado sugar
1 tbsp tomato ketchup
    (catsup)
1/2 tsp mild mustard
salt and pepper

green salad leaves, croûtons
    and fresh crusty bread, to
    serve

1 Place the lamb fillet on a large piece of double thickness kitchen foil. Season with salt and pepper to taste.

2 Heat the oil in a small pan and fry the onion and garlic for 2–3 minutes until softened but not browned. Stir in the grated ginger and cook for 1 minute, stirring occasionally.

3 Stir in the apple juice, apple sauce, sugar, ketchup (catsup) and mustard and bring to the boil. Boil rapidly for about 10 minutes until reduced by half. Stir the mixture occasionally so that it does not burn and stick to the base of the pan.

4 Brush half of the sauce over the lamb, then wrap up the lamb in the kitchen foil to completely enclose it. Barbecue (grill) over hot coals for about 25 minutes, turning the parcel over occasionally.

5 Open out the kitchen foil and brush the lamb with some of the sauce. Continue to barbecue (grill) for a further 15–20 minutes or until cooked through.

6 Place the lamb on a chopping board, remove the foil and cut into thick slices. Transfer to serving plates and spoon over the remaining sauce. Serve with green salad leaves, croûtons and fresh crusty bread.

Caribbean Pork

Serves 4

INGREDIENTS

4 pork loin chops
4 tbsp dark muscovado sugar
4 tbsp orange or pineapple
   juice
2 tbsp Jamaican rum
1 tbsp desiccated (shredded)
   coconut
1/2 tsp ground cinnamon

mixed salad leaves, to serve

COCONUT RICE:
225 g/8 oz/1 cup Basmati rice
450 ml/16 fl oz/2 cups water
150 ml/5 fl oz/2/3 cup coconut
   milk
4 tbsp raisins

4 tbsp roasted peanuts or
   cashew nuts
salt and pepper
2 tbsp desiccated (shredded)
   coconut, toasted

1 Trim any excess fat from the pork and place the chops in a shallow, non-metallic dish.

2 Combine the sugar, fruit juice, rum, coconut and cinnamon in a bowl, stirring until the sugar dissolves. Pour the mixture over the pork and leave to marinate in the refrigerator for at least 2 hours.

3 Remove the pork from the marinade, reserving the liquid for basting. Barbecue (grill) over hot coals for 15–20 minutes, basting with the marinade.

4 Meanwhile, make the coconut rice. Rinse the rice under cold water, place it in a pan with the water and coconut milk and bring gently to the boil. Stir, cover and reduce the heat. Simmer gently for 12 minutes or until the rice is tender and the liquid has been absorbed. Fluff up with a fork.

5 Stir the raisins and nuts into the rice, season with salt and pepper to taste and sprinkle with the coconut. Transfer the pork and rice to warm serving plates and serve with the mixed salad leaves.

Ham Steaks with Spicy Apple Rings

Serves 4

INGREDIENTS

4 ham steaks, each about
    175 g/6 oz
1–2 tsp wholegrain mustard
1 tbsp honey
2 tbsp lemon juice

1 tbsp sunflower oil

APPLE RINGS:
2 green dessert (eating) apples
2 tsp demerara sugar

1/4 tsp ground nutmeg
1/4 tsp ground cinnamon
1/4 tsp ground allspice
1–2 tbsp melted butter

1 Using a pair of scissors, make a few cuts around the edges of the ham steaks to prevent them from curling up as they cook. Spread a little wholegrain mustard over the steaks.

2 Mix together the honey, lemon juice and oil in a bowl.

3 To prepare the apple rings, core the apples and cut them into thick slices. Mix the sugar with the spices and press the apple slices in the mixture until they are well coated on both sides.

4 Barbecue (grill) the steaks over hot coals for 3–4 minutes on each side, frequently basting with the honey and lemon mixture to prevent the meat from drying out during cooking.

5 Brush the apple slices with a little melted butter and barbecue (grill) alongside the pork for 3–4 minutes, turning once and brushing with melted butter as they cook.

6 Serve with the apple slices as a garnish.

COOK'S TIP

If you have time, soak the steaks in cold water for 30–60 minutes before cooking – this process will remove the excess salt.

Honey-Glazed Pork Chops

Serves 4

INGREDIENTS

4 lean pork loin chops	4 tbsp orange juice	salt and pepper
4 tbsp clear honey	2 tbsp olive oil	
1 tbsp dry sherry	2.5 cm/1 inch piece root (fresh) ginger, grated	

1 Season the pork chops with salt and pepper to taste. Set aside while you make the glaze.

2 To make the glaze, place the honey, sherry, orange juice, oil and ginger in a small pan and heat gently, stirring continuously, until all of the ingredients are well blended.

3 Barbecue (grill) the chops on an oiled rack over hot coals for about 5 minutes on each side.

4 Brush the chops with the glaze and barbecue (grill) for a further 2–4 minutes on each side, basting frequently with the glaze.

5 Transfer the chops to warm serving plates and serve hot.

COOK'S TIP

To give the recipe a little more punch, stir ½ teaspoon of chilli sauce or 1 tablespoon of wholegrain mustard into the basting glaze.

VARIATION

This recipe works equally well with lamb chops and with chicken portions, such as thighs or drumsticks. Barbecue (grill) the meat in exactly the same way as in this recipe, basting frequently with the honey glaze – the result will be just as delicious!

Liver & Onion Kebabs (Kabobs)

Makes 4

INGREDIENTS

350 g/12 oz lamb's liver
2 tbsp seasoned plain (all-
 purpose) flour
1/2 tsp dried mixed herbs

125 g/4 1/2 oz rindless streaky
 bacon
2 medium onions
75 g/2 3/4 oz butter

2 tsp balsamic vinegar

TO SERVE:
mixed salad leaves
tomato quarters

1 Cut the lamb's liver into bite-sized pieces. Then mix the flour with the dried mixed herbs and toss the liver in the seasoned flour.

2 Stretch out the bacon rashers with the back of a knife. Cut each rasher in half and wrap the bacon around half of the liver pieces.

3 Thread the plain liver pieces on to skewers, alternating them with the bacon-wrapped liver pieces.

4 Cut the onions into rings and thread over the kebabs (kabobs). Finely chop the onion rings that are too small to thread over the kebabs (kabobs).

5 Heat the butter in a small pan and sauté the chopped onions for about 5 minutes until softened. Stir in the vinegar.

6 Brush the butter mixture over the kebabs (kabobs) and barbecue (grill) over hot coals for 8–10 minutes, basting occasionally with

the butter mixture, until the liver is just cooked but is still a little pink inside.

7 Transfer the kebabs (kabobs) to serving plates. Serve with mixed salad leaves and tomatoes.

COOK'S TIP

Choose thick slices of liver to give good-sized pieces. Use bacon to hold 2–3 pieces of thinner liver together if necessary.

Fish & Seafood

The wealth of species and flavours that the world's oceans
and rivers provide is immense. Each country combines its
local catch with the region's favourite herbs and spices to
create a variety of dishes. All of the recipes featured here are
easy to prepare and delicious to eat. Moreover, not only are
fish and seafood are quick to cook but they are packed full
with nutritional goodness. Naturally low in fat, yet rich in
minerals and proteins, fish and seafood are important to
help balance any diet.

The superb recipes in this chapter demonstrate the richness
of cooking with fish and seafood. Dishes include modern
variations of traditional recipes, such as Macaroni and
Prawn Bake and Potato-Topped Cod, and exotic flavours,
such as Shrimp Fu Yung and Terriyaki Stir-Fried Salmon
with Crispy Leeks. The variety of different fish and the
prices of fish and seafood allow you to choose a dish to
suit your mood and your pocket.

Sweet & Sour Fish Salad

Serves 4

INGREDIENTS

225 g/8 oz trout fillets	1 bunch spring onions (scallions), trimmed and shredded	fresh snipped chives, to garnish
225 g/8 oz white fish fillets (such as haddock or cod)	115 g/4 oz fresh pineapple flesh, diced	DRESSING:
300 ml/$^1/_2$ pint/1$^1/_4$ cups water	1 small red (bell) pepper, deseeded and diced	1 tbsp sunflower oil
1 stalk lemon grass	1 bunch watercress, washed and trimmed	1 tbsp rice wine vinegar
2 lime leaves		pinch of chilli powder
1 large red chilli		1 tsp clear honey
		salt and pepper

1 Rinse the fish, place in a frying pan (skillet) and pour over the water. Bend the lemon grass in half to bruise it and add to the pan with the lime leaves. Prick the chilli with a fork and add to the pan. Bring to the boil and simmer for 7–8 minutes. Let cool.

2 Drain the fish fillets, discarding the lemon grass, lime leaves and chilli.

Flake the flesh away from the skin of the fish and place in a bowl. Gently stir in the spring onions (scallions), pineapple and (bell) pepper.

3 Arrange the washed watercress on 4 serving plates, spoon the cooked fish mixture on top and set aside.

4 To make the dressing, mix all the ingredients together and season well. Spoon over the fish and serve garnished with chives.

VARIATION

This recipe also works very well if you replace the fish with 350 g/12 oz white crab meat. Add a dash of Tabasco sauce if you like it hot!

Pasta Vongole

Serves 4

INGREDIENTS

675 g/1½ lb fresh clams or	mussels, defrosted if frozen	2 tbsp chopped tarragon
1 x 290 g/ 10 oz can clams,	2 tbsp olive oil	salt and pepper
drained	2 cloves garlic, finely chopped	675 g/1½ lb fresh pasta or 350
400 g/14 oz mixed seafood, such	150 ml/5 fl oz/⅔ cup white wine	g/12 oz dried pasta
as prawns (shrimps), squid and	150 ml/5 fl oz/⅔ cup fish stock	

1 If you are using fresh clams, scrub them clean and discard any that are already open.

2 Heat the oil in a large frying pan (skillet). Add the garlic and the clams to the pan and cook for 2 minutes, shaking the pan to ensure that all of the clams are coated in the oil.

3 Add the remaining seafood mixture to the pan and cook for a further 2 minutes.

4 Pour the wine and stock over the mixed seafood and garlic and bring to the boil. Cover the pan, reduce the heat and leave to simmer for 8–10 minutes or until the shells open. Discard any clams or mussels that do not open.

5 Meanwhile, cook the pasta in a saucepan of boiling water according to the instructions on the packet or until it is cooked through, but still has 'bite'. Drain.

6 Stir the tarragon into the sauce and season to taste.

7 Transfer the pasta to a serving plate and pour over the sauce.

VARIATION

Red clam sauce can be made by adding 8 tablespoons of passata (tomato purée) to the sauce along with the stock in step 4. Follow the same cooking method.

Genoese Seafood Risotto

Serves 4

INGREDIENTS

1.2 litres/2 pints/5 cups hot fish
    or chicken stock
350 g/12 oz arborio (risotto) rice,
    washed
50 g/1¾ oz/3 tbsp butter

2 garlic cloves, chopped
250 g/9 oz mixed seafood,
    preferably raw, such as prawns
    (shrimp), squid, mussels, clams
    and (small) shrimps

2 tbsp chopped oregano, plus
    extra for garnishing
50 g/1¾ oz pecorino or
    Parmesan cheese, grated

1 In a large saucepan, bring the stock to the boil. Add the rice and cook for about 12 minutes, stirring, until the rice is tender or according to the instructions on the packet. Drain thoroughly, reserving any excess liquid.

2 Heat the butter in a large frying pan (skillet) and add the garlic, stirring.

3 Add the raw mixed seafood to the pan (skillet) and cook for 5 minutes. If the seafood is already cooked, fry for 2–3 minutes.

4 Stir the oregano into the seafood mixture in the frying pan (skillet).

5 Add the cooked rice to the pan and cook for 2–3 minutes, stirring, or until hot. Add the reserved stock if the mixture gets too sticky.

6 Add the pecorino or Parmesan cheese and mix well.

7 Transfer the risotto to warm serving dishes and serve immediately.

COOK'S TIP

The Genoese are excellent cooks, and they make particularly delicious fish dishes flavoured with the local olive oil.

Celery & Salt Cod Casserole

Serves 4

INGREDIENTS

250 g/9 oz salt cod, soaked
 overnight
1 tbsp oil
4 shallots, finely chopped
2 garlic cloves, chopped

3 celery sticks, chopped
1 x 400g/14 oz can tomatoes,
 chopped
150 ml/5 fl oz/⅔ cup fish stock

50 g/1¾ oz pine nuts
2 tbsp roughly chopped tarragon
2 tbsp capers
crusty bread or mashed potato,
 to serve

1 Drain the salt cod, rinse
it under plenty of
running water and drain again
thoroughly. Remove and
discard any skin and bones.
Pat the fish dry with paper
towels and cut it into chunks.

2 Heat the oil in a large
frying pan (skillet).
Add the shallots and garlic
and cook for 2–3 minutes.
Add the celery and cook for
a further 2 minutes, then
add the tomatoes and stock.

3 Bring the mixture to
the boil, reduce the
heat and leave to simmer
for 5 minutes.

4 Add the fish and
cook for 10 minutes
or until tender.

5 Meanwhile, place the
pine nuts on a baking
tray (cookie sheet). Place
under a preheated grill
(broiler) and toast for 2–3
minutes or until golden.

6 Stir the tarragon, capers
and pine nuts into the
fish casserole and heat
gently to warm through.

7 Transfer to serving
plates and serve with
fresh crusty bread or
mashed potato.

COOK'S TIP

*Salt cod is a useful ingredient
to keep in the storecupboard
and once soaked, can be
used in the same way as any
other fish. It does, however,
have a stronger flavour
than normal, and it is,
of course, slightly salty. It can
be found in fishmongers,
larger supermarkets
and delicatessens.*

Salt Cod Fritters

Makes 28 cakes

INGREDIENTS

100 g/3½ oz self-raising flour	1 small red onion, finely chopped	TO SERVE:
1 egg, beaten	1 small fennel bulb, finely chopped	crisp salad, chilli relish, cooked
150 ml/5 fl oz/⅔ cup milk	1 red chilli, finely chopped	rice and fresh vegetables
250 g/9 oz salt cod, soaked overnight	2 tbsp oil	

1 Sift the flour into a large bowl. Make a well in the centre of the flour and add the egg.

2 Using a wooden spoon, gradually draw in the flour, slowly adding the milk, and mix to form a smooth batter. Leave to stand for 10 minutes.

3 Drain the salt cod and rinse it under cold running water. Drain again thoroughly.

4 Remove and discard the skin and any bones from the fish, then mash the flesh with a fork.

5 Place the fish in a large bowl and combine with the onion, fennel and chilli. Add the mixture to the batter and blend together.

6 Heat the oil in a large frying pan (skillet) and, taking about 1 tablespoon of the mixture at a time, spoon it into the hot oil. Cook the fritters, in batches, for 3–4 minutes on each side until golden and slightly puffed. Keep warm while cooking the remaining mixture.

7 Serve with salad and a chilli relish for a light meal or with vegetables and rice.

COOK'S TIP

If you prefer larger fritters, use 2 tablespoons per fritter and cook for slightly longer.

Herrings with Hot Pesto Sauce

Serves 4

INGREDIENTS

4 whole herrings or small mackerel, cleaned and gutted	225 g/8 oz tomatoes, peeled, deseeded and chopped	about 30 fresh basil leaves
2 tbsp olive oil	8 canned anchovy fillets, chopped	50 g/1¾ oz pine nuts
		2 garlic cloves, crushed

1 Cook the herrings under a preheated grill (broiler) for about 8–10 minutes on each side, or until the skin is slightly charred on both sides.

2 Meanwhile, heat 1 tablespoon of the olive oil in a large saucepan.

3 Add the tomatoes and anchovies to the saucepan and cook over a medium heat for 5 minutes.

4 Meanwhile, place the basil, pine nuts, garlic and remaining oil into a food processor and blend to form a smooth paste.

Alternatively, pound the ingredients by hand in a mortar and pestle.

5 Add the pesto mixture to the saucepan containing the tomato and anchovy mixture, and stir to heat through.

6 Spoon some of the pesto sauce on to warm individual serving plates. Place the fish on top and pour the rest of the pesto sauce over the fish. Serve immediately.

COOK'S TIP

Try barbecuing (grilling) the fish for an extra chargrilled flavour, if you prefer.

Sole Fillets in Marsala & Cream

Serves 4

INGREDIENTS

STOCK:
600 ml/1 pint/2½ cups water
bones and skin from the sole fillets
1 onion, peeled and halved
1 carrot, peeled and halved
3 fresh bay leaves

SAUCE;
1 tbsp olive oil
15 g/½ oz/1 tbsp butter
4 shallots, finely chopped
100 g/ 3½ oz baby button
    mushrooms, wiped and halved

1 tbsp peppercorns, lightly crushed
8 sole fillets
100 ml/3½ fl oz/⅓ cup Marsala
150 ml/5 fl oz/⅔ pint double
    (heavy) cream

1 To make the stock, place the water, fish bones and skin, onion, carrot and bay leaves in a saucepan and bring to the boil.

2 Reduce the heat and leave the mixture to simmer for 1 hour or until the stock has reduced to about 150 ml/5 fl oz/⅔ cup. Drain the stock through a fine sieve, discarding the bones and vegetables, and set aside.

3 To make the sauce, heat the oil and butter in a frying pan (skillet).

Add the shallots and cook, stirring, for 2–3 minutes or until just softened.

4 Add the mushrooms to the frying pan (skillet) and cook, stirring, for a further 2–3 minutes or until they are just beginning to brown.

5 Add the peppercorns and sole fillets to the frying pan (skillet). Fry the sole fillets for 3–4 minutes on each side or until golden brown.

6 Pour the wine and stock over the fish and leave to simmer for 3 minutes. Remove the fish with a fish slice or a perforated spoon, set aside and keep warm.

7 Increase the heat and boil the mixture in the pan for about 5 minutes or until the sauce has reduced and thickened.

8 Pour in the cream, return the fish to the pan and heat through. Serve with the cooked vegetables of your choice.

Fresh Baked Sardines

Serves 4

INGREDIENTS

2 tbsp olive oil
2 large onions, sliced into rings
3 garlic cloves, chopped
2 large courgettes (zucchini), cut into sticks

3 tbsp fresh thyme, stalks removed
8 sardine fillets or about 1 kg/2 lb
4 oz whole sardines, filleted
75 g/2¾ oz Parmesan cheese, grated

4 eggs, beaten
150 ml/5 fl oz/⅔ pint milk
salt and pepper

1 Heat 1 tablespoon of the oil in a frying pan (skillet). Add the onions and garlic and sauté for 2–3 minutes.

2 Add the courgettes (zucchini) to the frying pan (skillet) and cook for about 5 minutes or until golden.

3 Stir 2 tablespoons of the thyme into the mixture.

4 Place half of the onions and courgettes (zucchini) in the base of a large ovenproof dish. Top

with the sardine fillets and half of the Parmesan cheese.

5 Place the remaining onions and courgettes (zucchini) on top and sprinkle with the remaining thyme.

6 Mix the eggs and milk together in a bowl and season to taste with salt and pepper. Pour the mixture over the vegetables and sardines in the dish. Sprinkle the remaining Parmesan cheese over the top.

7 Bake in a preheated oven at 180°C/350°F/ Gas Mark 4 for 20–25 minutes or until golden and set. Serve hot, straight from the oven.

VARIATION

If you cannot find sardines that are large enough to fillet, use small mackerel instead.

Marinated Fish

Serves 4

INGREDIENTS

4 whole mackerel, cleaned and gutted	2 tbsp extra virgin olive oil	2 garlic cloves, crushed
4 tbsp chopped marjoram	finely grated rind and juice of 1 lime	salt and pepper

1 Under gently running water, scrape the mackerel with the blunt side of a knife to remove any scales.

2 Using a sharp knife, make a slit in the stomach of the fish and cut horizontally along until the knife will go no further very easily. Gut the fish and rinse under water. You may prefer to remove the heads before cooking, but it is not necessary.

3 Using a sharp knife, cut 4–5 diagonal slashes on each side of the fish. Place the fish in a shallow, non-metallic dish.

4 To make the marinade, mix together the marjoram, olive oil, lime rind and juice, garlic and salt and pepper in a bowl.

5 Pour the mixture over the fish. Leave to marinate in the refrigerator for 30 minutes.

6 Cook the mackerel, under a preheated grill (broiler), for 5–6 minutes on each side, brushing occasionally with the reserved marinade, until golden.

7 Transfer the fish to serving plates. Pour over any remaining marinade before serving.

COOK'S TIP

If the lime is too hard to squeeze, microwave on high power for 30 seconds to release the juice. This dish is also excellent cooked on the barbecue (grill).

Mussel Casserole

Serves 4

INGREDIENTS

1 kg/2 lb 4 oz mussels	1 onion, finely chopped	100 g/3½ oz passata (tomato paste)
150 ml/5 fl oz/²⁄₃ cup white wine	3 garlic cloves, chopped	1 tbsp chopped marjoram
1 tbsp oil	1 red chilli, finely chopped	toast or crusty bread, to serve

1 Scrub the mussels to remove any mud or sand.

2 Remove the beards from the mussels by pulling away the hairy bit between the two shells. Rinse the mussels in a bowl of clean water. Discard any mussels that do not close when they are tapped – they are dead and should not be eaten.

3 Place the mussels in a large saucepan. Pour in the wine and cook for 5 minutes, shaking the pan occasionally until the shells open. Remove and discard any mussels that do not open.

4 Remove the mussels from the saucepan with a perforated spoon. Strain the cooking liquid through a fine sieve set over a bowl, reserving the liquid.

5 Heat the oil in a large frying pan (skillet). Add the onion, garlic and chilli and cook for 4–5 minutes or until softened.

6 Add the reserved cooking liquid to the pan and cook for 5 minutes or until reduced.

7 Stir in the passata (tomato paste), marjoram and mussels and cook until hot.

8 Transfer to serving bowls and serve with toast or plenty of crusty bread to mop up the juices.

COOK'S TIP

Finger bowls are individual bowls of warm water with a slice of lemon floating in them. They are used to clean your fingers at the end of a meal.

Sea Bass with Olive Sauce
on a Bed of Macaroni

Serves 4

INGREDIENTS

450 g/1 lb dried macaroni
1 tbsp olive oil
8 x 115 g/4 oz sea bass
    medallions

TO GARNISH:
lemon slices
shredded leek
shredded carrot

SAUCE:
25 g/1 oz/2 tbsp butter
4 shallots, chopped
2 tbsp capers
175 g/6 oz/1^1/2 cups stoned
    (pitted) green olives,
    chopped
4 tbsp balsamic vinegar

300 ml/^{1}/2 pint/1^1/4 cups fish
    stock
300 ml/^{1}/2 pint/1^1/4 cups
    double (heavy) cream
juice of 1 lemon
salt and pepper

1 For the sauce, melt the butter in a frying pan (skillet) and cook the shallots for 4 minutes. Add the capers and olives and cook for 3 minutes.

2 Stir in the balsamic vinegar and fish stock, bring to the boil and reduce by half. Stir in the cream and reduce again by half. Season to taste and stir in the lemon juice. Remove the pan from the heat, set aside and keep warm.

3 Bring a large pan of lightly salted water to the boil. Add the pasta and olive oil and cook for about 12 minutes, until tender but still firm to the bite.

4 Lightly grill (broil) the sea bass medallions for 3–4 minutes on each side, until cooked through, but still moist and delicate.

5 Drain the pasta and transfer to individual serving dishes. Top the pasta with the fish medallions and pour over the olive sauce. Garnish with lemon slices, shredded leek and shredded carrot and serve.

Vermicelli with Fillets of Red Mullet

Serves 4

INGREDIENTS

1 kg/2^1/4 lb red mullet fillets
300 ml/^{1}/2 pint/1^1/4 cups dry
    white wine
4 shallots, finely chopped
1 garlic clove, crushed
3 tbsp mixed fresh herbs
finely grated rind and juice of
    1 lemon

pinch of freshly grated
    nutmeg
3 anchovy fillets, roughly
    chopped
2 tbsp double (heavy) cream
1 tsp cornflour (cornstarch)
450 g/1 lb dried vermicelli
1 tbsp olive oil

salt and pepper

TO GARNISH:
1 fresh mint sprig
lemon slices
lemon rind

1 Put the red mullet fillets in a large casserole. Pour over the wine and add the shallots, garlic, herbs, lemon rind and juice, nutmeg and anchovies. Season with salt and pepper to taste. Cover and bake in a preheated oven at 180°C/350°F/Gas 4 for 35 minutes.

2 Carefully transfer the mullet and herbs to a warm dish. Set aside and keep warm.

3 Pour the cooking liquid into a pan and bring to the boil. Simmer for 25 minutes, until reduced by half. Mix the cream and cornflour (cornstarch) and stir into the sauce to thicken.

4 Bring a pan of salted water to the boil. Add the vermicelli and olive oil and cook until tender, but still firm to the bite. Drain the pasta and transfer to a warm serving dish.

5 Discard the herbs before arranging the red mullet fillets on top of the vermicelli; pour over the sauce. Garnish with a fresh mint sprig, slices of lemon and strips of lemon rind. Serve immediately.

COOK'S TIP

The best red mullet is sometimes called golden mullet, although it is bright red in colour.

Spaghetti al Tonno

Serves 4

INGREDIENTS

200 g/7 oz can tuna, drained
60 g/2 oz can anchovies, drained
250 ml/9 fl oz/1¹/₈ cups olive oil

60 g/2 oz/1 cup roughly chopped flat leaf parsley, plus extra to garnish
150 ml/¹/₄ pint/⁵/₈ cup crème fraîche

450 g/1 lb dried spaghetti
25 g/1 oz/2 tbsp butter
salt and pepper
black olives, to garnish
crusty bread, to serve

1 Remove any bones from the tuna. Put the tuna into a food processor or blender, together with the anchovies, 225 ml/8 fl oz/1 cup of the olive oil and the flat leaf parsley. Process until smooth.

2 Spoon the crème fraîche into the food processor or blender and process again for a few seconds to blend thoroughly. Season to taste.

3 Bring a large pan of lightly salted water to the boil. Add the spaghetti and the remaining olive oil and cook until tender, but still firm to the bite.

4 Drain the spaghetti, return to the pan and place over a medium heat. Add the butter and toss well to coat. Spoon in the sauce and quickly toss into the spaghetti, using 2 forks.

5 Remove the pan from the heat and divide the spaghetti between 4 warm individual serving plates. Garnish with olives and parsley and serve with warm, crusty bread.

VARIATION

If liked, you could add 1–2 garlic cloves to the sauce, substitute 25 g/1 oz/¹/₂ cup chopped fresh basil for half the parsley and garnish with capers instead of black olives.

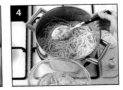

Casserole of Fusilli & Smoked Haddock with Egg Sauce

Serves 4

INGREDIENTS

25 g/1 oz/2 tbsp butter, plus
extra for greasing
450 g/1 lb smoked haddock
fillets, cut into 4 slices
600 ml/1 pint/2¹/2 cups milk
25 g/1 oz/¹/4 cup plain
(all purpose) flour

pinch of f eshly grated
nutmeg
3 tbsp double (heavy) cream
1 tbsp chopped fresh parsley,
plus extra to garnish
2 eggs, hard boiled (hard
cooked) and mashed

450 g/1 lb/4 cups dried fusilli
1 tbsp lemon juice
salt and pepper
boiled new potatoes and
beetroot (beet), to serve

1 Grease a casserole with butter. Put the haddock in the casserole and pour over the milk. Bake in a preheated oven at 200°C/400°G/Gas 6 for 15 minutes. Carefully pour the cooking liquid into a jug (pitcher) without breaking up the fish.

2 Melt the butter in a saucepan and stir in the flour. Gradually whisk in the reserved cooking liquid. Season with salt, pepper and nutmeg. Stir in the cream, parsley and mashed eggs and cook for 2 minutes.

3 Meanwhile, bring a large saucepan of salted water to the boil. Add the fusilli and lemon juice and cook until tender, but still firm to the bite.

4 Drain the pasta and tip it over the fish. Top with the sauce and return to the oven for 10 minutes.

5 Garnish and serve the casserole with boiled new potatoes and beetroot (beet).

VARIATION

You can use any type of dried pasta for this casserole. Try penne, conchiglie or rigatoni.

Poached Salmon Steaks with Penne

Serves 4

INGREDIENTS

4 x 275 g/10 oz fresh salmon
   steaks
60 g/2 oz/4 tbsp butter
175 ml/6 fl oz/³/4 cup dry
   white wine
sea salt
8 peppercorns
fresh dill sprig
fresh tarragon sprig

1 lemon, sliced
450 g/1 lb dried penne
2 tbsp olive oil
lemon slices and fresh
   watercress, to garnish

LEMON & WATERCRESS
   SAUCE:
25 g/1 oz/2 tbsp butter

25 g/1 oz/¹/4 cup plain (all
   purpose) flour
150 ml/¹/4 pint/⁵/8 cup warm
   milk
juice and finely grated rind of
   2 lemons
60 g/2 oz watercress, chopped
salt and pepper

1 Put the salmon in a large, non-stick pan. Add the butter, wine, a pinch of sea salt, the peppercorns, dill, tarragon and lemon. Cover, bring to the boil, and simmer for 10 minutes.

2 Using a slotted spoon, carefully remove the salmon. Strain and reserve the cooking liquid. Remove and discard the salmon skin and centre bones. Place on a warm dish, cover and keep warm.

3 Bring a pan of salted water to the boil. Add the penne and 1 tbsp of oil and cook for 12 minutes. Drain and sprinkle over the remaining oil. Place on a serving dish, top with the salmon and keep warm.

4 To make the sauce, melt the butter and stir in the flour for 2 minutes. Stir in the milk and about 7 tbsp of the reserved cooking liquid. Add the lemon juice and rind and cook, stirring, for a further 10 minutes.

5 Stir in the watercress and seasoning.

6 Pour the sauce over the salmon and penne, garnish with slices of lemon and fresh watercress and serve immediately.

Spaghetti with Smoked Salmon

Serves 4

INGREDIENTS

450 g/1 lb dried buckwheat
   spaghetti
2 tbsp olive oil
90 g/3 oz/^{1}/$_2$ cup crumbled
   feta cheese
salt
fresh coriander (cilantro) or
   parsley leaves, to garnish

SAUCE:
300 ml/^{1}/$_2$ pint/1^1/$_4$ cups
   double (heavy) cream
150 ml/^{1}/$_4$ pint/^{5}/$_8$ cup whisky
   or brandy
125 g/4^1/$_2$ oz smoked salmon
pinch of cayenne pepper
black pepper

2 tbsp chopped fresh coriander
   (cilantro) or parsley

1 Bring a large pan of lightly salted water to the boil. Add the spaghetti and 1 tbsp of the olive oil and cook until tender, but still firm to the bite. Drain and return to the pan with the remaining olive oil. Cover, set aside and keep warm.

2 Pour the cream into a small saucepan and bring to simmering point, but do not let it boil. Pour the whisky or brandy into another small saucepan and bring to simmering point, but do not allow it to boil. Remove both pans from the heat and mix together the cream and whisky or brandy.

3 Cut the smoked salmon into thin strips and add to the cream mixture. Season with cayenne and black pepper. Just before serving, stir in the fresh coriander (cilantro) or parsley.

4 Transfer the spaghetti to a warm serving dish, pour over the sauce and toss thoroughly with 2 large forks. Scatter over the crumbled feta cheese, garnish with the coriander (cilantro) or parsley leaves and serve immediately.

COOK'S TIP

Serve this rich and luxurious dish with a green salad tossed in a lemony dressing.

Spaghetti with Seafood Sauce

Serves 4

INGREDIENTS

225 g/8 oz dried spaghetti, broken into 15 cm/6 inch lengths
2 tbsp olive oil
300 ml/^{1}/2 pint/1^1/4 cups chicken stock
1 tsp lemon juice
1 small cauliflower, cut into florets (flowerets)
2 carrots, thinly sliced

115 g/4 oz mangetouts (snow peas)
60 g/2 oz/4 tbsp butter
1 onion, sliced
225 g/8 oz courgettes (zucchini), sliced
1 garlic clove, chopped
350 g/12 oz frozen, cooked, peeled prawns (shrimp), defrosted

2 tbsp chopped fresh parsley
25 g/1 oz/^{1}/3 cup freshly grated Parmesan cheese
^{1}/2 tsp paprika
salt and pepper
4 unpeeled, cooked prawns (shrimp), to garnish

1 Bring a pan of lightly salted water to the boil. Add the spaghetti and 1 tbsp of the olive oil and cook until tender, but still firm to the bite. Drain, toss with the remaining olive oil, cover and keep warm.

2 Bring the chicken stock and lemon juice to the boil. Add the cauliflower and carrots and cook for 3–4 minutes.

Remove from the pan and set aside. Cook the mangetouts (snow peas) for 1–2 minutes then set aside with the other vegetables.

3 Melt half the butter in a frying pan (skillet) and fry the onion and courgettes (zucchini) for 3 minutes. Add the garlic and prawns (shrimp) and cook for a further 2–3 minutes. Stir in the

reserved vegetables and heat through. Season to taste and stir in the remaining butter.

4 Transfer the spaghetti to a warm serving dish. Mix in the sauce and the chopped parsley until coated. Sprinkle over the Parmesan cheese and paprika, garnish with the unpeeled prawns (shrimp) and serve immediately.

Macaroni & Prawn (Shrimp) Bake

Serves 4

INGREDIENTS

350 g/12 oz/3 cups dried
  short-cut macaroni
1 tbsp olive oil, plus extra
  for brushing
90 g/3 oz/6 tbsp butter, plus
  extra for greasing
2 small fennel bulbs, thinly
  sliced and fronds reserved

175 g/6 oz mushrooms, thinly
  sliced
175 g/6 oz peeled, cooked
  prawns (shrimp)
pinch of cayenne pepper
300 ml/½ pint/1¼ cups
  Béchamel Sauce (see
  Cook's Tip, below)

60 g/2 oz/⅔ cup freshly
  grated Parmesan cheese
2 large tomatoes, sliced
1 tsp dried oregano
salt and pepper

1 Bring a pan of salted water to the boil. Add the pasta and oil and cook until tender, but still firm to the bite. Drain, return to the pan and toss in 25 g/1 oz/2 tbsp of the butter. Cover and keep warm.

2 Fry the fennel in the remaining butter for 3–4 minutes. Stir in the mushrooms and fry for 2 minutes. Stir in the prawns (shrimp), then remove the pan from the heat.

3 Stir the pasta, cayenne pepper and prawn (shrimp) mixture into the Béchamel sauce. Pour into a greased ovenproof dish. Sprinkle over the Parmesan cheese and arrange the tomato slices around the edge. Brush the tomatoes with olive oil and sprinkle over the oregano.

4 Bake in a preheated oven at 180°C/350°F/ Gas 4 for 25 minutes, until golden brown. Serve.

COOK'S TIP

For Béchamel sauce, melt 25 g/1 oz/2 tbsp butter. Stir in 25 g/1 oz/¼ cup flour and cook for 2 minutes. Gradually, stir in 300 ml/ ½ pint/1¼ cups warm milk. Add 2 tbsp finely chopped onion, 5 white peppercorns and 2 parsley sprigs. Season with salt, dried thyme and grated nutmeg. Simmer, stirring, for 15 minutes. Strain.

Pasta Parcels

Serves 4

INGREDIENTS

450 g/1 lb dried fettuccine
150 ml/¼ pint/⅝ cup Pesto
  Sauce
4 tsp extra virgin olive oil

750 g/1 lb 10 oz large raw
  prawns (shrimp), peeled
  and deveined
2 garlic cloves, crushed

125 ml/4 fl oz/½ cup dry
  white wine
salt and pepper
lemon wedges, to serve

1 Cut out 4 × 30 cm/ 12 inch squares of greaseproof (baking) paper.

2 Bring a large saucepan of lightly salted water to the boil. Add the fettuccine and cook for 2–3 minutes, until just softened. Drain and set aside.

3 Mix together the fettuccine and half of the Pesto Sauce. Spread out the paper squares and put 1 tsp olive oil in the middle of each. Divide the fettuccine between the squares, then divide the prawns (shrimp) and place on top of the fettuccine.

4 Mix together the remaining Pesto Sauce and the garlic and spoon it over the prawns (shrimp). Season each parcel with salt and black pepper and sprinkle with the white wine.

5 Dampen the edges of the greaseproof (baking) paper and wrap the parcels loosely, twisting the edges to seal.

6 Place the parcels on a baking (cookie) sheet and bake in a preheated oven at 200°C/400°F/ Gas 6 for 10–15 minutes. Transfer the parcels to 4 individual serving plates and serve immediately.

COOK'S TIP

Traditionally, these parcels are designed to look like money bags. The resemblance is more effective with greaseproof (baking) paper than with foil.

Pasta Shells with Mussels

Serves 4–6

INGREDIENTS

1.25 kg/2³/₄ lb mussels
225 ml/8 fl oz/1 cup dry white wine
2 large onions, chopped
115 g/4 oz/¹/₂ cup unsalted butter

6 large garlic cloves, finely chopped
5 tbsp chopped fresh parsley
300 ml/¹/₂ pint/1¹/₄ cups double (heavy) cream
400 g/14 oz dried pasta shells

1 tbsp olive oil
salt and pepper
crusty bread, to serve

1 Scrub and debeard the mussels under cold running water. Discard any that do not close immediately when tapped. Put the mussels in a pan with the wine and half of the onions. Cover and cook over a medium heat, shaking the pan frequently, until the shells open.

2 Remove from the heat. Drain the mussels and reserve the cooking liquid. Discard any mussels that have not opened. Strain the cooking liquid and reserve.

3 Fry the remaining onion in the butter for 2–3 minutes. Stir in the garlic and cook for 1 minute. Gradually stir in the reserved cooking liquid, parsley and cream. Season and leave to simmer.

4 Cook the pasta with the oil in a pan of salted water until just tender, but still firm to the bite. Drain, return to the pan, cover and keep warm.

5 Reserve a few mussels for the garnish and remove the remainder from their shells. Stir the shelled mussels into the cream sauce and warm briefly. Transfer the pasta to a serving dish. Pour over the sauce and toss well to coat. Garnish with the reserved mussels and serve with warm, crusty bread.

COOK'S TIP

Pasta shells are ideal because the sauce collects in the cavities and impregnates the pasta with flavour.

Saffron Mussel Tagliatelle

Serves 4

INGREDIENTS

1 kg/2^1/4 lb mussels	2 tsp cornflour (cornstarch)	450 g/1 lb dried tagliatelle
150 ml/^{1}/4 pint/^{5}/8 cup white wine	300 ml/^{1}/2 pint/1^1/4 cups double (heavy) cream	1 tbsp olive oil
1 medium onion, finely chopped	pinch of saffron threads or saffron powder	salt and pepper
25 g/1 oz/2 tbsp butter	1 egg yolk	3 tbsp chopped fresh parsley, to garnish
2 garlic cloves, crushed	juice of ^{1}/2 lemon	

1 Scrub and debeard the mussels under cold running water. Discard any that do not close when sharply tapped. Put the mussels in a pan with the wine and onion. Cover and cook over a high heat until the shells open.

2 Drain and reserve the cooking liquid. Discard any mussels that are still closed. Reserve a few mussels for the garnish and remove the remainder from their shells.

3 Strain the cooking liquid into a saucepan. Bring to the boil and reduce by about a half. Remove from the heat.

4 Melt the butter in a saucepan and fry the garlic for 2 minutes, until golden brown. Stir in the cornflour (cornstarch) and cook, stirring, for 1 minute. Gradually stir in the cooking liquid and the cream. Crush the saffron threads and add to the pan. Season to taste and simmer over a low heat for 2–3 minutes, until thickened.

5 Stir in the egg yolk, lemon juice and shelled mussels. Do not allow the mixture to boil.

6 Bring a pan of salted water to the boil. Add the pasta and oil and cook until tender. Drain and transfer to a serving dish. Add the mussel sauce and toss. Garnish with the parsley and reserved mussels and serve.

Vermicelli with Clams

Serves 4

INGREDIENTS

400 g/14 oz dried vermicelli, spaghetti or other long pasta
2 tbsp olive oil
25 g/1 oz/2 tbsp butter
2 onions, chopped
2 garlic cloves, chopped

2 x 200 g/7 oz jars clams in brine
125 ml/4 fl oz/$^1/_2$ cup white wine
4 tbsp chopped fresh parsley
$^1/_2$ tsp dried oregano
pinch of freshly grated nutmeg

salt and pepper

TO GARNISH:
fresh basil sprigs

1 Bring a large pan of lightly salted water to the boil. Add the pasta and half the olive oil and cook until tender, but still firm to the bite. Drain, return to the pan and add the butter. Cover the pan, shake well and keep warm.

2 Heat the remaining oil in a saucepan over a medium heat. Add the onions and fry until they are translucent. Stir in the garlic and cook for 1 minute.

3 Strain the liquid from 1 jar of clams and add the liquid to the pan, together with the wine. Stir, bring to simmering point and simmer for 3 minutes. Drain the second jar of clams and discard the liquid.

4 Add the clams, parsley and oregano to the saucepan and season with pepper and nutmeg. Lower the heat and cook until the sauce is completely heated through.

5 Transfer the pasta to a serving dish and pour over the sauce. Garnish with the basil and serve.

COOK'S TIP

There are many different types of clams found along almost every coast in the world. Those traditionally used in this dish are the tiny ones – only 2.5–5 cm/ 1–2 inches across – known in Italy as vongole.

Squid & Macaroni Stew

Serves 4–6

INGREDIENTS

225 g/8 oz/2 cups dried short-cut macaroni or other small pasta shapes

7 tbsp olive oil

2 onions, sliced

350 g/12 oz prepared squid, cut into 4 cm/1¹/₂ inch strips

225 ml/8 fl oz/1 cup fish stock

150 ml/¹/₄ pint/⁵/₈ cup red wine

2 tbsp tomato purée (paste)

350 g/12 oz tomatoes, skinned and thinly sliced

1 tsp dried oregano

2 bay leaves

2 tbsp chopped fresh parsley

salt and pepper

crusty bread, to serve

1 Bring a large pan of salted water to the boil. Add the pasta and 1 tbsp of oil and cook for 3 minutes. Drain and keep warm.

2 Heat the remaining oil in a pan and fry the onions until translucent. Add the squid and stock and simmer for 5 minutes. Pour in the wine and add the tomato purée (paste), tomatoes, oregano and bay leaves. Bring the sauce to the boil, season to taste and cook for 5 minutes.

3 Stir the pasta into the pan, cover and simmer for 10 minutes, or until the squid and macaroni are tender and the sauce has thickened. If the sauce remains too liquid, uncover the pan and continue cooking for a few minutes.

4 Discard the bay leaves. Reserve a little parsley and stir the remainder into the pan. Transfer to a warm serving dish and sprinkle over the remaining parsley. Serve with crusty bread.

COOK'S TIP

To prepare squid, peel off the outer skin, then cut off the head and tentacles. Extract the transparent flat oval bone from the body and discard. Remove the sac of black ink, then turn the body sac inside out. Wash in cold water. Cut off the tentacles and discard the rest; wash thoroughly.

Steamed Fish with Black Bean Sauce

Serves 4

INGREDIENTS

900 g/2 lb whole snapper,
cleaned and scaled
3 garlic cloves, crushed
2 tbsp black bean sauce
1 tsp cornflour (cornstarch)

2 tsp sesame oil
2 tbsp light soy sauce
2 tsp caster (superfine) sugar
2 tbsp dry sherry
1 small leek, shredded

1 small red (bell) pepper,
seeded and cut into thin
strips
shredded leek and lemon
wedges, to garnish
boiled rice or noodles, to serve

1 Rinse the fish inside and out with cold running water and pat dry with kitchen paper (paper towels). Make 2-3 diagonal slashes in the flesh on each side of the fish, using a sharp knife. Rub the garlic into the fish.

2 Thoroughly mix the black bean sauce, cornflour (cornstarch), sesame oil, light soy sauce, sugar and dry sherry together in a bowl. Place the fish in a shallow heatproof dish and pour the sauce mixture over the top.

3 Sprinkle the leek and (bell) pepper strips on top of the sauce. Place the dish in the top of a steamer, cover and steam for 10 minutes, or until the fish is cooked through.

4 Transfer to a serving dish, garnish with shredded leek and lemon wedges and serve with boiled rice or noodles.

VARIATION

Whole sea bream or sea bass may be used in this recipe instead of snapper, if you prefer.

COOK'S TIP

Insert the point of a sharp knife into the fish to test if it is cooked. The fish is cooked through if the knife goes into the flesh easily.

Trout with Pineapple

Serves 4

INGREDIENTS

4 trout fillets, skinned
2 tbsp vegetable oil
2 garlic cloves, cut into slivers
4 slices fresh pineapple, peeled and diced
1 celery stick, sliced
1 tbsp light soy sauce

50 ml/2 fl oz/¼ cup fresh or unsweetened pineapple juice
150 ml/¼ pint/⅔ cup fish stock
1 tsp cornflour (cornstarch)
2 tsp water

shredded celery leaves and fresh red chilli strips, to garnish

1 Cut the trout fillets into strips. Heat 1 tbsp of the oil in a preheated wok until almost smoking. Reduce the heat slightly, add the fish and sauté for 2 minutes. Remove from the wok and set aside.

2 Add the remaining oil to the wok, reduce the heat and add the garlic, pineapple and celery. Stir-fry for 1–2 minutes.

3 Add the soy sauce, pineapple juice and fish stock to the wok. Bring to the boil and cook, stirring, for 2–3 minutes, or until the sauce has reduced.

4 Blend the cornflour (cornstarch) with the water to form a paste and stir it into the wok. Bring the sauce to the boil and cook, stirring constantly, until the sauce thickens and clears.

5 Return the fish to the wok, and cook, stirring gently, until heated through. Transfer to a warmed serving dish and serve, garnished with shredded celery leaves and red chilli strips.

COOK'S TIP

Use canned pineapple instead of fresh pineapple if you wish, choosing slices in unsweetened, natural juice in preference to a syrup.

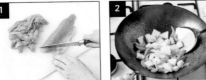

Mullet with Ginger

Serves 4

INGREDIENTS

1 whole mullet, cleaned and
    scaled
2 spring onions (scallions),
    chopped
1 tsp grated fresh root ginger
125 ml/4 fl oz/^{1}/2 cup garlic
    wine vinegar

125 ml/4 fl oz/^{1}/2 cup light
    soy sauce
3 tsp caster (superfine) sugar
dash of chilli sauce
125 ml/4 fl oz/^{1}/2 cup fish
    stock
1 green (bell) pepper, seeded
    and thinly sliced

1 large tomato, skinned,
    seeded and cut into thin
    strips
salt and pepper
sliced tomato, to garnish

1 Rinse the fish inside
and out and pat dry
with kitchen paper (paper
towels).

2 Make 3 diagonal slits
in the flesh on each
side of the fish. Season
with salt and pepper inside
and out.

3 Place the fish on a
heatproof plate and
scatter the spring onions
(scallions) and ginger over
the top. Cover and steam

for 10 minutes, or until the
fish is cooked through.

4 Place the vinegar, soy
sauce, sugar, chilli
sauce, fish stock, (bell)
pepper and tomato in a
saucepan and bring to the
boil, stirring occasionally.
Cook over a high heat until
the sauce has slightly
reduced and thickened.

5 Remove the fish from
the steamer and
transfer to a warm serving

dish. Pour the sauce over
the fish, garnish with
tomato slices and serve
immediately.

COOK'S TIP

*Use fillets of fish for this
recipe if preferred, and
reduce the cooking time
to 5–7 minutes.*

Seafood Medley

Serves 4

INGREDIENTS

2 tbsp dry white wine
1 egg white, lightly beaten
1/2 tsp Chinese five-spice
   powder
1 tsp cornflour (cornstarch)
300 g/10 1/2 oz raw prawns
   (shrimp), peeled and
   deveined

125 g/4 1/2 oz prepared squid,
   cut into rings
125 g/4 1/2 oz white fish fillets,
   cut into strips
vegetable oil, for deep-frying
1 green (bell) pepper, seeded
   and cut into thin strips
1 carrot, cut into thin strips

4 baby corn cobs, halved
   lengthways

1 Mix together the wine, egg white, Chinese five-spice powder and cornflour (cornstarch) in a large bowl. Add the prawns (shrimp), squid rings and fish fillets and stir to coat evenly. Remove the fish and seafood with a slotted spoon, reserving any leftover cornflour (cornstarch) mixture.

2 Heat the oil in a preheated wok and deep-fry the prawns (shrimp), squid and fish for 2–3 minutes. Remove the seafood mixture from the wok with a slotted spoon and set aside.

3 Pour off all but 1 tablespoon of oil from the wok and return to the heat. Add the (bell) pepper, carrot and corn cobs and stir-fry for 4–5 minutes.

4 Return the seafood mixture to the wok and add any remaining cornflour mixture. Cook, stirring and tossing well, to heat through. Transfer to a serving plate and serve immediately.

COOK'S TIP

Open up the squid rings and using a sharp knife, score a lattice pattern on the flesh to make them look more attractive.

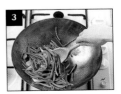

Fried Prawns (Shrimp) with Cashews

Serves 4

INGREDIENTS

2 garlic cloves, crushed	1 leek, sliced	SAUCE:
1 tbsp cornflour (cornstarch)	125 g/4 1/2 oz broccoli florets	175 ml/6 fl oz/3/4 cup fish
pinch of caster (superfine)	1 orange (bell) pepper, seeded	stock
sugar	and diced	1 tbsp cornflour (cornstarch)
450 g/1 lb raw tiger prawns	75 g/2 3/4 oz/3/4 cup unsalted	dash of chilli sauce
(jumbo shrimp)	cashew nuts	2 tsp sesame oil
4 tbsp vegetable oil		1 tbsp Chinese rice wine

1 Mix together the garlic, cornflour (cornstarch) and sugar in a bowl. Peel and devein the prawns (shrimp). Stir the prawns (shrimp) into the mixture to coat.

2 Heat the oil in a preheated wok and add the prawn (shrimp) mixture. Stir-fry over a high heat for 20–30 seconds until the prawns (shrimp) turn pink. Remove the prawns (shrimp) from the wok

with a slotted spoon and set aside.

3 Add the leek, broccoli and (bell) pepper to the wok and stir-fry for 2 minutes.

4 To make the sauce, mix together the fish stock, cornflour (cornstarch), chilli sauce to taste, the sesame oil and Chinese rice wine. Add the mixture to the wok, together with the cashew nuts. Return the prawns (shrimp) to the

wok and cook for 1 minute to heat through. Transfer to a warm serving dish and serve immediately.

VARIATION

This recipe also works well with chicken, pork or beef strips instead of the prawns (shrimp). Use 225 g/8 oz meat instead of 450 g/1 lb prawns (shrimp).

(Small) Shrimp Fu Yong

Serves 4

INGREDIENTS

2 tbsp vegetable oil
1 carrot, grated
5 eggs, beaten
225 g/8 oz raw (small) shrimp,
    peeled

1 tbsp light soy sauce
pinch of Chinese five-spice
    powder
2 spring onions (scallions),
    chopped

2 tsp sesame seeds
1 tsp sesame oil

1 Heat the vegetable oil in a preheated wok.

2 Add the carrot and stir-fry for 1–2 minutes.

3 Push the carrot to one side of the wok and add the eggs. Cook, stirring gently, for 1–2 minutes.

4 Stir the (small) shrimp, soy sauce and five-spice powder into the mixture in the wok. Stir-fry the mixture for 2–3 minutes, or until the (small) shrimps change colour and the mixture is almost dry.

5 Turn the (small) shrimp fu yong out on to a warm plate and sprinkle the spring onions (scallions), sesame seeds and sesame oil on top. Serve immediately.

VARIATION

For a more substantial dish, you could add 225 g/8 oz/ 1 cup cooked long-grain rice with the (small) shrimp in step 4. Taste and adjust the quantities of soy sauce, Chinese five-spice powder and sesame oil if necessary.

COOK'S TIP

If only cooked prawns (shrimp) are available, add them just before the end of cooking, but make sure that they are fully incorporated into the fu yong. They require only heating through – overcooking will make them chewy and tasteless.

Cantonese Prawns (Shrimp)

Serves 4

INGREDIENTS

5 tbsp vegetable oil
4 garlic cloves, crushed
675 g/1^1/2 lb raw prawns
   (shrimp), shelled and
   deveined
5-cm/2-inch piece fresh root
   ginger, chopped
175 g/6 oz lean pork, diced

1 leek, sliced
3 eggs, beaten
shredded leek and red (bell)
   pepper matchsticks, to
   garnish

SAUCE:
2 tbsp dry sherry
2 tbsp light soy sauce
2 tsp caster (superfine) sugar
150 ml/^{1}/4 pint/^{2}/3 cup fish
   stock
4^1/2 tsp cornflour (cornstarch)
3 tbsp water

1 Heat 2 tablespoons of the oil in a preheated wok. Add the garlic and stir-fry for 30 seconds. Add the prawns (shrimp) and stir-fry for 5 minutes, or until they change colour. Remove the prawns (shrimp) from the wok with a slotted spoon, set aside and keep warm.

2 Add the remaining oil to the wok and heat. Add the ginger, diced pork and leek and stir-fry over a medium heat for 4–5 minutes, or until the pork is lightly coloured.

3 Add the sherry, soy, sugar and fish stock to the wok. Blend the cornflour (cornstarch) with the water to form a smooth paste and stir it into the wok. Cook, stirring, until the sauce thickens and clears.

4 Return the prawns (shrimp) to the wok and add the beaten eggs.

Cook for 5–6 minutes, gently stirring occasionally, until the eggs set. Transfer to a warm serving dish, garnish with shredded leek and pepper matchsticks and serve at once.

COOK'S TIP

If possible, use Chinese rice wine instead of the sherry.

Squid with Oyster Sauce

Serves 4

INGREDIENTS

450 g/1 lb squid
150 ml/¼ pint/²/₃ cup
　vegetable oil
1-cm/½-inch piece fresh root
　ginger, grated

60 g/2 oz mangetout (snow
　peas)
5 tbsp hot fish stock
red (bell) pepper triangles, to
　garnish

SAUCE:
1 tbsp oyster sauce
1 tbsp light soy sauce
pinch of caster (superfine)
　sugar
1 garlic clove, crushed

1 To prepare the squid, cut down the centre of the body lengthways. Flatten the squid out, inside uppermost, and score a lattice design deep into the flesh, using a sharp knife.

2 To make the sauce, combine the oyster sauce, soy sauce, sugar and garlic in a small bowl. Stir to dissolve the sugar and set aside until required.

3 Heat the oil in a preheated wok until almost smoking. Lower the heat slightly, add the squid and stir-fry until they curl up. Remove with a slotted spoon and drain thoroughly on kitchen paper (paper towels).

4 Pour off all but 2 tablespoons of the oil and return the wok to the heat. Add the ginger and mangetout (snow peas) and stir-fry for 1 minute.

5 Return the squid to the wok and pour in the sauce and hot fish stock.

Leave the mixture to simmer for 3 minutes, or until thickened.

6 Transfer to a warm serving dish, garnish with (bell) pepper triangles and serve immediately.

COOK'S TIP

Take care not to overcook the squid, otherwise it will be rubbery and unappetizing.

Scallops in Ginger Sauce

Serves 4

INGREDIENTS

2 tbsp vegetable oil
450 g/1 lb scallops, cleaned
    and halved
2.5-cm/1-inch piece fresh root
    ginger, finely chopped
3 garlic cloves, crushed

2 leeks, shredded
75 g/2³/₄ oz/³/₄ cup shelled
    peas
125 g/4¹/₂ oz canned bamboo
    shoots, drained and rinsed
2 tbsp light soy sauce

2 tbsp unsweetened orange
    juice
1 tsp caster (superfine) sugar
orange zest, to garnish

1 Heat the oil in a wok. Add the scallops and stir-fry for 1–2 minutes. Remove the scallops from the wok with a slotted spoon and set aside.

2 Add the ginger and garlic to the wok and stir-fry for 30 seconds. Stir in the leeks and peas and cook, stirring, for 2 minutes.

3 Add the bamboo shoots and return the scallops to the wok. Stir gently to mix without breaking up the scallops.

4 Stir in the soy sauce, orange juice and sugar and cook for 1–2 minutes. Transfer to a serving dish, garnish and serve.

COOK'S TIP

The edible parts of a scallop are the round white muscle and the orange and white coral or roe. The frilly skirt surrounding the muscle – the gills and mantle – may be used for making shellfish stock. All other parts should be discarded.

COOK'S TIP

Frozen scallops may be thawed and used in this recipe, adding them at the end of cooking to prevent them from breaking up. If you are buying scallops already shelled, check whether they are fresh or frozen. Fresh scallops are cream coloured and more translucent, while frozen scallops tend to be pure white.

Crab in Ginger Sauce

Serves 4

INGREDIENTS

2 small cooked crabs	1 green (bell) pepper, seeded	1/2 tsp sesame oil
2 tbsp vegetable oil	and cut into thin strips	150 ml/1/4 pint/2/3 cup fish
9-cm/3-inch piece fresh root	6 spring onions (scallions), cut	stock
ginger, grated	into 2.5-cm/1-inch lengths	1 tsp light brown sugar
2 garlic cloves, thinly sliced	2 tbsp dry sherry	2 tsp cornflour (cornstarch)
		150 ml/1/4 pint/2/3 cup water

1 Rinse the crabs and gently loosen around the shell at the top. Using a sharp knife, cut away the grey tissue and discard. Rinse the crabs again.

2 Twist off the legs and claws from the crabs. Using a pair of crab claw crackers or a cleaver, crack the claws to break through the shell to expose the flesh. Remove and discard any loose pieces of shell.

3 Separate the body and discard the inedible lungs and sac. Cut down the centre of each crab to separate the body into two pieces and then cut each of these in half again.

4 Heat the oil in a preheated wok. Add the ginger and garlic and stir-fry for 1 minute. Add the crab pieces and stir-fry for 1 minute.

5 Stir in the (bell) pepper, spring onions (scallions), sherry, sesame oil, stock and sugar. Bring to the boil, reduce the heat, cover and simmer for 3–4 minutes.

6 Blend the cornflour (cornstarch) with the remaining water and stir it into the wok. Bring to the boil, stirring, until the sauce is thickened and clear. Serve.

COOK'S TIP

If preferred, remove the crabmeat from the shells prior to stir-frying and add to the wok with the (bell) pepper.

Potato-Topped Cod

Serves 4

INGREDIENTS

60 g/2 oz/¼ cup butter	pinch of chilli powder	50 g/1¾ oz Gruyère cheese,
4 waxy potatoes, sliced	1 tbsp chopped fresh dill	grated
1 large onion, finely chopped	75 g/2¾ oz/1¼ cups fresh	salt and pepper
1 tsp wholegrain mustard	breadcrumbs	fresh dill sprigs, to garnish
1 tsp garam masala	4 cod fillets, about 175 g/6 oz each	

1 Melt half of the butter in a frying pan (skillet). Add the potatoes and fry for 5 minutes, turning until they are browned all over. Remove the potatoes from the pan with a perforated spoon.

2 Add the remaining butter to the frying pan (skillet) and stir in the onion, mustard, garam masala, chilli powder, chopped dill and breadcrumbs. Cook for 1–2 minutes, stirring and mixing well.

3 Layer half of the potatoes in the base of an ovenproof dish and place the cod fillets on top. Cover the cod fillets with the rest of the potato slices. Season to taste with salt and pepper.

4 Spoon the spicy mixture from the frying pan (skillet) over the potato and sprinkle with the grated cheese.

5 Cook in a preheated oven, 200°C/400°F/ Gas Mark 6, for 20–25 minutes or until the topping is golden and crisp and the fish is cooked through. Garnish with fresh dill sprigs and serve at once.

COOK'S TIP

This dish is ideal served with baked vegetables which can be cooked in the oven at the same time.

VARIATION

You can use any fish for this recipe: for special occasions use salmon steaks or fillets.

Seafood Stir-Fry

Serves 4

INGREDIENTS

100 g/3½ oz small, thin asparagus spears, trimmed	100 g/3½ oz baby sweetcorn cobs, quartered lengthwise	freshly cooked egg noodles, to serve
1 tbsp sunflower oil	2 tbsp light soy sauce	
2.5 cm/1 inch piece root (fresh) ginger, cut into thin strips	1 tbsp oyster sauce	TO GARNISH:
	1 tsp clear honey	4 large cooked prawns
1 medium leek, shredded	450 g/1 lb cooked, assorted shellfish, thawed if frozen	small bunch fresh chives, freshly snipped
2 medium carrots, julienned		

1 Bring a small pan of water to the boil and blanch the asparagus for 1–2 minutes. Drain, set aside and keep warm.

2 Heat the oil in a wok or large frying pan (skillet) and stir-fry the ginger, leek, carrots and sweetcorn for 3 minutes.

3 Add the soy sauce, oyster sauce and honey to the wok or frying pan (skillet). Stir in the shellfish and stir-fry for 2–3 minutes until the vegetables are just tender and the shellfish are heated through. Add the blanched asparagus and stir-fry for about 2 minutes.

4 To serve, pile the cooked noodles on to 4 warm serving plates and spoon over the seafood and vegetable stir fry. Serve garnished with a large prawn and freshly snipped chives.

COOK'S TIP

When you are preparing dense vegetables, such as carrots and other root vegetables, for stir frying, slice them into thin, evenly sized pieces so that they cook quickly and at the same rate. Delicate vegetables, such as (bell) peppers, leeks and spring onions (scallions), do not need to be cut as thinly.

Citrus Fish Skewers

Serves 4

INGREDIENTS

450 g/1 lb firm white fish
fillets (such as cod or
monkfish)
450 g/1 lb thick salmon fillet
2 large oranges
1 pink grapefruit

1 bunch fresh bay leaves
1 tsp finely grated lemon rind
3 tbsp lemon juice
2 tsp clear honey
2 garlic cloves, crushed
salt and pepper

TO SERVE:
crusty bread
mixed salad

1 Skin the white fish and the salmon, rinse and pat dry on absorbent kitchen paper. Cut each fillet into 16 pieces.

2 Using a sharp knife, remove the skin and pith from the oranges and grapefruit. Cut out the segments of flesh, removing all remaining traces of the pith and dividing membrane.

3 Thread the pieces of fish alternately with the orange and grapefruit segments and the bay leaves on to 8 skewers. Place the kebabs (kabobs) in a shallow dish.

4 Mix together the lemon rind and juice, the honey and garlic. Pour over the fish kebabs (kabobs) and season well. Cover and chill for 2 hours, turning occasionally.

5 Preheat the grill (broiler) to medium. Remove the skewers from the marinade and place on the rack. Cook for 7–8 minutes, turning once, until cooked through.

6 Drain, transfer to serving plates and serve with crusty bread and a fresh salad.

VARIATION

This dish makes an unusual starter. Try it with any firm fish – swordfish or shark, for example – or with tuna for a meatier texture.

Five-Spice Salmon with Ginger Stir-Fry

Serves 4

INGREDIENTS

4 salmon fillets, skinned, 115 g/4 oz each	2.5 cm/1 inch piece root (fresh) ginger	TO GARNISH:
2 tsp five-spice powder	2 tbsp ginger wine	shredded leek
1 large leek	2 tbsp light soy sauce	shredded root (fresh) ginger
1 large carrot	1 tbsp vegetable oil	shredded carrot
115 g/4 oz mangetout (snow peas)	salt and pepper	
	freshly boiled noodles, to serve	

1 Wash the salmon and pat dry on absorbent kitchen paper. Rub the five-spice powder into both sides of the fish and season with salt and pepper. Set aside until required.

2 Trim the leek, slice it down the centre and rinse under cold water to remove any dirt. Finely shred the leek. Peel the carrot and cut it into very thin strips. Top and tail the mangetout (snow peas) and cut them into shreds. Peel the ginger and slice thinly into strips.

3 Place all of the vegetables into a large bowl and toss in the ginger wine and 1 tablespoon of soy sauce. Set aside.

4 Preheat the grill (broiler) to medium. Place the salmon fillets on the rack and brush with the remaining soy sauce. Cook for 2–3 minutes on each side until cooked through.

5 While the salmon is cooking, heat the oil in a non-stick wok or large frying pan (skillet) and stir-fry the vegetables for 5 minutes until just tender. Take care that you do not overcook the vegetables – they should still have bite. Transfer to serving plates.

6 Drain the salmon on kitchen paper and serve on a bed of stir-fried vegetables. Garnish with shredded leek, ginger and carrot and serve.

404

Skewered Oriental Shellfish

Makes 12

INGREDIENTS

350 g/12 oz raw tiger prawns (jumbo shrimp), peeled leaving tails intact
350 g/12 oz scallops, cleaned, trimmed and halved
1 bunch spring onions (scallions), sliced into 2.5 cm/1 inch pieces
1 red (bell) pepper, deseeded and cubed

100 g/3^1/$_2$ oz baby corn, trimmed and sliced into 1 cm/^{1}/$_2$ inch pieces
3 tbsp dark soy sauce
1^1/$_2$ tsp hot chilli powder
^{1}/$_2$ tsp ground ginger
1 tbsp sunflower oil
1 red chilli, deseeded and sliced

DIP:
4 tbsp dark soy sauce
4 tbsp dry sherry
2 tsp clear honey
2.5 cm/1 inch piece root (fresh) ginger, peeled and grated
1 spring onion (scallion), trimmed and very finely sliced

1 Soak 12 wooden skewers in cold water for 10 minutes to prevent them from burning.

2 Divide the prawns (shrimp), scallops, spring onions (scallions), (bell) pepper and baby corn cobs into 12 portions and thread on to the skewers. Cover the ends with foil so that they do not burn and place in a shallow dish.

3 Mix the soy sauce, chilli powder and ground ginger and coat the shellfish and vegetable kebabs (kabobs). Cover and leave to chill for about 2 hours.

4 Preheat the grill (broiler) to hot. Place the kebabs (kabobs) on the rack, brush the shellfish and vegetables with oil and cook for 2–3 minutes on

each side until the prawns (shrimp) turn pink, the scallops become opaque and the vegetables are soft.

5 Mix together the dip ingredients.

6 Remove the foil and transfer the kebabs (kabobs) to a warm serving platter. Garnish with sliced chilli and serve with the dip.

Tuna Steaks with Fragrant Spices & Lime

Serves 4

INGREDIENTS

4 tuna steaks, 175 g/6 oz each
1/2 tsp finely grated lime rind
1 garlic clove, crushed
2 tsp olive oil
1 tsp ground cumin

1 tsp ground coriander
pepper
1 tbsp lime juice
fresh coriander (cilantro), to
  garnish

TO SERVE:
avocado relish (see Cook's Tip,
  below)
lime wedges
tomato wedges

1 Trim the skin from the tuna steaks, rinse and pat dry on absorbent kitchen paper.

2 In a small bowl, mix together the lime rind, garlic, olive oil, cumin, ground coriander and pepper to make a paste.

3 Spread the paste thinly on both sides of the tuna. Heat a non-stick, ridged frying pan (skillet) until hot and press the tuna steaks into the pan to seal them. Lower the heat and cook for 5 minutes. Turn the fish over and cook for a further 4–5 minutes until the fish is cooked through. Drain on absorbent kitchen paper and transfer to a serving plate.

4 Sprinkle the lime juice and chopped coriander (cilantro) over the fish.

5 Serve with freshly made avocado relish (see Cook's Tip, right), lime wedges and tomatoes.

COOK'S TIP

For low-fat avocado relish to serve with tuna, peel and remove the stone from one small ripe avocado. Toss in 1 tbsp lime juice. Mix in 1 tbsp freshly chopped coriander (cilantro) and 1 small finely chopped red onion. Stir in some chopped fresh mango or a chopped medium tomato and season well.

Teriyaki Stir-Fried Salmon with Crispy Leeks

Serves 4

INGREDIENTS

450 g/1 lb salmon fillet, skinned	1 tsp rice wine vinegar	4 tbsp corn oil
2 tbsp sweet soy sauce	1 tbsp demerara sugar	450 g/1 lb leeks, thinly shredded
2 tbsp tomato ketchup	1 clove garlic, crushed	finely chopped red chillies, to garnish

1 Using a sharp knife, cut the salmon into slices. Place the slices of salmon in a shallow non-metallic dish.

2 Mix together the soy sauce, tomato ketchup, rice wine vinegar, sugar and garlic.

3 Pour the mixture over the salmon, toss well and leave to marinate for about 30 minutes.

4 Meanwhile, heat 3 tablespoons of the corn oil in a large preheated wok.

5 Add the leeks to the wok and stir-fry over a medium high heat for about 10 minutes, or until the leeks become crispy and tender.

6 Using a slotted spoon, carefully remove the leeks from the wok and transfer to warmed serving plates.

7 Add the remaining oil to the wok. Add the salmon and the marinade to the wok and cook for 2 minutes. Spoon over the leeks, garnish and serve immediately.

VARIATION

You can use a fillet of beef instead of the salmon, if you prefer.

Stir-Fried Salmon with Pineapple

Serves 4

INGREDIENTS

100 g/3¾ oz/1 cup baby corn cobs, halved	1 green (bell) pepper, deseeded and sliced	100 g/3½ oz/1 cup beansprouts
2 tbsp sunflower oil	450 g/1 lb salmon fillet, skin removed	2 tbsp tomato ketchup
1 red onion, sliced	1 tbsp paprika	2 tbsp soy sauce
1 orange (bell) pepper, deseeded and sliced	225 g/8 oz can cubed pineapple, drained	2 tbsp medium sherry
		1 tsp cornflour (cornstarch)

1 Using a sharp knife, cut the baby corn cobs in half.

2 Heat the sunflower oil in a large preheated wok. Add the onion, (bell) peppers and baby corn cobs to the wok and stir-fry for 5 minutes.

3 Rinse the salmon fillet under cold running water and pat dry with absorbent kitchen paper.

4 Cut the salmon flesh into thin strips and place in a large bowl.

Sprinkle with the paprika and toss until well coated.

5 Add the salmon to the wok together with the pineapple and stir-fry for a further 2–3 minutes or until the fish is tender.

6 Add the beansprouts to the wok and toss well.

7 Mix together the tomato ketchup, soy sauce, sherry and cornflour (cornstarch). Add the mixture to the wok and cook until the juices start to thicken. Transfer to warm

serving plates and serve immediately.

VARIATION

You can use trout fillets instead of the salmon as an alternative, if you prefer.

Stir-Fried Cod with Mango

Serves 4

INGREDIENTS

175 g/6 oz carrots	1 green (bell) pepper, deseeded and	1 tbsp soy sauce
2 tbsp vegetable oil	sliced	100 ml/3½ fl oz/1⅓ cup tropical fruit
1 red onion, sliced	450 g/1 lb skinless cod fillet	juice
1 red (bell) pepper, deseeded and	1 ripe mango	1 tbsp lime juice
sliced	1 tsp cornflour (cornstarch)	1 tbsp chopped coriander (cilantro)

1 Using a sharp knife, slice the carrots into thin sticks.

2 Heat the vegetable oil in a preheated wok.

3 Add the onions, carrots and (bell) peppers to the wok and stir-fry for 5 minutes.

4 Using a sharp knife, cut the cod into small cubes.

5 Peel the mango, then carefully remove the flesh from the centre stone. Cut the flesh into thin slices.

6 Add the cod and mango to the wok and stir-fry for a further 4–5 minutes, or until the fish is cooked through. Do not stir the mixture too much or you may break the fish up.

7 Mix the cornflour (cornstarch), soy sauce, fruit juice and lime juice in a small bowl.

8 Pour the cornflour (cornstarch) mixture over the stir-fry and allow the mixture to bubble and the juices to thicken. Scatter with coriander (cilantro) and serve immediately.

VARIATION

You can use paw-paw (papaya) as an alternative to the mango, if you prefer.

Stir-Fried Gingered Monkfish

Serves 4

INGREDIENTS

450 g/1 lb monkfish
1 tbsp freshly grated root ginger
2 tbsp sweet chilli sauce

1 tbsp corn oil
100 g/3½ oz/1 cup fine asparagus

3 spring onions (scallions), sliced
1 tsp sesame oil

1 Using a sharp knife, slice the monkfish into thin flat rounds.

2 Mix the ginger with the chilli sauce in a small bowl.

3 Brush the ginger and chilli sauce mixture over the monkfish pieces.

4 Heat the corn oil in a large preheated wok.

5 Add the monkfish, asparagus and spring onions (scallions) to the wok and stir-fry for about 5 minutes.

6 Remove the wok from the heat, drizzle the sesame oil over the stir-fry and toss well to combine.

7 Transfer to warm serving plates and serve immediately.

VARIATION

Monkfish is quite expensive, but it is well worth using it as it has a wonderful flavour and texture. At a push you could use cubes of chunky cod fillet instead.

COOK'S TIP

Some recipes specify to grate ginger before it is cooked with other ingredients. To do this, just peel the flesh and rub it at a 45° angle up and down on the fine section of a metal grater, or use a special wooden or ceramic ginger grater.

Fried Fish with Coconut & Basil

Serves 4

INGREDIENTS

2 tbsp vegetable oil
450 g/1 lb skinless cod fillet
25 g/1 oz/¼ cup seasoned flour
1 clove garlic, crushed

2 tbsp red Thai curry paste
1 tbsp fish sauce
300 ml/½ pint/1¼ cups coconut milk
175 g/6 oz cherry tomatoes, halved

20 fresh basil leaves
fragrant rice, to serve

1 Heat the vegetable oil in a large preheated wok.

2 Using a sharp knife, cut the fish into large cubes, taking care to remove any bones with a pair of tweezers.

3 Place the seasoned flour in a bowl. Add the cubes of fish and mix until well coated.

4 Add the coated fish to the wok and stir-fry over a high heat for 3–4 minutes, or until the fish just begins to brown at the edges.

5 Mix together the garlic, curry paste, fish sauce and coconut milk in a bowl. Pour the mixture over the fish and bring to the boil.

6 Add the tomatoes to the mixture in the wok and leave to simmer for 5 minutes.

7 Roughly chop or tear the fresh basil leaves. Add the basil to the wok, stir carefully to combine, taking care not to break up the cubes of fish.

8 Transfer to serving plates and serve hot with fragrant rice.

COOK'S TIP

Take care not to overcook the dish once the tomatoes are added, otherwise they will break down and the skins will come away.

Prawn (Shrimp) Omelette

Serves 4

INGREDIENTS

2 tbsp sunflower oil	100 g/3½ oz/1 cup beansprouts	1 tbsp light soy sauce
4 spring onions (scallions), sliced	1 tsp cornflour (cornstarch)	6 eggs
350 g/12 oz peeled prawns (shrimp)		

1 Heat the sunflower oil in a large preheated wok.

2 Using a sharp knife, trim the spring onions (scallions) and cut into slices.

3 Add the prawns (shrimp), spring onions (scallions) and beansprouts to the wok and stir-fry for 2 minutes.

4 Mix together the cornflour (cornstarch) and soy sauce in a bowl.

5 Beat the eggs with 3 tablespoons of cold water and then blend with the cornflour (cornstarch) and soy mixture.

6 Add the egg mixture to the wok and cook for 5–6 minutes, or until the mixture sets.

7 Transfer the omelette to a serving plate and cut into quarters to serve.

VARIATION

Add any other vegetables of your choice, such as grated carrot or cooked peas, to the omelette in step 3, if you wish.

COOK'S TIP

It is important to use fresh beansprouts for this dish as the canned ones don't have the crunchy texture necessary.

Prawns (Shrimp) with Spicy Tomatoes

Serves 4

INGREDIENTS

2 tbsp corn oil	1 tbsp demerara sugar	450 g/1 lb peeled king prawns
1 onion	400 g/14 oz can chopped tomatoes	(shrimp)
2 cloves garlic, crushed	1 tbsp sundried tomato purée	salt and pepper
1 tsp cumin seeds	1 tbsp chopped fresh basil	

1 Heat the corn oil in a large preheated wok.

2 Using a sharp knife, finely chop the onion.

3 Add the onion and garlic to the wok and stir-fry for 2–3 minutes, or until softened.

4 Stir in the cumin seeds and stir-fry for 1 minute.

5 Add the sugar, chopped tomatoes and sundried tomato purée to the wok. Bring the mixture to the boil, then reduce the heat and leave the sauce to simmer for 10 minutes.

6 Add the basil, prawns (shrimp) and salt and pepper to taste to the mixture in the wok. Increase the heat and cook for a further 2–3 minutes or until the prawns (shrimp) are completely cooked through.

COOK'S TIP

Always heat your wok before you add oil or other ingredients. This will prevent anything from sticking to it.

COOK'S TIP

Sun-dried tomato purée has a much more intense flavour than that of normal tomato purée. It adds a distinctive intensity to any tomato-based dish.

Chinese Leaves with Shiitake Mushrooms & Crab Meat

Serves 4

INGREDIENTS

225 g/8 oz shiitake mushrooms	1 head Chinese leaves, shredded	200 g/7 oz can white crab meat,
2 tbsp vegetable oil	1 tbsp mild curry paste	drained
2 cloves garlic, crushed	6 tbsp coconut milk	1 tsp chilli flakes
6 spring onions (scallions), sliced		

1 Using a sharp knife, cut the the mushrooms into slices.

2 Heat the vegetable oil in a large preheated wok.

3 Add the mushrooms and garlic to the wok and stir-fry for 3 minutes or until the mushrooms have softened.

4 Add the spring onions (scallions) and shredded Chinese leaves to the wok and stir-fry until the leaves have wilted.

5 Mix together the mild curry paste and coconut milk in a small bowl.

6 Add the curry paste and coconut milk mixture to the wok together with the crab meat and chilli flakes. Mix together until well combined and heat through until the juices start to bubble.

7 Transfer to warm serving bowls and then serve immediately.

COOK'S TIP

Shiitake mushrooms are now readily available in the fresh vegetable section of most large supermarkets.

Seared Scallops with Butter Sauce

Serves 4

INGREDIENTS

450 g/1 lb scallops, without roe	2 tbsp vegetable oil	3 tbsp sweet soy sauce
6 spring onions (scallions)	1 green chilli, deseeded and sliced	50 g/1¾ oz/1½ tbsp butter, cubed

1 Rinse the scallops under cold running water, then pat the scallops dry with absorbent kitchen paper.

2 Using a sharp knife, slice each scallop in half horizontally.

3 Using a sharp knife, trim and slice the spring onions (scallions).

4 Heat the vegetable oil in a large preheated wok.

5 Add the chilli, spring onions (scallions) and scallops to the wok and stir-fry over a high heat for 4–5 minutes, or until the scallops are just cooked through.

6 Add the soy sauce and butter to the scallop stir-fry and heat through until the butter melts.

7 Transfer to warm serving bowls and serve hot.

COOK'S TIP

If you buy scallops on the shell, slide a knife underneath the membrane to loosen and cut off the tough muscle that holds the scallop to the shell. Discard the black stomach sac and intestinal vein.

COOK'S TIP

Use frozen scallops if preferred, but make sure they are completely defrosted before cooking. In addition, do not overcook them as they will easily disintegrate.

Stir-Fried Squid with Green (Bell) Peppers & Black Bean Sauce

Serves 4

INGREDIENTS

450 g/1 lb squid rings
2 tbsp plain (all-purpose) flour
½ tsp salt

1 green (bell) pepper
2 tbsp groundnut oil

1 red onion, sliced
160 g/5¾ oz jar black bean sauce

1 Rinse the squid rings under cold running water and pat dry with absorbent kitchen paper.

2 Place the plain (all-purpose) flour and salt in a bowl and mix together. Add the squid rings and toss until they are finely coated.

3 Using a sharp knife, deseed the (bell) pepper. Slice the (bell) pepper into thin strips.

4 Heat the groundnut oil in a large preheated wok.

5 Add the (bell) pepper and red onion to the wok and stir-fry for about 2 minutes, or until the vegetables are just beginning to soften.

6 Add the squid rings to the wok and cook for a further 5 minutes, or until the squid is cooked through.

7 Add the black bean sauce to the wok and heat through until the juices are bubbling. Transfer to warm serving bowls and serve immediately.

COOK'S TIP

Serve this recipe with fried rice or noodles tossed in soy sauce, if you wish.

Prawns (Shrimp) with (Bell) Peppers

Serves 4

INGREDIENTS

450 g/1 lb frozen prawns (shrimp) fresh coriander (cilantro) leaves	1 tsp fresh garlic, crushed 1 tsp salt 1 medium green (bell) pepper, sliced	1 medium red (bell) pepper 75 g/2³/4 oz/5¹/2 tbsp unsalted butter

1 Defrost the prawns (shrimp). Once they are completely thawed, rinse them under cold running water twice. Drain the prawns (shrimp) thoroughly and place in a large mixing bowl.

2 Using a sharp knife, finely chop the bunch of fresh coriander (cilantro) leaves.

3 Add the garlic, salt and fresh, chopped coriander (cilantro) leaves to the prawns (shrimp), then set the bowl aside until required.

4 Deseed the (bell) peppers and cut into thin slices, using a sharp knife.

5 Melt the butter in a large frying pan (skillet). Add the prawns (shrimp) to the pan and stir-fry, stirring and tossing the prawns (shrimp) gently, for 10-12 minutes.

6 Add the (bell) peppers to the pan and fry for a further 3-5 minutes, stirring occasionally.

7 Transfer the prawns (shrimp) and (bell)

pepper to a serving dish and serve hot.

VARIATION

You could use large tiger prawns (shrimp) in this dish, if you prefer.

Prawns (Shrimp) with Tomatoes

Serves 4-6

INGREDIENTS

3 medium onions
1 green (bell) pepper
1 tsp fresh ginger root, finely
   chopped
1 tsp fresh garlic, crushed

1 tsp salt
1 tsp chilli powder
2 tbsp lemon juice
350 g/12 oz frozen prawns
   (shrimp)

3 tbsp oil
400 g/14 oz can tomatoes
fresh coriander (cilantro)
   leaves, to garnish

1 Using a sharp knife, slice the onions and the green (bell) pepper.

2 Place the ginger, garlic, salt and chilli powder in a small bowl and mix. Add the lemon juice and mix to form a paste.

3 Place the prawns (shrimp) in a bowl of cold water and set aside to defrost. Drain thoroughly.

4 Heat the oil in a medium-sized saucepan. Add the onions and fry until golden brown.

5 Add the spice paste to the onions, reduce the heat to low and cook, stirring and mixing well, for about 3 minutes.

6 Add the tomatoes, tomato juice and the green (bell) pepper, and cook for 5-7 minutes, stirring occasionally.

7 Add the defrosted prawns (shrimp) to the pan and cook the mixture for about 10 minutes, stirring. Garnish with fresh coriander (cilantro) leaves and serve hot with plain boiled rice and a crisp green salad.

COOK'S TIP

Fresh ginger root looks rather like a knobbly potato. The skin should be peeled, then the flesh either grated, finely chopped or sliced. Ginger is also available ground: this can be used as a substitute for fresh root ginger, but the fresh root is far superior.

Bacon & Scallop Skewers

Makes 4

INGREDIENTS

grated rind and juice of $^1/_2$ lemon	12 scallops	1 yellow (bell) pepper
4 tbsp sunflower oil	1 red (bell) pepper	6 rashers smoked streaky
$^1/_2$ tsp dried dill	1 green (bell) pepper	bacon

1 Mix together the lemon rind and juice, oil and dill in a non-metallic dish. Add the scallops and mix thoroughly to coat in the marinade. Leave to marinate for 1–2 hours.

2 Cut the red, green and yellow (bell) peppers in half and deseed them. Cut the (bell) pepper halves into 2.5 cm/1 inch pieces and then set aside until required.

3 Carefully remove the rind from the bacon. Stretch the bacon rashers with the back of a knife, then cut each bacon rasher in half.

4 Remove the scallops from the marinade, reserving any excess marinade. Wrap a piece of bacon around each scallop.

5 Thread the bacon-wrapped scallops on to skewers, alternating with the (bell) pepper pieces.

6 Barbecue (grill) the bacon and scallop skewers over hot coals for about 5 minutes, basting with the marinade.

7 Transfer the bacon and scallop skewers to serving plates and serve at once.

VARIATION

Peel 4–8 raw prawns (shrimp) and add them to the marinade with the scallops. Thread them on to the skewers alternately with the scallops and (bell) peppers.

Caribbean Prawns (Shrimp)

Serves 4

INGREDIENTS

16 cooked king (tiger) prawns (shrimp)
1 small pineapple
flaked coconut, to garnish (optional)

MARINADE:
150 ml/5 fl oz/^{2}/3 cup pineapple juice
2 tbsp white wine vinegar
2 tbsp dark muscovado sugar

2 tbsp desiccated (shredded) coconut

1 Peel the prawns (shrimp), leaving the tails attached if preferred.

2 Peel the pineapple and cut it in half lengthwise. Cut one pineapple half into wedges then into chunks.

3 To make the marinade, mix together half of the pineapple juice and the vinegar, sugar and coconut in a shallow, non-metallic dish. Add the peeled prawns (shrimp) and pineapple chunks and toss until well coated. Leave to marinate for at least 30 minutes.

4 Remove the pineapple and prawns (shrimp) from the marinade and thread them on to skewers. Reserve the marinade.

5 Strain the marinade and place in a food processor. Roughly chop the remaining pineapple and add to the processor with the remaining pineapple juice. Process the pineapple for a few seconds to produce a thick sauce.

6 Pour the sauce into a small saucepan. Bring to the boil then simmer for about 5 minutes.

7 Transfer the kebabs (kabobs) to the barbecue (grill) and brush with some of the sauce. Barbecue (grill) for about 5 minutes until the kebabs (kabobs) are piping hot. Turn the kebabs (kabobs), brushing occasionally with the sauce. Serve with extra sauce, sprinkled with flaked coconut (if using), on the side.

Herb & Garlic Prawns (Shrimp)

Serves 4

INGREDIENTS

350 g/12 oz raw prawns (shrimp), peeled	4 tbsp lemon juice	2 cloves garlic, chopped
2 tbsp chopped, fresh parsley	2 tbsp olive oil	salt and pepper
	65 g/2 1/4 oz butter	

1 Place the prepared prawns (shrimp) in a shallow, non-metallic dish with the parsley, lemon juice and salt and pepper to taste. Leave the prawns (shrimp) to marinate in the herb mixture for at least 30 minutes.

2 Heat the oil and butter in a small pan with the garlic until the butter melts. Stir to mix thoroughly.

3 Remove the prawns (shrimp) from the marinade with a perforated spoon and add them to the pan containing the garlic butter. Stir the prawns (shrimp) into the garlic butter until well coated, then thread the prawns (shrimp) on to skewers.

4 Barbecue (grill) the kebabs (kabobs) over hot coals for 5–10 minutes, turning the skewers occasionally, until the prawns (shrimp) turn pink and are cooked through. Brush the prawns (shrimp) with the remaining garlic butter during the cooking time.

5 Transfer the herb and garlic prawn (shrimp) kebabs (kabobs) to serving plates. Drizzle over any of the remaining garlic butter and serve at once.

VARIATION

If raw prawns (shrimp) are unavailable, use cooked prawns (shrimp) but reduce the cooking time. Small cooked prawns (shrimp) can also be cooked in a kitchen foil parcel istead of on the skewers. Marinate and toss the cooked prawns (shrimp) in the garlic butter, wrap in kitchen foil and cook for about 5 minutes, shaking the parcels once or twice.

Desserts & Puddings

For many people the favourite part of any meal, the desserts and puddings that have been selected here will be a treat for all palettes. Whether you are a chocolate-lover or are on a diet there is a recipe here to tempt you. Choose from a light summer delicacy or a hearty hot winter treat, you will find desserts to indulge in all year round. If you are looking for a chilled sweet, choose the Granita or rich Vanilla Ice Cream, or if a warm pudding takes your fancy, Baked Bananas or Pan-Cooked Apples in Red Wine will do the trick.

If you are after a low-fat dessert, fresh fruit and fromage frais is the ideal way to finish off your meal. Fruit contains no fat and is naturally sweet and full of vitamins. However, if you are looking for a special treat for the children's lunch box, choose from No-Cook Fruit and Nut Chocolate Fudge and Nutty Chocolate Clusters. All of the recipes are easy to prepare and are packed full flavour.

Chocolate Banana Sundae

Serves 4

INGREDIENTS

GLOSSY CHOCOLATE SAUCE:
60 g/2 oz dark chocolate
4 tbsp golden (light corn) syrup
15 g/$^1/_2$ oz/1 tbsp butter
1 tbsp brandy or rum (optional)

SUNDAE:
4 bananas
150 ml/$^1/_4$ pint/$^2/_3$ cup double (heavy) cream
8–12 scoops of good quality vanilla ice cream

75 g/2$^3/_4$ oz/$^2/_3$ cup flaked (slivered) or chopped almonds, toasted
grated or flaked chocolate, to sprinkle
4 fan wafer biscuits (cookies)

1 To make the chocolate sauce, break the chocolate into small pieces and place in a heatproof bowl with the syrup and butter. Heat over a pan of hot water until melted, stirring until combined. Remove the bowl from the heat and stir in the brandy or rum, if using.

2 Slice the bananas and whip the cream until just holding its shape. Place a scoop of ice cream in the bottom of 4 tall sundae dishes. Top with slices of banana, some chocolate sauce, a spoonful of cream and a good sprinkling of nuts.

3 Repeat the layers, finishing with a good dollop of cream, sprinkled with nuts and a little grated or flaked chocolate. Serve with fan wafer biscuits (cookies).

VARIATION

Use half vanilla ice cream and half chocolate ice cream, if you like.

VARIATION

For a traditional banana split, halve the bananas lengthways and place on a plate with two scoops of ice cream between. Top with cream and sprinkle with nuts. Serve with the glossy chocolate sauce poured over the top.

Black Forest Trifle

Serves 6-8

INGREDIENTS

6 thin slices chocolate butter
  cream Swiss roll
2 x 400 g/14 oz can black
  cherries
2 tbsp kirsch
1 tbsp cornflour (cornstarch)

2 tbsp caster (superfine) sugar
425 ml/3/4 pint/13/4 cups milk
3 egg yolks
1 egg
75 g/23/4 oz dark chocolate
300 ml/1/2 pint/11/4 cups double

(heavy) cream, lightly
  whipped
TO DECORATE:
dark chocolate, melted
maraschino cherries (optional)

1 Place the slices of chocolate Swiss roll in a glass serving bowl.

2 Drain the black cherries, reserving 6 tbsp of the juice. Place the cherries and the reserved juice on top of the cake. Sprinkle with the kirsch.

3 In a bowl, mix the cornflour (cornstarch) and caster (superfine) sugar. Stir in enough of the milk to mix to a smooth paste. Beat in the egg yolks and the whole egg.

4 Heat the remaining milk in a small saucepan until almost boiling, then pour it on to the egg mixture, whisking well until it is combined.

5 Place the bowl over a pan of hot water and cook over a low heat until the custard thickens, stirring. Add the chocolate and stir until melted.

6 Pour the chocolate custard over the cherries and cool. When cold, spread the cream over the custard, swirling with the back of a spoon. Chill before decorating.

7 To make chocolate caraque, spread the melted dark chocolate on a marble or acrylic board. As it begins to set, pull a knife through the chocolate at a 45°C angle, working quickly. Remove each caraque as you make it and chill firmly before using.

Raspberry Shortcake

Serves 8

INGREDIENTS

175 g/6 oz/1¹/2 cups self-
raising flour
100 g/3¹/2 oz/¹/3 cup butter,
cut into cubes
75 g/2³/4 oz/¹/3 cup caster
(superfine) sugar

1 egg yolk
1 tbsp rose water
600 ml/1 pint/2¹/2 cups
whipping cream, whipped
lightly

225 g/8 oz raspberries, plus a
few for decoration

TO DECORATE:
icing (confectioners') sugar
mint leaves

1 Lightly grease 2 baking trays (cookie sheets).

2 To make the shortcakes, sieve (strain) the flour into a bowl.

3 Rub the butter into the flour with your fingers until the mixture resembles breadcrumbs.

4 Stir the sugar, egg yolk and rose water into the mixture and bring together to form a soft dough. Divide the dough in half.

5 Roll each piece of dough to a 20 cm/ 8 inch round and lift each one on to a prepared baking tray (cookie sheet). Crimp the edges of the dough.

6 Bake in a preheated oven, 190°C/375°F/Gas Mark 5, for 15 minutes until lightly golden. Transfer the shortcakes to a wire rack and leave to cool.

7 Mix the cream with the raspberries and spoon on top of one of the shortcakes. Top with the

other shortcake round, dust with a little icing (confectioners') sugar and decorate with the extra raspberries and mint leaves.

COOK'S TIP

The shortcake can be made a few days in advance and stored in an airtight container until required.

One Roll Fruit Pie

Serves 8

INGREDIENTS

PASTRY (PIE DOUGH):
175 g/6 oz/1^1/$_2$ cups plain
    (all-purpose) flour
100 g/3^1/$_2$ oz/^{1}/$_3$ cup butter,
    cut into small pieces
1 tbsp water
1 egg, separated

sugar cubes, crushed, for
    sprinkling

FILLING:
600 g/1^1/$_2$ lb prepared fruit
    (rhubarb, gooseberries,
    plums, damsons)

75 g/3 oz/6 tbsp soft brown
    sugar
1 tbsp ground ginger

1 Grease a large baking
tray (cookie sheet).

2 To make the pastry
(pie dough), place the
flour and butter in a
mixing bowl and rub in the
butter with your fingers.
Add the water and work
the mixture together until a
soft pastry (pie dough) has
formed. Wrap and leave to
chill in the refrigerator for
30 minutes.

3 Roll out the chilled
pastry (pie dough)

to a round about 35 cm/
14 inches in diameter.

4 Transfer the round to
the centre of the greased
baking sheet (cookie sheet).
Brush the pastry (pie dough)
with the egg yolk.

5 To make the filling,
mix the prepared fruit
with the brown sugar and
ginger and pile it into the
centre of the pastry.

6 Turn in the edges of
the pastry (pie dough)

all the way around. Brush
the surface of the pastry
(pie dough) with the
egg white and sprinkle
evenly with the crushed
sugar cubes.

7 Bake in a preheated
oven, 200°C/400°F/Gas,
Mark 6 for 35 minutes, or
until golden brown. Serve.

Treacle Tart

Serves 8

INGREDIENTS

250 g/ 9 oz fresh ready-made
shortcrust pastry
350 g/12 oz/1 cup golden
(light corn) syrup
125 g/4^1/2 oz/2 cups fresh
white breadcrumbs

125 ml/4 fl oz/^{1}/2 cup double
(heavy) cream
finely grated rind of ^{1}/2 lemon
or orange

2 tbsp lemon or orange juice
custard, to serve

1 Roll out the pastry
(pie dough) to line a
20 cm/8 inch loose-
bottomed quiche/flan tin
(pan), reserving the pastry
(pie dough) trimmings.
Prick the base of the pastry
(pie dough) with a fork and
chill in the refrigerator.

2 Using a shaped pastry
cutter or a sharp knife,
cut out small shapes from
the reserved pastry (pie
dough) trimmings, such as
leaves, stars or hearts, to
decorate the top of the tart.

3 In a bowl, mix together
the golden (light corn)
syrup, breadcrumbs, cream
and grated lemon or orange
rind and juice.

4 Pour the mixture into
the pastry case (pie
shell) and decorate the
edges of the tart with the
pastry (pie dough) cut-outs.

5 Bake in a preheated
oven, 190°C/375°F/Gas
Mark 5, for 35-40 minutes
or until the filling is set.

6 Leave the tart to cool
slightly in the tin.
Turn out and serve with
hot custard.

VARIATION

*Use the pastry
(pie dough) trimmings to
create a lattice pattern on top
of the tart, if preferred.*

Pear Tarts

Makes 6

INGREDIENTS

250 g/9 oz fresh ready-made
puff pastry
25 g/1 oz/8 tsp soft brown
sugar

25 g/1 oz/6 tsp butter (plus
extra for brushing)
1 tbsp stem (candied) ginger,
finely chopped

3 pears, peeled, halved and
cored
cream, to serve

1 On a lightly floured surface, roll out the pastry (pie dough). Cut out six 10 cm/4 inch rounds.

2 Place the circles on to a large baking tray (cookie sheet) and leave to chill for 30 minutes.

3 Cream together the brown sugar and butter in a small bowl, then stir in the chopped stem (candied) ginger.

4 Prick the pastry circles with a fork and spread a little of the ginger mixture on to each one.

5 Slice the pear halves lengthways, keeping the pears intact at the tip. Fan out the slices slightly.

6 Place a fanned-out pear half on top of each pastry (pie dough) circle. Make small flutes around the edge of the pastry (pie dough) circles and brush each pear half with melted butter.

7 Bake in a preheated oven, 200°C/400°F/Gas Mark 6, for 15-20 minutes until the pastry is well risen and golden. Serve warm with a little cream.

COOK'S TIP

If you prefer, serve these tarts with vanilla ice cream for a delicious dessert.

Orange & Grapefruit Salad

Serves 4

INGREDIENTS

2 grapefruit, ruby or plain
4 oranges
pared rind and juice of 1 lime

4 tbsp runny honey
2 tbsp warm water

1 sprig of mint, roughly chopped
50 g/1¾ oz chopped walnuts

1 Using a sharp knife, slice the top and bottom from the grapefruits, then slice away the rest of the skin and pith.

2 Cut between each segment of the grapefruit to remove the fleshy part only.

3 Using a sharp knife, slice the top and bottom from the oranges, then slice away the rest of the skin and pith.

4 Cut between each segment of the oranges to remove the fleshy part. Add to the grapefruit.

5 Place the lime rind, 2 tablespoons of lime juice, the honey and the warm water in a small bowl. Whisk with a fork to mix the dressing.

6 Pour the dressing over the segmented fruit, add the chopped mint and mix well. Leave to chill in the refrigerator for 2 hours for the flavours to mingle.

7 Place the chopped walnuts on a baking tray (cookie sheet). Lightly toast the walnuts under a preheated medium grill (broiler) for 2–3 minutes until browned.

8 Sprinkle the toasted walnuts over the fruit and serve.

VARIATION

Instead of the walnuts, you could sprinkle toasted almonds, cashew nuts, hazelnuts or pecans over the fruit, if you prefer.

Zabaglione

Serves 4

INGREDIENTS

5 egg yolks
100 g/3½ oz caster (superfine) sugar

150 ml/ 5 fl oz/⅔ cup Marsala or
sweet sherry

amaretti biscuits, to serve
(optional)

1 Place the egg yolks in a large mixing bowl.

2 Add the caster (superfine) sugar to the egg yolks and whisk until the mixture is thick and very pale and has doubled in volume.

3 Place the bowl containing the egg yolk and sugar mixture over a saucepan of gently simmering water.

4 Add the Marsala or sherry to the egg yolk and sugar mixture and continue whisking until the foam mixture becomes warm. This process may take as long as 10 minutes.

5 Pour the mixture, which should be frothy and light, into 4 wine glasses.

6 Serve the zabaglione warm with fresh fruit or amaretti biscuits, if you wish.

VARIATION

Any other type of liqueur may be used instead of the Marsala or sweet sherry, if you prefer. Serve soft fruits, such as strawberries or raspberries, with the zabaglione – it's a delicious combination!

VARIATION

Iced or Semifreddo Zabaglione can be made by following the method here, then continuing to whisk the foam while standing the bowl in cold water. Beat 150 ml/¼ pint/⅔ cup whipping (light) cream until it just holds its shape. Fold into the foam and freeze for about 2 hours, until just frozen.

Sweet Mascarpone Mousse

Serves 4

INGREDIENTS

450 g/1 lb mascarpone cheese
100 g/3½ oz caster (superfine) sugar
4 egg yolks

400 g/14 oz frozen summer fruits,
such as raspberries and
redcurrants

redcurrants, to garnish
amaretti biscuits, to serve

1 Place the mascarpone cheese in a large mixing bowl. Using a wooden spoon, beat the mascarpone cheese until smooth.

2 Stir the egg yolks and sugar into the mascarpone cheese, mixing well. Leave the mixture to chill in the refrigerator for about 1 hour.

3 Spoon a layer of the mascarpone mixture into the bottom of 4 individual serving dishes. Spoon a layer of the summer fruits on top. Repeat the layers in the same order, reserving some of the mascarpone mixture for the top.

4 Leave the mousses to chill in the refrigerator for about 20 minutes. The fruits should still be slightly frozen.

5 Serve the mascarpone mousses with amaretti biscuits.

VARIATION

Try adding 3 tablespoons of your favourite liqueur to the mascarpone cheese mixture in step 1, if you prefer.

COOK'S TIP

Mascarpone (sometimes spelled mascherpone) *is a soft, creamy cheese from Italy. It is becoming increasingly more available, and you should have no difficulty finding cartons in your local supermarket, or Italian delicatessen.*

Rich Chocolate Loaf

Makes 16 Slices

INGREDIENTS

150 g/5½ oz dark chocolate
75 g/2¾ oz/6 tbsp butter, unsalted
1 x 210 g/7¼ oz tin condensed milk

2 tsp cinnamon
75 g/2¾ oz almonds
75 g/2¾ oz amaretti biscuits, broken

50 g/1¾ oz dried no-need-to-soak
apricots, roughly chopped

1 Line a 675 g/1½ lb loaf tin (pan) with a sheet of kitchen foil.

2 Using a sharp knife, roughly chop the almonds.

3 Place the chocolate, butter, milk and cinnamon in a heavy-based saucepan. Heat gently over a low heat for 3–4 minutes, stirring with a wooden spoon, until the chocolate has melted. Beat the mixture well.

4 Stir the almonds, biscuits and apricots into the chocolate mixture in the pan, stirring with a wooden spoon, until well mixed.

5 Pour the mixture into the prepared tin (pan) and leave to chill in the refrigerator for about 1 hour or until set.

6 Cut the rich chocolate loaf into slices to serve.

COOK'S TIP

To melt chocolate, first break it into manageable pieces. The smaller the pieces, the quicker it will melt.

COOK'S TIP

When baking or cooking with fat, butter has the finest flavour. If possible, it is best to use unsalted butter as an ingredient in puddings and desserts, unless stated otherwise in the recipe. Low-fat spreads are not suitable for cooking.

Peaches in White Wine

Serves 4

INGREDIENTS

4 large ripe peaches
2 tbsp icing (confectioners')
  sugar, sifted

pared rind and juice of 1 orange

200 ml/7 fl oz/³⁄₄ cup medium or
  sweet white wine, chilled

1 Using a sharp knife,
halve the peaches,
remove the stones and
discard them. Peel the
peaches, if you prefer. Slice
the peaches into thin wedges.

2 Place the peach wedges
in a glass serving bowl
and sprinkle over the sugar.

3 Using a sharp knife,
pare the rind from the
orange. Cut the orange rind
into matchsticks, place
them in a bowl of cold
water and set aside.

4 Squeeze the juice from
the orange and pour
over the peaches together
with the wine.

5 Leave the peaches to
marinate and chill in
the refrigerator for at least
1 hour.

6 Remove the orange
rind from the cold
water and pat dry with
paper towels.

7 Garnish the peaches
with the strips of
orange rind and serve
immediately.

COOK'S TIP

*There is absolutely no need
to use expensive wine in this
recipe, so it can be quire
economical to make*

COOK'S TIP

*The best way to pare the
rind thinly from citrus fruits
is to use a potato peeler.*

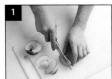

Vanilla Ice Cream

Serves 4–6

INGREDIENTS

600 ml/1 pint/2½ cups double (heavy) cream	pared rind of 1 lemon	2 egg, yolks
1 vanilla pod	4 eggs, beaten	175 g/6 oz caster (superfine) sugar

1 Place the cream in a heavy-based saucepan and heat gently, whisking. Add the vanilla pod, lemon rind, eggs and egg yolks and heat until the mixture reaches just below boiling point.

2 Reduce the heat and cook for 8–10 minutes, whisking the mixture continuously, until thickened.

3 Stir the sugar into the cream mixture, set aside and leave to cool.

4 Strain the cream mixture through a sieve.

5 Slit open the vanilla pod, scoop out the tiny black seeds and stir them into the cream.

6 Pour the mixture into a shallow freezing container with a lid and freeze overnight until set. Serve when required.

COOK'S TIP

Ice cream is one of the traditional dishes of Italy. Everyone eats it and there are numerous gelato stalls selling a wide variety of flavours, usually in a cone. It is also served in scoops, and even sliced!

COOK'S TIP

To make tutti frutti ice cream, soak 100 g/3½ oz mixed dried fruit, such as sultanas, cherries, apricots, candied peel and pineapple, in 2 tablespoons of Marsala or sweet sherry for 20 minutes. Follow the method for vanilla ice cream, omitting the vanilla pod, and stir in the Marsala or sherry-soaked fruit in step 5, just before freezing.

Granita

Serves 4

INGREDIENTS

LEMON GRANITA:

3 lemons

200 ml/7 fl oz/³⁄₄ cup lemon juice

100 g/3¹⁄₂ oz caster (superfine) sugar

500 ml/18 fl oz/2¹⁄₄ cups cold water

COFFEE GRANITA:

2 tbsp instant coffee

2 tbsp sugar

2 tbsp hot water

600 ml/1 pint/2¹⁄₂ cups cold water

2 tbsp rum or brandy

1 To make lemon granita, finely grate the lemon rind. Place the lemon rind, juice and caster (superfine) sugar in a pan. Bring the mixture to the boil and leave to simmer for 5-6 minutes or until thick and syrupy. Leave to cool.

2 Once cooled, stir in the cold water and pour into a shallow freezer container with a lid. Freeze the granita for 4–5 hours, stirring occasionally to break up the ice. Serve as a palate cleanser between dinner courses.

3 To make coffee granita, place the coffee and sugar in a bowl and pour over the hot water, stirring until dissolved.

4 Stir in the cold water and rum or brandy.

5 Pour the mixture into a shallow freezer container with a lid. Freeze the granita for at least 6 hours, stirring every 1–2 hours in order to create a grainy texture. Serve with cream after dinner, if you wish.

COOK'S TIP

If you would prefer a non-alcoholic version of the coffee granita, simply omit the rum or brandy and add extra instant coffee instead.

Almond Trifles

Serves 4

INGREDIENTS

8 Amaretti di Saronno biscuits
4 tbsp brandy or Amaretti
    liqueur
225 g/8 oz raspberries

300 ml/¹/₂ pint/1¹/₄ cups
    low-fat custard
300 ml/¹/₂ pint/1¹/₄ cups low-
    fat natural fromage frais
    (unsweetened yogurt)

1 tsp almond essence (extract)
15 g/¹/₂ oz toasted almonds,
    flaked (slivered)
1 tsp cocoa powder

1 Place the biscuits in a mixing bowl and using the end of a rolling pin, carefully crush the biscuits into small pieces.

2 Divide the crushed biscuits among 4 serving glasses. Sprinkle the brandy or liqueur over the crushed biscuits and leave to stand for about 30 minutes to allow the biscuits to soften.

3 Top the layer of crushed biscuits with a layer of raspberries, reserving a few raspberries for decoration, and spoon over enough custard to just cover.

4 Mix the fromage frais (unsweetened yogurt) with the almond essence (extract) and spoon over the custard. Leave to chill in the refrigerator for about 30 minutes.

5 Just before serving, sprinkle over the toasted almonds and dust with cocoa powder. Decorate with the reserved raspberries and serve at once.

VARIATION

Try this trifle with assorted summer fruits. If they are a frozen mix, use them frozen and allow them to thaw so that the juices soak into the biscuit base – it will taste truly delicious.

Red Fruits with Foaming Sauce

Serves 4

INGREDIENTS

225 g/8 oz redcurrants,
washed and trimmed,
thawed if frozen
225 g/8 oz cranberries
75 g/3 oz light muscovado
sugar

200 ml/7 fl oz/³/4 cup
unsweetened apple juice
1 cinnamon stick, broken
300 g/10¹/2 oz small
strawberries, washed,
hulled and halved

SAUCE:
225 g/8 oz raspberries, thawed
if frozen
2 tbsp fruit cordial
100 g/3¹/2 oz marshmallows

1 Place the redcurrants,
cranberries and sugar
in a saucepan. Pour in the
apple juice and add the
cinnamon stick. Bring the
mixture to the boil and
simmer gently for 10
minutes until the fruit has
just softened.

2 Stir the strawberries
into the cranberry and
sugar mixture and mix
well. Transfer the mixture
to a bowl, cover and leave
to chill for about 1 hour.
Remove and discard the
cinnamon stick.

3 Just before serving,
make the sauce. Place
the raspberries and fruit
cordial in a small pan, bring
to the boil and simmer for
2–3 minutes until the fruit
is just beginning to soften.
Stir the marshmallows into
the raspberry mixture and
heat through, stirring,
until the marshmallows
begin to melt.

4 Transfer the fruit salad
to serving bowls.
Spoon over the raspberry
and marshmallow sauce
and serve.

VARIATION

*This sauce is delicious
poured over low-fat ice
cream. For an extra-colourful
sauce, replace the raspberries
with an assortment of
summer berries.*

Citrus Meringue Crush

Serves 4

INGREDIENTS

8 ready-made meringue nests
300 ml/^{1}/2 pint/1^1/4 cups low-
 fat natural (unsweetened)
 yogurt
^{1}/2 tsp finely grated orange
 rind
^{1}/2 tsp finely grated lemon
 rind
^{1}/2 tsp finely grated lime rind

2 tbsp orange liqueur or
 unsweetened orange juice

TO DECORATE:
sliced kumquat
lime rind, grated

SAUCE:
60 g/2 oz kumquats

8 tbsp unsweetened orange
 juice
2 tbsp lemon juice
2 tbsp lime juice
2 tbsp water
2–3 tsp caster (superfine)
 sugar
1 tsp cornflour (cornstarch)
 mixed with 1 tbsp water

1 Place the meringues in a clean plastic bag, seal the bag and using a rolling pin, crush the meringues into small pieces. Transfer to a mixing bowl.

2 Stir the yogurt, grated citrus rinds and the liqueur or juice into the crushed meringue. Spoon the mixture into 4 mini-basins, smooth over the tops and freeze for 1^1/2–2 hours until firm.

3 To make the sauce, thinly slice the kumquats and place them in a small pan with the fruit juices and water. Bring gently to the boil and then simmer over a low heat for 3–4 minutes until the kumquats have just softened.

4 Sweeten with sugar to taste, stir in the cornflour (cornstarch) mixture and cook, stirring, until thickened. Pour into a small bowl, cover the surface with a layer of cling film (plastic wrap) and leave to cool – the film will help prevent a skin forming. Leave to chill.

5 To serve, dip the meringue basins in hot water for 5 seconds or until they loosen, and turn on to serving plates. Spoon over a little sauce, decorate with slices of kumquat and lime rind and serve immediately.

Tropical Fruit Fool

Serves 4

INGREDIENTS

1 medium ripe mango
2 kiwi fruit
1 medium banana
2 tbsp lime juice

$1/2$ tsp finely grated lime rind,
     plus extra to decorate
2 medium egg whites
425 g/15 oz can low-fat
     custard

$1/2$ tsp vanilla essence
     (extract)
2 passion fruit

1 To peel the mango, slice either side of the smooth, flat central stone. Roughly chop the flesh and blend the fruit in a food processor or blender until smooth. Alternatively, mash the chopped mango flesh with a fork.

2 Peel the kiwi fruit, chop the flesh into small pieces and place in a bowl. Peel and chop the banana and add to the bowl. Toss all of the fruit in the lime juice and rind and mix well to prevent discoloration.

3 In a grease-free bowl, whisk the egg whites until stiff and then gently fold in the custard and vanilla essence (extract) until thoroughly mixed.

4 In 4 tall glasses, alternately layer the chopped fruit, mango purée and custard mixture, finishing with the custard on top. Leave to chill in the refrigerator for 20 minutes.

5 Halve the passion fruits, scoop out the seeds and spoon the passion fruit over the fruit fools.

6 Decorate each serving with the extra lime rind and serve.

VARIATION

Other tropical fruits to try include papaya purée, with chopped pineapple and dates, and tamarillo or pomegranate seeds to decorate. Or make a summer fruit fool by using strawberry purée, topped with raspberries and blackberries, with cherries to finish.

Brown Sugar Pavlovas

Serves 4

INGREDIENTS

2 large egg whites
1 tsp cornflour (cornstarch)
1 tsp raspberry vinegar
100 g/3^1/2 oz light muscovado
 sugar, crushed free of
 lumps

2 tbsp redcurrant jelly
2 tbsp unsweetened orange
 juice
150 ml/5 fl oz/^{3}/4 cup low-fat
 natural fromage frais
 (unsweetened yogurt)

175 g/6 oz raspberries, thawed
 if frozen
rose-scented geranium leaves,
 to decorate (optional)

1 Preheat the oven to 150°C/300°F/Gas Mark 2. Line a large baking sheet (cookie sheet) with baking parchment. In a large, grease-free bowl, whisk the egg whites until very stiff and dry. Fold in the cornflour (cornstarch) and vinegar.

2 Gradually whisk in the sugar, a spoonful at a time, until the mixture is thick and glossy.

3 Divide the mixture into 4 and spoon on to the baking sheet (cookie sheet), spaced well apart. Smooth each into a round, about 10 cm/4 inch across, and bake in the oven for 40–45 minutes until lightly browned and crisp; let cool.

4 Place the redcurrant jelly and orange juice in a small pan and heat, stirring, until melted. Leave to cool for 10 minutes.

5 Using a palette knife (spatula), carefully remove each pavlova from the baking parchment and transfer to a serving plate. Top with fromage frais (unsweetened yogurt) and raspberries. Spoon over the redcurrant jelly mixture to glaze. Decorate and serve.

VARIATION

Make a large pavlova by forming the meringue into a round, measuring 18 cm/ 7 inches across, on a lined baking sheet (cookie sheet) and bake for 1 hour.

Sticky Sesame Bananas

Serves 4

INGREDIENTS
---

4 ripe medium bananas
3 tbsp lemon juice
115 g/4 oz caster (superfine)
   sugar
4 tbsp cold water

2 tbsp sesame seeds
150 ml/5 fl oz/²/3 cup low-fat
   natural fromage frais
   (unsweetened yogurt)

1 tbsp icing (confectioner's)
   sugar
1 tsp vanilla essence (extract)
lemon and lime rind, shredded,
   to decorate

---

1 Peel the bananas and cut into 5 cm/2 inch pieces. Place the banana in a bowl, spoon over the lemon juice and stir well to coat – this will prevent the bananas from discoloring.

2 Place the sugar and water in a small pan and heat gently, stirring, until the sugar dissolves. Bring to the boil and cook for 5–6 minutes until the mixture caramelizes.

3 Drain the bananas and blot with absorbent kitchen paper to dry. Line a baking sheet (cookie sheet) or board with parchment and arrange the bananas, well spaced out, on top.

4 Drizzle the caramel over the bananas, working quickly because the caramel sets almost instantly. Sprinkle over the sesame seeds and leave to cool for 10 minutes.

5 Meanwhile, mix the fromage frais (unsweetened yogurt) with the icing (confectioner's) sugar and vanilla essence (extract).

6 Peel the bananas away from the paper and arrange on serving plates. Serve the fromage frais (unsweetened yogurt) as a dip, decorated with the lemon and lime rind.

COOK'S TIP

For best results, use a cannelle knife or a potato peeler to peel away thin strips of rind from the fruit, taking care not to include any bitter pith. Blanch the shreds in boiling water for 1 minute, then refresh in cold water.

Fruit & Fibre Layers

Serves 4

INGREDIENTS

115 g /4 oz no-need-to-soak dried apricots	60g /2 oz dried apple	1 cinnamon stick, broken
115 g /4 oz no-need-to-soak dried prunes	25 g/1 oz dried cherries	300 ml/^{1}/2 pint/1^1/4 cups low-fat natural yogurt
115 g /4 oz no-need-to-soak dried peaches	450 ml/16 fl oz/2 cups unsweetened apple juice	115 g/4 oz crunchy oat cereal
	6 cardamom pods	apricot slices, to decorate
	6 cloves	

1 To make the fruit compote, place the dried apricots, prunes, peaches, apple and cherries in a saucepan and pour in the apple juice.

2 Add the cardamom pods, cloves and cinnamon stick to the pan, bring to the boil and simmer for 10–15 minutes until the fruits are plump and tender.

3 Leave the mixture to cool completely in the pan. Remove and discard the spices from the fruits, then transfer the mixture to a bowl and leave to chill in the refrigerator for 1 hour.

4 Spoon the compote into 4 dessert glasses, layering it alternately with yogurt and oat cereal, finishing with the oat cereal on top.

5 Decorate each dessert with slices of apricot and serve at once.

COOK'S TIP

There are many dried fruits available, including mangoes and pears, some of which need soaking, so read the instructions on the packet before use. Also, check the ingredients label, because several types of dried fruit have added sugar or are rolled in sugar, and this will affect the sweetness of the dish that you use them in.

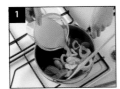

Pan-Cooked Apples in Red Wine

Serves 4

INGREDIENTS

4 eating (dessert) apples
2 tbsp lemon juice
40 g/1½ oz low-fat spread
60 g/2 oz light muscovado
   sugar

1 small orange
1 cinnamon stick, broken
150 ml/5 fl oz/⅔ cup red
   wine

225 g/8 oz raspberries, hulled
   and thawed if frozen
sprigs of fresh mint, to
   decorate

1 Peel and core the apples, then cut them into thick wedges. Place the apples in a bowl and toss in the lemon juice to prevent the fruit from discoloring.

2 In a frying pan (skillet), gently melt the low-fat spread over a low heat, add the sugar and stir to form a paste.

3 Stir the apple wedges into the pan and cook, stirring occasionally, for 2 minutes until well coated in the sugar paste.

4 Using a vegetable peeler, pare off a few strips of orange rind. Add the orange rind to the pan along with the cinnamon pieces. Extract the juice from the orange and pour into the pan with the red wine. Bring to the boil, then simmer for 10 minutes, stirring.

5 Add the raspberries to the pan and cook for 5 minutes until the apples are tender.

6 Discard the orange rind and cinnamon

pieces. Transfer the apple and raspberry mixture to a serving plate together with the wine sauce. Decorate with a sprig of fresh mint and serve hot.

VARIATION

For other fruity combinations, cook the apples with blackberries, blackcurrants or redcurrants. You may need to add more sugar if you use currants as they are not as sweet as raspberries.

Grilled Fruit Platter with Lime Butter

Serves 4

INGREDIENTS

1 baby pineapple	4 tbsp dark rum	LIME 'BUTTER':
1 ripe papaya	1 tsp ground allspice	60 g/2 oz low-fat spread
1 ripe mango	2 tbsp lime juice	1/2 tsp finely grated lime rind
2 kiwi fruit	4 tbsp dark muscovado sugar	1 tbsp icing (confectioner's)
4 apple (finger) bananas		sugar

1 Quarter the pineapple, trimming away most of the leaves, and place in a shallow dish. Peel the papaya, cut it in half and scoop out the seeds. Cut the flesh into thick wedges and place in the same dish as the pineapple.

2 Peel the mango, cut either side of the smooth, central flat stone and remove the stone. Slice the flesh into thick wedges. Peel the kiwi fruit and cut in half. Peel the bananas. Add all of these fruits to the dish.

3 Sprinkle over the rum, allspice and lime juice, cover and leave at room temperature for 30 minutes, turning occasionally, to allow the flavours to develop.

4 Meanwhile, make the 'butter'. Place the low-fat spread in a small bowl and beat in the lime rind and sugar until well mixed. Leave to chill in the refrigerator until required.

5 Preheat the grill (broiler) to hot. Drain the fruit, reserving the juices, and arrange in the grill (broiler) pan. Sprinkle with the sugar and grill (broil) for 3–4 minutes until hot, bubbling and just beginning to char.

6 Transfer the fruit to a serving plate and spoon over the juices. Serve with the lime 'butter'.

VARIATION

Serve with a light sauce of 300 ml/ 1/2 pint/1 1/4 cups tropical fruit juice thickened with 2 tsp arrowroot.

Baked Pears with Cinnamon & Brown Sugar

Serves 4

INGREDIENTS
---

4 ripe pears
2 tbsp lemon juice
4 tbsp light muscovado sugar

1 tsp ground cinnamon
60 g/2 oz low-fat spread
low-fat custard, to serve

lemon rind, finely grated, to decorate

---

1 Preheat the oven to 200°C/400°F/Gas Mark 6. Core and peel the pears, then slice them in half lengthwise and brush all over with the lemon juice to prevent the pears from discoloring. Place the pears, cored side down, in a small non-stick roasting tin (pan).

2 Place the sugar, cinnamon and low-fat spread in a small saucepan and heat gently, stirring, until the sugar has melted. Keep the heat low to stop too much water evaporating from the low-fat spread as it gets hot. Spoon the mixture over the pears.

3 Bake for 20–25 minutes or until the pears are tender and golden, spooning the sugar mixture over the fruit during the cooking time.

4 To serve, heat the custard until it is piping hot and spoon over the bases of 4 warm dessert plates. Arrange 2 pear halves on each plate. Decorate with grated lemon rind and serve.

VARIATION

This recipe also works well if you use cooking apples. For alternative flavours, replace the cinnamon with ground ginger and serve the pears sprinkled with chopped stem ginger in syrup. Alternatively, use ground allspice and spoon over some warmed dark rum to serve.

Baked Apples with Blackberries

Serves 4

INGREDIENTS

4 medium-sized cooking
    apples
1 tbsp lemon juice
100 g/3¹/₂ oz prepared
    blackberries, thawed if
    frozen

15 g/¹/₂ oz flaked (slivered)
    almonds
¹/₂ tsp ground allspice
¹/₂ tsp finely grated lemon
    rind
2 tbsp demerara (brown
    crystal) sugar

300 ml/¹/₂ pint/1¹/₄ cups ruby
    port
1 cinnamon stick, broken
2 tsp cornflour (cornstarch)
    blended with 2 tbsp cold
    water
low-fat custard, to serve

1 Preheat the oven to 200°C/400°F/Gas Mark 6. Wash and dry the apples. Make a shallow cut through the skin around the middle of each apple – this will help the apples to cook through.

2 Core the apples, brush the centres with the lemon juice to prevent browning and stand in a shallow ovenproof dish.

3 In a bowl, mix the blackberries, almonds, allspice, lemon rind and sugar. Using a teaspoon, spoon the mixture into the centre of each apple.

4 Pour the port into the dish, add the cinnamon stick and bake the apples in the oven for 35–40 minutes or until tender and soft. Drain the cooking juices into a pan and keep the apples warm.

5 Discard the cinnamon and add the cornflour (cornstarch) mixture to the cooking juices. Heat, stirring, until thickened.

6 Heat the custard until piping hot. Pour the sauce over the apples and serve with the custard.

VARIATION

Use raspberries instead of blackberries and, if you prefer, replace the port with unsweetened orange juice.

Fruity Skewers with Chocolate Dipping Sauce

Serves 4

INGREDIENTS

Selection of fruit (choose from oranges, bananas, strawberries, pineapple chunks (fresh or canned), apricots (fresh or canned), dessert (eating) apples, pears, kiwi fruit)	1 tbsp lemon juice CHOCOLATE SAUCE: 50 g/1¾ oz butter 50 g/1¾ oz dark chocolate, broken into small cubes ½ tbsp cocoa powder	2 tbsp golden syrup BASTE: 4 tbsp clear honey grated rind and juice of ½ orange

1 To make the chocolate sauce, place the butter, chocolate, cocoa powder and golden syrup in a small pan. Heat gently on a stove or at the side of the barbecue (grill), stirring continuously, until all of the ingredients have melted and are well combined.

2 To prepare the fruit, peel and core if necessary, then cut into large, bite-size pieces or wedges as appropriate. Dip apples, pears and bananas in lemon juice to prevent discoloration. Thread the fruit on to skewers.

3 To make the baste, mix the honey, orange juice and rind, heat gently and brush over the fruit.

4 Barbecue (grill) the fruit skewers over warm coals for 5–10 minutes until hot. Serve with the chocolate dipping sauce.

COOK'S TIP

If the coals are too hot raise the rack so that it is about 15 cm/6 inches above the coals or spread out the coals a little to reduce the heat. Do not assemble the skewers more than 1-2 hours before they are required.

Toffee Fruit Kebabs (Kabobs)

Serves 4

INGREDIENTS

2 dessert (eating) apples
2 firm pears, cored and cut
into wedges
juice of $^1/_2$ lemon

25 g/1 oz light muscovado
sugar
$^1/_4$ tsp ground allspice
25 g/1 oz unsalted butter,
melted

SAUCE:
125 g/4$^1/_2$ oz butter
100 g/3$^1/_2$ oz light
muscovado sugar
6 tbsp double (heavy) cream

1 Core the apples and cut them into wedges. Toss the apple and pears in the lemon juice to prevent any discoloration.

2 Mix the sugar and allspice together and sprinkle over the fruit.

3 Thread the fruit pieces on to skewers.

4 To make the toffee sauce, place the butter and sugar in a saucepan and heat, stirring gently, until the butter has melted and the sugar has dissolved.

5 Add the cream to the pan and bring to the boil. Boil for 1–2 minutes, then set aside.

6 Meanwhile, place the fruit kebabs (kabobs) over hot coals and barbecue (grill) for about 5 minutes, turning and basting frequently with the melted butter, until the fruit is just tender.

7 Transfer the fruit kebabs (kabobs) to warm serving plates and serve with the slightly cooled toffee sauce.

COOK'S TIP

Firm apples that will keep their shape are needed for this dish – varieties such as Golden Delicious, Granny Smith and Braeburn are a good choice. Soft apples and pears will become mushy as they cook.

VARIATION

Sprinkle the fruit kebabs (kabobs) with chopped walnuts or pecan nuts before serving, if you wish.

Baked Bananas

Serves 4

INGREDIENTS

4 bananas
2 passion fruit
4 tbsp orange juice
4 tbsp orange-flavoured
   liqueur

ORANGE-FLAVOURED CREAM:
150 ml/5 fl oz/²/3 cup double
   (heavy) cream
3 tbsp icing (confectioners')
   sugar

2 tbsp orange-flavoured
   liqueur

1 Peel the bananas and place each one on to a sheet of kitchen foil.

2 Cut the passion fruit in half and squeeze the pulp of each half over each banana. Spoon over the orange juice and liqueur.

3 Fold the kitchen foil over the top of the bananas to enclose them completely.

4 Barbecue (grill) the bananas over hot coals for about 10 minutes or until they are just tender.

5 To make the orange-flavoured cream, pour the double (heavy) cream into a mixing bowl and sprinkle over the icing (confectioners') sugar. Whisk the mixture until it is standing in soft peaks. Carefully fold in the orange-flavoured liqueur and leave to chill in the refrigerator until required.

6 Transfer the foil parcel containing the bananas to warm, individual serving plates. Open out the foil parcels at the table and then serve the bananas

immediately with the orange-flavoured cream.

VARIATION

Leave the bananas in their skins for a really quick dessert. Split the banana skins and pop in 1–2 cubes of chocolate. Wrap the bananas in kitchen foil and barbecue (grill) for 10 minutes, or until the chocolate just melts.

Rocky Road Bites

Makes 18

INGREDIENTS

125 g/4¹/2 oz milk chocolate
50 g/2¹/2 oz mini multi-coloured
    marshmallows

25 g/1 oz/¹/4 cup chopped
walnuts

25 g/1 oz no-soak apricots,
chopped

1 Line a baking tray (cookie sheet) with baking parchment and set aside.

2 Break the milk chocolate into small pieces and place in a large mixing bowl. Set the bowl over a pan of simmering water and stir until the chocolate has melted.

3 Stir in the marshmallows, walnuts and apricots and toss in the melted chocolate until well covered.

4 Place heaped teaspoons of the mixture on to the prepared baking tray (cookie sheet).

5 Leave the sweets (candies) to chill in the refrigerator until set.

6 Once set, carefully remove the sweets from the baking parchment.

7 The chewy bites can be placed in paper sweet (candy) cases to serve.

COOK'S TIP

These sweets (candies) can be stored in a cool, dry place for up to 2 weeks.

VARIATION

Light, fluffy marshmallows are available in white or pastel colours. If you cannot find mini marshmallows, use large ones and snip them into smaller pieces with kitchen scissors before mixing them into the melted chocolate in step 3.

Easy Chocolate Fudge

Makes 25–30 pieces

INGREDIENTS

500 g/1 lb 2 oz dark chocolate
75 g/2³⁄₄ oz/¹⁄₃ cup unsalted
   butter

400 g/14 oz can sweetened
   condensed milk

¹⁄₂ tsp vanilla flavouring (extract)

1 Lightly grease a 20 cm/
8 inch square cake tin
(pan).

2 Break the chocolate
into pieces and place in
a large saucepan with the
butter and condensed milk.

3 Heat gently, stirring
until the chocolate
and butter melts and the
mixture is smooth. Do
not allow to boil.

4 Remove from the
heat. Beat in the vanilla
flavouring (extract), then
beat the mixture for a few
minutes until thickened.
Pour it into the prepared
tin (pan) and level the top.

5 Chill the mixture in the
refrigerator until firm.

6 Tip the fudge out on to
a chopping board and
cut into squares to serve.

VARIATION

*For chocolate peanut fudge,
replace 50 g/1¹⁄₂ oz/4 tbsp of
the butter with crunchy
peanut butter.*

COOK'S TIP

*Store the fudge in an airtight
container in a cool, dry place
for up to 1 month. Do
not freeze.*

COOK'S TIP

*Don't use milk chocolate as
the results will be too sticky.*

No-Cook Fruit & Nut Chocolate Fudge

Makes about 25 pieces

INGREDIENTS

250 g/9 oz dark chocolate	(confectioners') sugar, sieved	50 g/1³/4 oz/¹/3 cup sultanas
25 g/1 oz/2 tbsp butter	(strained)	(golden raisins)
4 tbsp evaporated milk	50 g/1³/4 oz/¹/2 cup roughly	
450 g/1 lb/3 cups icing	chopped hazelnuts	

1 Lightly grease a 20 cm/8 inch square cake tin (pan).

2 Break the chocolate into pieces and place it in a bowl with the butter and evaporated milk. Set the bowl over a pan of gently simmering water and stir until the chocolate and butter have melted and the ingredients are well combined.

3 Remove the bowl from the heat and gradually beat in the icing (confectioners') sugar. Stir the hazelnuts and sultanas (golden raisins) into the mixture. Press the fudge into the prepared tin (pan) and level the top. Chill until firm.

4 Tip the fudge out on to a chopping board and cut into squares. Place in paper sweet (candy) cases. Chill until required.

VARIATION

Vary the nuts used in this recipe; try making the fudge with almonds, brazil nuts, walnuts or pecans.

COOK'S TIP

The fudge can be stored in an airtight container for up to 2 weeks.

Nutty Chocolate Clusters

Makes about 30

INGREDIENTS

175 g/6 oz white chocolate
100 g/3 1/2 oz digestive biscuits
(graham crackers)

100 g/3 1/2 oz macadamia nuts or
brazil nuts, chopped

25 g/1 oz stem ginger, chopped
(optional)
175 g/6 oz dark chocolate

1 Line a baking tray (cookie sheet) with a sheet of baking parchment. Break the white chocolate into small pieces and place in a large mixing bowl set over a pan of gently simmering water; stir until melted.

2 Break the digestive biscuits (graham crackers) into small pieces. Stir the biscuits (graham crackers) into the melted chocolate with the chopped nuts and stem ginger, if using.

3 Place heaped teaspoons of the mixture on to the prepared baking tray (cookie sheet).

4 Chill the mixture until set, then carefully remove from the baking parchment.

5 Melt the dark chocolate and leave it to cool slightly. Dip the clusters into the melted chocolate, allowing the excess to drip back into the bowl. Return the clusters to the baking tray (cookie sheet) and chill in the refrigerator until set.

COOK'S TIP

The clusters can be stored for up to 1 week in a cool, dry place.

COOK'S TIP

Macadamia and brazil nuts are both rich and high in fat, which makes them particularly popular for confectionery, but other nuts can be used, if preferred.

Chocolate Cherries

Makes 24

INGREDIENTS

12 glacé (candied) cherries
2 tbsp rum or brandy

250 g/9 oz marzipan
125 g/5 1/2 oz dark chocolate

extra milk, dark or white
chocolate, to decorate
(optional)

1 Line a baking tray (cookie sheet) with a sheet of baking parchment.

2 Cut the cherries in half and place in a small bowl. Add the rum or brandy and stir to coat. Leave the cherries to soak for at least 1 hour, stirring occasionally.

3 Divide the marzipan into 24 pieces and roll each piece into a ball. Press half a cherry into the top of each marzipan ball.

4 Break the chocolate into pieces, place in a bowl and set over a pan of hot water. Stir until the chocolate has melted.

5 Dip each sweet (candy) into the melted chocolate, allowing the excess to drip back into the bowl. Place the coated cherries on the baking parchment and chill until set.

6 If liked, melt a little extra chocolate and drizzle it over the top of the coated cherries. Leave to set.

VARIATION

Flatten the marzipan and use it to mould (mold) around the cherries to cover them, then dip in the chocolate as above.

VARIATION

Use a whole almond in place of the halved glacé (candied) cherries and omit the rum or brandy.

Chocolate Marzipans

Makes about 30

INGREDIENTS

450 g/1 lb marzipan
25 g/1 oz/¹⁄₃ cup glacé (candied)
cherries, chopped very finely

25 g/1 oz stem ginger, chopped
very finely
50 g/1³⁄₄ oz no-soak dried
apricots, chopped very finely

350 g/12 oz dark chocolate
25 g/1 oz white chocolate
icing (confectioners') sugar, to
dust

1 Line a baking tray (cookie sheet) with a sheet of baking parchment. Divide the marzipan into 3 balls and knead each ball to soften it.

2 Work the glacé (candied) cherries into one portion of the marzipan by kneading on a surface lightly dusted with icing (confectioners') sugar.

3 Do the same with the stem ginger and another portion of marzipan and then the apricots and the third portion of marzipan.

4 Form each flavoured portion of marzipan into small balls, keeping the different flavours separate.

5 Melt the dark chocolate. Dip one of each flavoured ball of marzipan into the chocolate by spiking each one with a cocktail stick (toothpick) or small skewer, allowing the excess chocolate to drip back into the bowl.

6 Carefully place the balls in clusters of the three flavours on the prepared baking tray (cookie sheet). Repeat with the

remaining marzipan balls. Chill until set.

7 Melt the white chocolate and drizzle a little over the tops of each cluster of marzipan balls. Chill until hardened, then remove from the baking parchment and dust with sugar to serve.

VARIATION

Coat the marzipan balls in white or milk chocolate and drizzle with dark chocolate, if you prefer.

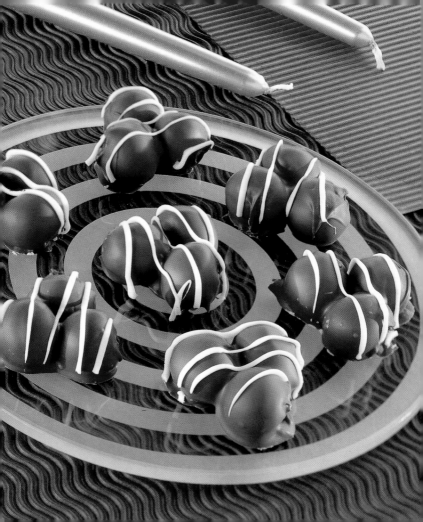

Cold Chocolate Drinks

Serves 2

INGREDIENTS

CHOCOLATE MILK SHAKE:
450 ml/16 fl oz/2 cups ice cold
   milk
3 tbsp drinking chocolate
   powder

3 scoops chocolate ice cream
cocoa powder, to dust (optional)

CHOCOLATE ICE CREAM SODA:
5 tbsp chocolate dessert sauce
soda water
2 scoops of chocolate ice cream
double (heavy) cream, whipped
dark or milk chocolate, grated

1 To make Chocolate
Milk Shake, place half
of the ice-cold milk in a
blender.

2 Add the drinking
chocolate powder to
the blender and 1 scoop of
the chocolate ice cream.
Blend until the mixture is
frothy and well mixed. Stir
in the remaining milk.

3 Place the remaining 2
scoops of chocolate ice
cream in 2 serving glasses
and carefully pour the
chocolate milk over the ice
cream.

4 Sprinkle a little cocoa
powder (if using) over
the top of each drink and
serve at once.

5 To make Chocolate Ice
Cream Soda, divide the
chocolate dessert sauce
between 2 glasses.

6 Add a little soda water
to each glass and stir to
combine the sauce and soda
water. Place a scoop of ice
cream in each glass and top
up with more soda water.

7 Place a dollop of
whipped heavy (double)

cream on the top, if
liked, and sprinkle with
a little grated dark or
milk chocolate.

COOK'S TIP

*Served in a tall glass, a milk
shake or an ice cream soda
makes a scrumptious snack
in a drink. Serve with
straws, if wished.*

Index

Almond Trifles 468

Bacon and Scallop Skewers 434
Baked Apples with Blackberries 488
Baked Bananas 494
Baked Pears with Cinnamon and Brown Sugar 486
Beef dishes:
  Beef and Beans 276
  Beef and Broccoli Stir-Fry 272
  Beef and Vegetable Noodle Soup 46
  Beef with Green Peas and Black Bean Sauce 304
  Egg Noodles with Beef 250
  Spicy Beef 274
  Steak and Kidney Kebabs 328
  Stir-Fry Beef and Vegetables with Sherry and Soy Sauce 302
Beef with Green Peas and Black Bean Sauce 304
Beetroot and Orange Rice Salad 148
Black Forest Trifle 442
Brown Lentil Soup with Pasta 18
Brown Sugar Pavlova 476
Bruschetta with Tomatoes 82

Cabbage and Walnut Stir-Fry 186
Calabrian Mushroom Soup 32
Cantonese Prawns 390
Caribbean Pork 322
Caribbean Shrimps 436
Carrot, Fennel and Potato Medley 106
Casserole of Beans in Tomato Sauce 84
Casserole of Fusilli and Smoked Haddock with Egg Sauce 358
Celery and Salt Cod Casserole 338
Celery, Stilton and Walnut Soup 66
Chargrilled Mediterranean Vegetable Skewers 160
Chick Peas with Parma Ham 78
Chicken dishes:
  Chicken and Pasta Broth 12
  Chicken and Spinach Salad 202
  Chicken and Sweetcorn Soup 34

Chicken Chop Suey 262
Chicken Lady Jayne 228
Chicken Pan Bagna 110
Chicken Risotto alla Milanese 210
Chicken Strips and Dips 226
Chicken with Two-Pepper Sauce 208
Chicken, Corn and Mangetout Sauté 234
Chicken, Pepper and Orange Stir-Fry 296
Chicken, Spring Green and Yellow Bean Stir-Fry 294
Chilli Chicken 258
Chinese Chicken Salad 266
Clear Chicken and Egg Soup 40
Cream of Chicken and Tomato Soup 16
Cream of Chicken Soup 14
Curried Chicken and Sweetcorn Soup 42
Devilled Chicken 220
Elizabethan Chicken 212
Garlic Chicken Cushions 224
Golden Chicken Risotto 238
Golden Glazed Chicken 230
Harlequin Chicken 204
Indonesian Potato and Chicken Salad 140
Indonesian Potato and Chicken Salad 140
Italian Chicken Spirals 222
Lemon Chicken 260
Mediterranean Chicken Parcels 232
Old English Spicy Chicken Salad 128
Parma-Ham-Wrapped Chicken Cushions 216
Poached Breast of Chicken with Whiskey Sauce 218
Quick Chicken Bake 240
Savoury Chicken Sausages 236
Speedy Chicken Pan-Fry 214
Spicy Chicken Livers with Pak Choi 96
Spicy Peanut Chicken 242
Steamed Chicken and Spring Vegetable Parcels 206
Stir-Fried Ginger Chicken 292
Thai Chicken Noodle Soup 10
Tuscan Chicken Livers on Toast 86
Chilli Fish Soup 56
Chinese Cabbage Soup 52
Chinese Chicken Salad 266

Chinese Leaves with Shiitake Mushrooms and Crab Meat 424
Chinese Omelette 90
Chinese Potato and Pork Broth 64
Chinese Prawn Salad 126
Chocolate Banana Sundae 440
Chocolate Cherries 504
Chocolate Marzipans 506
Ciabatta Rolls 190
Citrus Fish Skewers 402
Citrus Meringue Crush 472
Clear Chicken and Egg Soup 40
Coconut and Crab Soup 54
Coconut Couscous Salad 154
Cold Chocolate Drinks 508
Crab and Ginger Soup 50
Crab in Ginger Sauce 396
Cream of Chicken and Tomato Soup 16
Cream of Chicken Soup 14
Creamed Strips of Sirloin with Rigatoni 248
Creamy Tomato Soup 22
Crispy Seaweed 94
Cured Meats with Olives and Tomatoes 76
Curried Chicken and Sweetcorn Soup 42

Deep-Fried Seafood 80
Devilled Chicken 220
Dhal Soup 70
Duck with Baby Corn and Pineapple 298

Easy Chocolate Fudge 498
Egg Noodles with Beef 250
Elizabethan Chicken 212
Escalopes with Italian Sausage and Capers 246

Fish dishes:
  Casserole of Fusilli and Smoked Haddock with Egg Sauce 358
  Celery and Salt Cod Casserole 338
  Chilli Fish Soup 56
  Citrus Fish Skewers 402
  Five-Spice Salmon with Ginger Stir-Fry 404
  Fresh Baked Sardines 346
  Fried Fish with Coconut and Basil 418
  Herring with Hot Pesto Sauce 342
  Italian Fish Soup 38
  Lentil and Tuna Salad 124
  Marinated Fish 348
  Mullet with Ginger 382
  Poached Salmon Steaks with Penne 360

Potato-Topped Cod 398
Salt Cod Fritters 340
Sea Bass with Olive Sauce on a Bed of Macaroni 352
Skewered Oriental Shellfish 406
Sole Fillets with Marsala and Cream 344
Spaghetti al Tonno 356
Spaghetti with Smoked Salmon 362
Steamed Fish with Black Bean Sauce 378
Stir-Fried Cod with Mango 414
Stir-Fried Ginger Monkfish 416
Stir-Fried Salmon with Pineapple 412
Sweet and Sour Fish Salad 332
Teriyaki Stir-Fried Salmon with Crispy Leeks 410
Trout with Pineapple 380
Tuna Steaks with Fragrant Spices and Lime 414
Tuscan Bean Salad with Tuna 114
Vermicelli with Fillets of Red Mullet 354
Five-Spice Salmon with Ginger Stir-Fry 404
Fresh Baked Sardines 346
Fresh Figs with Parma Ham 74
Fried Fish with Coconut and Basil 418
Fried Kidneys 290
Fried Prawns with Cashews 386
Fruit and Fibre Layers 480
Fruity Skewers with Chocolate Dipping Sauce 490

Garlic Chicken Cushions 224
Garlic Mushrooms on Toast 174
Genoese Seafood Risotto 336
Ginger dishes:
  Crab and Ginger Soup 50
  Crab in Ginger Sauce 396
  Five-Spice Salmon with Ginger Stir-Fry 404
  Mullet with Ginger 382
  Scallops in Ginger Sauce 394
  Stir-Fried Ginger Chicken 292
  Stir-Fried Ginger Monkfish 416
Golden Chicken Risotto 238
Golden Glazed Chicken 230

Granita 466
Green Soup 26
Grilled Fruit Platter with
  Lime Butter 484
Grilled Minced Lamb 282
Grilled New Potato Salad 142

Ham Steaks with Spicy
  Apple Rings 324
Harlequin Chicken 204
Herb and Garlic Prawns 438
Herring with Hot Pesto Sauce
  342
Honey-Glazed Duck 268
Honey-Glazed Pork Chops 326
Hot and Sour Soup 44
Hummus and Garlic Toasts 102

Indian Potato and Pea Soup 60
Indonesian Potato and
  Chicken Salad 140
Italian Chicken Spirals 222
Italian Fish Soup 38
Italian Potato Salad 116

Lamb dishes:
  Grilled Minced Lamb 282
  Lamb and Rice Soup 48
  Lamb Cutlets with
    Rosemary 318
  Lamb with Mushroom
    Sauce 278
  Lean Lamb Cooked in
    Spinach 286
  Minced Lamb with Peas 284
  Sesame Lamb Stir-Fry 280
  Spring Onion and Lamb
    Stir-Fry with Oyster Sauce
    312
  Stir-Fried Lamb with
    Orange 314
  Sweet Lamb Fillet 320
Lemon Chicken 260
Lentil and Tuna Salad 124

Macaroni and Prawn Bake
  366
Marinated Fish 348
Marinated Grilled Fennel 188
Mediterranean Chicken
  Parcels 232
Mexican-Style Pizzas 162
Minced Lamb with Peas 284
Minestrone 30
Minted Fennel Salad 118
Mixed Bean Pan-Fry 180
Mixed Bean Pâté 104
Mullet with Ginger 382
Mushroom dishes:
  Chinese Leaves with
    Shiitake Mushrooms and
    Crab Meat 424
  Garlic Mushrooms on Toast
    174

Lamb with Mushroom
  Sauce 278
Mushroom Salad 120
Mushroom Soup 32
Potato, Pepper and
  Mushroom Hash 176
Mussel and Potato Soup 36
Mussel Casserole 350

Neapolitan Pork Steaks 244
No-Cook Fruit and Nut
  Chocolate Fudge 500
Nutty Chocolate Clusters 502

Old English Spicy Chicken
  Salad 128
Olive, Pepper and Cherry
  Tomato Pasta 194
One Roll Fruit Pie 448
Orange and Grapefruit Salad
  454
Orange, Thyme and Pumpkin
  Soup 28
Orecchioni with Pork in
  Cream Sauce, Garnished
  with Quail Eggs 254

Pan-Cooked Apples in Red
  Wine 482
Paprika Crisps 108
Parma-Ham-Wrapped
  Chicken Cushions 216
Pasta dishes:
  Brown Lentil Soup with
    Pasta 18
  Casserole of Fusilli and
    Smoked Haddock with
    Egg Sauce 358
  Chicken and Pasta Broth 12
  Creamed Strips of Sirloin
    with Rigatoni 248
  Egg Noodles with Beef 250
  Macaroni and Prawn Bake
    366
  Olive, Pepper and Cherry
    Tomato Pasta 194
  Orecchioni with Pork in
    Cream Sauce, Garnished
    with Quail Eggs 254
  Pasta Niçoise Salad 152
  Pasta Parcels 368
  Pasta Provençale 172
  Pasta Shells with Mussels
    370
  Pasta Vongole 334
  Poached Salmon Steaks
    with Penne 360
  Saffron Mussel Tagliatelle
    372
  Sea Bass with Olive Sauce
    on a Bed of Macaroni 352
  Sliced Breast of Duckling
    with Linguine 256
  Spaghetti al Tonno 356

Spaghetti with Anchovy and
  Pesto Sauce 158
Spaghetti with Ricotta
  Cheese 166
Spaghetti with Seafood
  Sauce 364
Spaghetti with Smoked
  Salmon 362
Spinach and Pine Nut Pasta
  196
Squid and Macaroni Stew
  376
Stir-Fried Pork with Pasta
  and Vegetables 252
Tagliarini with Gorgonzola
  164
Tagliatelle with Courgette
  Sauce 192
Vegetable Pasta Nests 182
Vegetable Spaghetti with
  Lemon Dressing 168
Vermicelli with Clams 374
Vermicelli with Fillets of
  Red Mullet 354
Peaches in White Wine 462
Pear Tarts 452
Pepper dishes:
  Chicken with Two-Pepper
    Sauce 208
  Chicken, Pepper and
    Orange Stir-Fry 296
  Olive, Pepper and Cherry
    Tomato Pasta 194
  Potato, Pepper and
    Mushroom Hash 176
  Prawns with Peppers 430
  Red Pepper and Chilli
    Soup 68
  Stir-Fried Squid with Green
    Peppers and Black Bean
    Sauce 428
  Twice-Cooked Pork with
    Peppers 310
  Yellow Pepper Salad 122
Poached Breast of Chicken
  with Whiskey Sauce 218
Poached Salmon Steaks with
  Penne 360
Pork dishes:
  Caribbean Pork 322
  Chinese Potato and Pork
    Broth 64
  Honey-Glazed Pork Chops
    326
  Neapolitan Pork Steaks
    244
  Orecchioni with Pork in
    Cream Sauce, Garnished
    with Quail Eggs 254
  Pork Fillet Stir-Fry with
    Crunchy Satay Sauce 306
  Pork Fry with Vegetables
    270
  Spicy Pork Balls 308

Twice-Cooked Pork with
  Peppers 310
Potato dishes:
  Carrot, Fennel and Potato
    Medley 106
  Chinese Potato and Pork
    Broth 64
  Grilled New Potato Salad
    142
  Indian Potato and Pea
    Soup 60
  Indonesian Potato and
    Chicken Salad 140
  Italian Potato Salad 116
  Mussel and Potato Soup
    36
  Potato and Italian Sausage
    Salad 144
  Potato and Mixed Vegetable
    Salad with Lemon
    Mayonnaise 138
  Potato, Mixed Bean and
    Apple Salad 130
  Potato, Pepper and
    Mushroom Hash 176
  Potato, Cabbage and
    Chorizo Soup 62
  Potato, Radish and
    Cucumber Salad 132
  Potato, Rocket and Apple
    Salad 136
  Potato-Topped Cod 398
  Sweet Potato and Nut Salad
    134
  Sweet Potato and Onion
    Soup 58
Prawn and Mushroom
  Omelette 98
Prawn Omelette 420
Prawns with Spicy Tomatoes
  422
Prawns with Peppers 430
Prawns with Tomatoes 432

Quick Chicken Bake 240

Raspberry Shortcake 446
Red Fruits with Foaming
  Sauce 470
Red Hot Slaw 150
Red Pepper and Chilli
  Soup 68
Refried Beans with Tortillas
  184
Rich Chocolate Loaf 460
Rocky Road Bites 496
Root Vegetable Salad 146
Rosy Melon and Strawberries
  156

Saffron Mussel Tagliatelle 372
Salad dishes:
  Beetroot and Orange Rice
    Salad 148

Chicken and Spinach Salad 202
Chinese Chicken Salad 266
Chinese Prawn Salad 126
Coconut Couscous Salad 154
Grilled New Potato Salad 142
Indonesian Potato and Chicken Salad 140
Italian Potato Salad 116
Lentil and Tuna Salad 124
Minted Fennel Salad 118
Mushroom Salad 120
Old English Spicy Chicken Salad 128
Orange and Grapefruit Salad 454
Pasta Niçoise Salad 152
Potato and Italian Sausage Salad 144
Potato and Mixed Vegetable Salad with Lemon Mayonnaise 138
Potato, Mixed Bean and Apple Salad 130
Potato, Radish and Cucumber Salad 132
Potato, Rocket and Apple Salad 136
Red Hot Slaw 150
Root Vegetable Salad 146
Sweet and Sour Fish Salad 332
Sweet Potato and Nut Salad 134
Tuscan Bean Salad with Tuna 114
Yellow Pepper Salad 122
Salt and Pepper Prawns 100
Salt Cod Fritters 340
Savoury Chicken Sausages 236
Scallops in Ginger Sauce 394
Scrambled Tofu on Toasted Rolls 178
Sea Bass with Olive Sauce on a Bed of Macaroni 352
Seafood dishes:
  Bacon and Scallop Skewers 434
  Cantonese Prawns 390
  Caribbean Shrimps 436
  Chinese Leaves with Shiitake Mushrooms and Crab Meat 424
  Chinese Prawn Salad 126
  Coconut and Crab Soup 54
  Crab in Ginger Sauce 396
  Deep-Fried Seafood 80
  Fried Prawns with Cashews 386
  Genoese Seafood Risotto 336

Herb and Garlic Prawns 438
Macaroni and Prawn Bake 366
Mussel and Potato Soup 36
Mussel Casserole 350
Pasta Shells with Mussels 370
Prawn and Mushroom Omelette 98
Prawn Omelette 100
Prawns with Spicy Tomatoes 422
Prawns with Peppers 430
Prawns with Tomatoes 432
Saffron Mussel Tagliatelle 372
Salt and Pepper Prawns 100
Scallops in Ginger Sauce 394
Seafood Medley 384
Seafood Stir-Fry 400
Seared Scallops with Butter Sauce 426
Sesame Prawn Toasts 88
Shrimp Fu Yung 388
Skewered Oriental Shellfish 406
Spaghetti with Seafood Sauce 364
Spring Onion and Lamb Stir-Fry with Oyster Sauce 312
Squid and Macaroni Stew 376
Squid with Oyster Sauce 392
Stir-Fried Squid with Green Peppers and Black Bean Sauce 428
Vermicelli with Clams 374
Sesame Lamb Stir-Fry 280
Sesame Prawn Toasts 88
Seven-Spice Aubergine 92
Shish Kebabs 316
Shrimp Fu Yung 388
Skewered Oriental Shellfish 406
Sliced Breast of Duckling with Linguine 256
Sole Fillets with Marsala and Cream 344
Soups:
  Beef and Vegetable Noodle Soup 46
  Brown Lentil Soup with Pasta 18
  Calabrian Mushroom Soup 32
  Celery, Stilton and Walnut Soup 56
  Chicken and Pasta Broth 12
  Chicken and Sweetcorn Soup 34
  Chilli Fish Soup 56
  Chinese Cabbage Soup 52
  Chinese Potato and Pork Broth 64
  Clear Chicken and Egg Soup 40

Coconut and Crab Soup 54
Crab and Ginger Soup 50
Cream of Chicken and Tomato Soup 16
Cream of Chicken Soup 14
Creamy Tomato Soup 22
Curried Chicken and Sweetcorn Soup 42
Dhal Soup 70
Green Soup 26
Hot and Sour Soup 44
Indian Potato and Pea Soup 60
Italian Fish Soup 38
Lamb and Rice Soup 48
Mussel and Potato Soup 36
Orange, Thyme and Pumpkin Soup 28
Potato, Cabbage and Chorizo Soup 62
Red Pepper and Chilli Soup 68
Sweet Potato and Onion Soup 58
Thai Chicken Noodle Soup 10
Tuscan Bean and Vegetable Soup 72
Tuscan Onion Soup 24
Vegetable Soup with Cannellini Beans 20
Spaghetti al Tonno 356
Spaghetti with Anchovy and Pesto Sauce 158
Spaghetti with Ricotta Cheese 166
Spaghetti with Seafood Sauce 364
Spaghetti with Smoked Salmon 362
Speedy Chicken Pan-Fry 214
Spicy Beef 274
Spicy Chicken Livers with Pak Choi 96
Spicy Peanut Chicken 264
Spicy Pork Balls 308
Spinach and Pine Nut Pasta 196
Spring Onion and Lamb Stir-Fry with Oyster Sauce 312
Squid and Macaroni Stew 376
Squid with Oyster Sauce 392
Steak and Kidney Kebabs 328
Steamed Chicken and Spring Vegetable Parcels 206
Steamed Fish with Black Bean Sauce 378
Sticky Sesame Bananas 478
Stir-Fried Cod with Mango 414
Stir-Fried Ginger Chicken 292
Stir-Fried Ginger Monkfish 416

Stir-Fried Lamb with Orange 314
Stir-Fried Salmon with Pineapple 412
Stir-Fried Squid with Green Peppers and Black Bean Sauce 428
Stir-Fried Tofu with Peanut and Chilli Sauce 170
Stir-Fried Pork with Pasta and Vegetables 252
Stir-Fry Beef and Vegetables with Sherry and Soy Sauce 302
Stir-Fry Turkey with Cranberry Glaze 300
Stuffed Tomatoes 288
Sweet and Sour Fish Salad 332
Sweet Lamb Fillet 320
Sweet Mascarpone Mousse 458
Sweet Potato and Nut Salad 134
Sweet Potato and Onion Soup 58

Tagliarini with Gorgonzola 164
Tagliatelle with Courgette Sauce 192
Terriyaki Stir-Fried Salmon with Crispy Leeks 410
Thai Chicken Noodle Soup 10
Toffee Fruit Kebabs 492
Tofu and Vegetable Stir-Fry 198
Tom's Toad-in-the-Hole 242
Treacle Tart 450
Tropical Fruit Fool 474
Trout with Pineapple 380
Tuna Steaks with Fragrant Spices and Lime 408
Tuscan Bean and Vegetable Soup 72
Tuscan Bean Salad with Tuna 114
Tuscan Chicken Livers on Toast 86
Tuscan Onion Soup 24
Twice-Cooked Pork with Peppers 310

Vanilla Ice Cream 464
Vegetable Pasta Nests 182
Vegetable Soup with Cannellini Beans 20
Vegetable Spaghetti with Lemon Dressing 168
Vermicelli with Clams 374
Vermicelli with Fillets of Red Mullet 354

Yellow Pepper Salad 122

Zabaglione 456